A Taste of Canada

In Search of a Reasonably Priced Sandwich

A Taste of Canada

In Search of a Reasonably Priced Sandwich

Special Grey Stripe Edition!

Chris Ambrose

Copyright © Chris Ambrose 2010

ISBN 978-0-9564473-1-9

Published by Chris Ambrose

ambrosebook@gmail.com

Cover Design by Richard Wood

Search *'A Taste of Canada*
In search of a reasonably priced sandwich'
on *Facebook*

"One man's eyebrow is another man's comedy act."

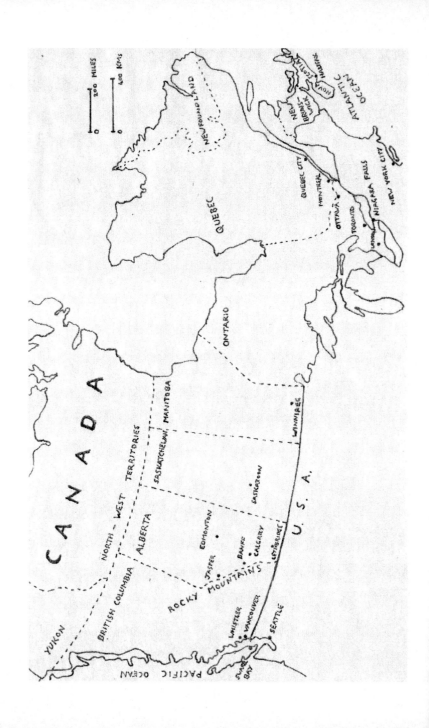

Author's ramble

Hello, I'm Chris Ambrose, and I wrote this book. Now, if that hasn't already put you off, then please continue reading.

This is a detailed geology textbook specialising in sedimentary rock analyses and soil formation...

Oh okay, so that's not *strictly* true. This is actually the story of a journey. A journey through time...and space! But mainly through Canada. Via Northamptonshire.

This is a tale of discovery and of adventure. A tale of how one moment of frustration can lead to a search in a far away land; a search that would span thousands of miles. A search that would lead across vast oceans, baron plains, and snow capped mountains. A search that would ultimately involve eating a lot of bread.

There will be parts that make you smile, parts that will surprise you, and even parts that will make your stomach churn!

Sorry, I meant *yearn*. There will be parts that make your stomach *yearn*. For sandwiches.

Now, a little about the book. No, I mean literally – about the *physical book.*

Firstly I would like to congratulate you on purchasing the *special grey stripe edition* of this publication! That grey stripe took some real artistic flare to create, so I hope it is appreciated.

Throughout this book I have used a font that I hope you find pleasing on the eye and easy to read. I've also broken the book down into short chapters so that you don't get too overloaded with information and excitement and pass out. However, some chapters are a *little* longer than others, so it might be best to check how long each one is before you go careering off into the book, especially if you are one of those 'night-time readers', in which case you can adjust your bedtime accordingly. I'd hate to disrupt your sleep pattern. Aren't I nice?

The brighter crayons amongst you will also notice a jump from *Chapter 12* to *Chapter 14*. This is because when I was in an apartment block in Canada I noticed that it didn't have a floor '13', and so I omitted a corresponding chapter in this book to show sensitivity to the apparently superstitious nature of the Canadian market. I've even added a Canadian-English translation section at the back of the book to help you decipher unusual words and terms.

So basically, if you can find a more thoughtful and considerate author then I'd like to meet them. And give them a prod in the side.

Anyway, enough talk – on with the show!

Chris Ambrose,
watching the World Cup and playing with Lego,
July 2010

Chapter 1

The lunch and Judy show

That woman casually glancing through the passing shop windows whilst carrying a large and colourful array of carrier bags – s*he* didn't know. The man wearing the tightly wrapped rain jacket standing expectantly at the pelican crossing – *he* didn't know either. The line of people queuing in an orderly and patient fashion at the bus stop – I'm sure none of *them* knew. No one did. And e*specially* not me.

Or maybe they did? Maybe it was just me being naive to the ways of the world. Maybe my blissful ignorance of how certain areas of society operate was the underlying factor to the outrageousness that was about to follow.

They could have warned me though, or at least been there to soften the blow. But no. Everyone was too busy. Too busy fighting their way along the bustling streets to their lunchtime appointments. Too busy weaving in between the lanes of hectic city traffic to get back to the office in time for the afternoon slog. Too busy diving in and out of shops in a desperate attempt to snap up a new outfit for the weekend. Too busy conversing on their fancy "smart" phones to care.

But then again, why would they? They *probably* thought I was one of them. I mean *I* was hurriedly making my way through the early afternoon chaos that is part and parcel of Oxford Street life. *I* was also navigating my way through any breaks in the chain of vehicles that linked up the backstreets in an attempt to shave a few seconds off my journey. *I* even had a "smart" phone for god's sake! I wasn't frantically looking for a heavily-sequined cocktail dress to impress the Friday night champagne-sipping fraternity though, and maybe that was my saving grace.

But the truth was that I was one of them – at least for now - and I was loving it. I had smart black shoes on (that I had *even* polished for the first time in months), I had my Oyster card in position for rapid-deployment should a transport turnstile present itself, I had a fancy key-fob attached to my wallet to gain entry to a smart office block, I had my *ItouchPodPhone* slipped into my inside jacket pocket, and I was patrolling the streets of Soho. I was yuppified to the max. It was great. But this still didn't prepare me for that day's lunchtime encounter. An encounter that would leave me red-faced and reeling. An encounter that would leave me shaken to my very core. An encounter that would leave me stranded in the gym changing room in a dazed state of despair. An encounter that would ultimately lead me on an adventure...

* * *

I was spending a week working in central London. I had joined the masses casually gripping the handrails as we were packed on to the rush-hour main line train service into Euston. I was one of the ones ducking and swerving to avoid the fierce jabbing action of the metal prongs being thrust about carelessly by the umbrella-army as we battled through the evening rain back to the station. But this was nevertheless the dream.

So there I was on a Thursday lunchtime, meandering along Oxford Street with another hour of exploration ahead of me. It was my fourth day of Soho-central employment, and although I was only there for the week, I was keen to make the most of my time in this trendy world of suited city-types.

I took a left down Regent Street and crossed over at the lights as I noticed the pavement on the other side of the road was slightly less congested. It also gave my nose a break from the incessant waves of chip-grease that were being constantly blasted up my nasal passages from the countless McDonald's restaurants that dominate this urban landscape. I passed Hamley's toy shop on the other side, where I used to go to look at the latest *Lego* sets when I was younger. I passed many stylish clothing boutiques, whose windows were filled with fashions I still have clearly yet to recognise.

And then I realised it was lunchtime, and that I should probably eat something. Busy mornings in this new environment had left me in need of stomach-replenishment, and after making a break off Regent Street into a far-less populated side road, I found a small sandwichatorium that looked like the classic lunchtime hang-out for the young urban professional. And it was here that it happened.

I stepped through the glass door with all the professionalism of a regular lunchtime diner. It was all a lie of course - I don't usually go flashing my (limited amount of) cash about in such places, but trying to pull-off the image that this was my usual lunchtime routine was all part of the course.

Once through the entrance I confidently strode over to the chilled cabinets and began assessing the options. Now I'm not a fussy eater, and nor do I get particularly excited about food. As far as I'm concerned it's a means to an ends, and a time (and stomach) filler, but I wanted to look like I had an acquired taste and my selection had to reflect this.

After a few seconds of deliberation I reached out and picked up a sandwich. It looked like it had cheese in it, and tomatoes, and lettuce, and possibly an onion. Exciting stuff. I read the description on the packaging for confirmation. Apparently it also contained homemade pickle! *And* it was served on a rustic malted wholegrain baguette. If it takes four words to describe bread (none of which

5

even being the word 'bread') then it must be good. So I headed to the counter.

'Would you like anything else?' the lady on the till with a shiny name badge that read "Judy" enquired, as she hurriedly took the sandwich from me.

Why? Was my choice that bad? Will this malted wholegrain offering leave me so disappointed I'll have to return to buy something else to make up for it? Or was I supposed to ask for something else in addition as part of some unwritten urban custom. Maybe there was some form of city-sandwich etiquette that I was inadvertently giving the middle finger to! I was almost panicking now, and I was worried that this may have come across in my response.

'No thanks.'

She moved on unfazed, tapping some buttons on the cash register. Phew, my nonplussed retort had done the trick. I'd dodged a bullet there.

But no, she wasn't done yet - more questions!

'Eat in or take away?'

Ah, this was a little easier. I had just spied a previous customer vacating a table at the front of the shop. It was nicely positioned with a view out onto the street, and was currently bathed in a slice of homemade London malted wholegrain sunshine. It *even* came with a tabloid newspaper. Brilliant! I could buff up on the weeks "hot gossip" that I have absolutely no interest in. This was working out nicely.

'Eat in.' I replied, confidently.

And *that's* when she dropped the bombshell.

'Three fifty-five.'

'...'

Yes. That was my stunned silence. And no, this wasn't because the lady hadn't added a 'please' on the end because I'm particularly offended by impoliteness, *or* because I had just noticed out of the corner of my eye someone pinching one of the inserts out of the newspaper on the table I had been planning on occupying. No, my utter bemusement was in fact at the amount she was saying.

What I hadn't mentioned before was that when I was selecting a sandwich, I had actually based my decision largely on the price. I wasn't really fussed about contents or quality. The fact that it had '£2.99' printed on the label was what had sold it for me. That seemed reasonable. It could have been filled with squirrel meat and pondweed for all I cared. Yet here I was being charged fifty-six pence more. The *one* determining factor in this purchase had revealed itself to be false.

So you know what I did next? I paid for it. That's right. I went into my wallet and got an extra pound coin out and handed it over along with the other three I had already prepared. Because that's what people do. They pretend not to be confused or wrong, act like everything's fine, and get on with it.

'Would you like a serviette?' she then enquired.

Gah! Was there any end to her questions?! No I bloody wouldn't! Because I dread to think how much you'll charge me for it, you heartless, corporate finger-puppet!

'No thank you.'

She then placed my sandwich on a silver tray. Great. Was that what I was paying an extra fifty-six pence for? A stupid, shiny tray. Presumably so I could see my miserable expression reflected back at me as I ate the sandwich. They were taunting me, and they were all in on it!

I took my now *over-priced* sandwich over to the table by the window. The sun had now disappeared, and the part of the newspaper that bastard had taken turned out to be the only part that wasn't filled with mindless, inaccurate conjecture. Things had taken a turn for the worse.

I ate the damn sandwich. No longer was I amused by the excessive use of words to describe it though. I now considered it pretentious. I also found that it had cress in it. And we all know that nothing is as uninspiring as a cress sandwich. I chewed on the dull, straggly shoots of cress and read all the shocking news stories of the day (that invariably revolved around B-list celebrities being caught out shopping without make-up on, and other such important issues) with an air of despondency hanging over me.

Having finished my slice of homemade malted wholegrain disappointment I got up to leave, but as I made my way to the door I glanced back at the label on the shelf and noticed the small print that showed the price if you were eating in. The higher price. The *unreasonable* price.

So that's how it works is it? You pay more to eat in. Now I know why park benches are always full between twelve and two every afternoon, *even* in mid-winter.

And I don't want to hear any of that 'VAT' business either. I don't care if 'eating in' makes the food subject to restaurant taxes. I worked it out. It would still have only made it £3.51, which for what it's worth *still* crosses the threshold of reasonable pricing in my opinion.

* * *

Okay, so maybe I over dramatised that event a bit. You may have expected me to start a petition to the government against unreasonably-priced sandwiching based on my over-zealous description of that lunchtime, but actually I didn't. If I'm being honest it was barely even a stand out moment of my week, but the following evening I found myself in the gym changing room without a pound coin for the locker, so I had to trek all the way down to the reception desk to get change. I was caught without the pound coin I *keep aside* for the locker at the gym. The pound coin that I had to hand over to afford that stupid over-priced sandwich. It had returned to haunt me.

8

Chapter 2

Scanning for ideas

It was a sunny March morning, which in itself was unusual. Not that it was March, because yesterday had been February 28th, and I'm pretty up to scratch with my understanding of the calendar, and so the fact that today was the 1st of March (knowing that it wasn't a leap year of course) came as very little surprise. No, what *was* unusual was the sun, because it hadn't been making much of an appearance lately. This was actually the first day that showed any sign that the long, cold winter we had been enduring might finally be coming to a close. A winter in which I suspect snow had well and truly ruined its reputation.

Normally Britain (or at least the less northern parts) experiences very little of the white stuff. There might be the odd couple of days where you wake up to a light dusting on the driveway, but that gradually turns to an inconvenient slush by the following day. Nothing major – the trains are a little delayed, a couple of schools close for the day, a few people build snowmen and send photos of them into the local newspaper, and a few cats are left in need of light vetinary attention having had their whiskers frozen onto the neighbours' pond. It happens – we move on.

But this winter was different. This winter featured a pre-Christmas covering, followed by a January of prolonged snow-based disruption. The novelty of snow had certainly worn off by February, and I fear that this will be remembered, and should it dare to make a come-back bid next winter, no one will be hugely impressed or excited.

So it was a sunny morning, and all was well… Except it wasn't. My spirits were temporarily lifted by the rays of light sneakily piercing their way through the office blinds, but ultimately I was bored. Bored of work. Bored of filing. Bored of filing files that would inevitably be taken out of the filing cabinet where I had just filed them, and then returned shortly after for me to re-file. It was a vicious circ-file of life. But that's administration for you. No frills – just filing. Actually I also had other tasks to do that rivalled the excitement of filing. I also got to scan things. I got to scan things from files, which once scanned I would then return to the file, and then I'd file the file. Oh, and sometimes I would mark the file as 'scanned'. But I would never mark the file as 'filed'…just in case someone took the file out, making the file *un*filed. That would be reckless. No, I think I can safely say that my enthusiasm for work was slowly being filed away with every file I saw (or filed). I appreciate that reading this has probably lowered *your* tolerance of filing too, so just imagine what seven months of it had done to *me*!

Over the past few weeks I had come up with numerous ingenious challenges and schemes as a distraction from this inane line of work, and to occupy myself with once I had finished my daily scanning and filing. On one particularly dull afternoon I created a work-themed crossword that ended up making it into the office newsletter. On another slow day I had decided to become an origami expert, and set about following online instructions on how to make a swan out of a piece of paper. I got pretty good at it, and soon my stationary draw was full of swans...but then one evening in the pub when I was bragging about my paper-based achievements, one of my friends took a piece of paper we had been using to try and work out the 'anagram' question in the pub quiz and he made a flower with it. It was very pretty and complicated, and it well and truly trumped my swan. That was the end of *that* master plan.

10

Another such day I had decided that I would become a pilot, and I thought I'd get ahead of the competition by learning the phonetic alphabet. I did this with surprising ease, so after mastering it I looked into flight schools that would surely be keen to snap me up now I was presumably halfway through the training course anyway. I found a nice looking flight school in New Zealand with a package that even included your flight uniform! This was tremendously exciting, and a real bonus as I didn't know where I was going to buy my aeroplane outfit from. Sadly I then noticed the price. £71,000. Sierra Hotel India Tango. That ended that dream. My friend then replied to my text that I had sent him earlier to show-off my new alphabet skills. It turns out that *he also* knew his aeroplane alphabet. That phonetic, flower-folding bastard.

The most committed scheme I had embarked on involved making use of my available resources. In admin you are usually surrounded by a healthy supply of paperclips, and so over several weeks I began attaching these paperclips together, hoping to eventually break the world record for the longest paperclip chain. A flawless plan I'm sure you'll agree, but sadly, having clipped together a chain that *I* considered to be very impressive (at an estimated seven metres long) I chose to do a little interweb research, and it quickly became apparent that I was not destined for this title, as some school children in Utah had made one that was over twenty-two miles long. Losers. To rub insult into injury I also discovered that there are lots of rules and regulations into paperclip chain making, such as needing to do it within a twenty-four hour period, the requirement to use regulation-sized paperclips, and *even* the need to staple them apparently. Oh, and all of this had to be done in a team of no more than sixty people. I had failed on several counts. This was most demoralising, but I suppose it was just as well really, as I walked into the office one morning to discover my paperclip chain had been used as a very tacky (and not remotely festive) Christmas decoration. Things were not going well.

11

This job wasn't a career choice I'd like to point out; it was a very convenient means of raising funds in between university terms, and more recently for my travels. But I was back now, and this job was merely serving the purpose of filling time (and my bank account) until I could find more career-based employment. But cleverly, I had arrived back from my round-the-world adventures in mid recession – yes, there's that buzz word of 2009 – and as a result I was getting nowhere. Endless CV sending and job site searching was proving fruitless. Despite their claims, the jobs that these "specialist" websites and agencies "match specifically to you" are all rubbish, and bear no relation to your skills or preferred fields. It turns out that most of these employment sources firmly believe that you are perfectly suited to a career in media sales, and will bombard you with such opportunities until you crack and send a CV to one of them. Then you hear nothing back. You can't win. You also find job opportunities listed that say they require someone "asap". I clearly have been misinformed as to what this stands for, because on submitting an application in response, you are invariably told that you *may* hear something within three months if they are interested in you, and if not, your details will be "kept on file for future opportunities." B******s will they. I bet they don't even *have* a proper filing system. I could show them a thing or two about that...

So I was getting hugely frustrated as the employment sector was asap-ing my hopes of ever getting a proper career job. I was also developing ever stronger urges to go out in search of more adventures. People talk about 'getting the travel bug', and I certainly had it. And it was growing. All I needed was a sign. Some direction. A *mission*!

And it presented itself that sunny Monday morning...

I had finished my morning filing, and was spending a few minutes on the interweb, trawling the regular haunts for any half relevant jobs. Having carefully concluded that I probably wasn't the best candidate for the managerial production vacancy at a Dutch picture-frame wholesaler I turned my attention to my phone, which had just alerted me to the fact that I had a message. It was from my good friend the gym, telling me that I could join up for only £1! This was fantastic news, and I certainly would have been appreciative of the offer...had I not already been a member of the gym. The gym that I had been a member of for the past six months. The gym that only had my contact details *because* I was already a member. The gym that had charged me £25 to join up. I deleted the message.

£1 membership. It was undeniably reasonable. I had a pound in my wallet right now; I could have signed up right there and then if I hadn't been conned by the colourful banners and sparkly changing rooms that had lured me in to joining when it had first opened. I checked my wallet to confirm that I did in fact have a pound in my wallet. No, I wasn't *actually* considering joining the gym I was already a member of, but I was planning on putting in a session that evening, and I wanted to make sure I had change for the locker.

And that's when I remembered my five days working in London that I had completed a couple of weeks ago. The fancy entry mechanism on all the floors. The slick office environment and racks of hi-tech equipment. There wasn't a paper file in sight. It was good. Then I remembered that lunchtime. That sandwich. The anger at the unreasonable pricing structure. The annoyance of having to hand over that extra £1 coin. The £1 coin I found myself in desperate need of at the gym the following evening. The same gym I could now have *joined* for £1!

I found myself staring at the computer screen in front of me. The web browser was open and it had defaulted to the *Google* home page. I impulsively typed into it.

Now, I can't exactly be sure what I was hoping to discover from this. Maybe I was hoping to be told about a local outlet that specialised in averagely-made sandwiches served with excessive amounts of ambivalence and all at a non descript price, or maybe I would be presented with a link that if I followed it I would be offered a special discount card that made every sandwich in London reasonably priced - *just* because I had been desperate enough to conduct such a ridiculous search. This was all testament to the mind-numbing state I was sometimes left in after a morning of filing and scanning.

Although maybe it wasn't such a ridiculous search, because it came up with over 116,000 results. That's a lot of places to go for a reasonably priced-sandwich. I could *comfortably* fill all the lunchtimes that would accompany full-time employment exploring all of those. I started clicking my mouse at the top of the list of search results.

The first link was blocked. Oh how I love the protective and restrictive nature of large-scale office interwebbing. I moved on. The second link was a site going on about the 'best' sandwich. No, no, no! I didn't want the *best* sandwich! I wanted a *reasonably priced* one! I continued. Number three and four were lists of cafes. There was no thought put into these – lists were no good. Time for search result number five. Now this was just some self-promoting advert spiel by some newly set-up franchise. That was no good either. *Google* had failed me. I was rapidly losing confidence in my carefully thought through approach to economic lunchtime dining. I grudgingly decided to try one last search result. Number six.

Trusty number six...

I clicked on the title without extensive reading of the limited information that is usually found under the link heading. Past experience of *"Googling"* has taught me that these are often not a true reflection of the page that it leads to, and therefore relying on these excerpts can be risky and lead to immense disappointment. I had seen the words "sandwich" and "reasonably priced" highlighted in the brief passage though, so I was confident I was hitting in the right zone.

After a few seconds (my office suffered from a gloriously slow interweb connection) a page appeared, and immediately I was drawn to it. There was a nice photograph of a decking area, with benches positioned looking out across an expanse of water onto a distant hilly landscape on the horizon beneath clear blue skies. It looked nice. I fancied being there. But did this place serve sandwiches? And more importantly, were they reasonably priced? I scrolled down the page. And there it was. A fantastically constructed photograph of a sandwich. The *reasonably priced* sandwich. This was it, I could feel it. This was the sandwich I needed to purchase...but where was it?!

Underneath the photograph was a paragraph of text, but conveniently certain words were highlighted; Swartz Bay Terminal. Vancouver Island. British Columbia.

I knew what this meant; I was going to Canada!

Chapter 3

A sandwich too far?

This was massively exciting. I'd never been to Canada before, and *especially* not for lunch! It made so much sense too – because *everyone* knows that places and words where every other letter is an 'a' are great; banana, Sahara, taramasalata, abracadabra...okay, maybe that last one doesn't quite work, but *certainly* Canada! I could even try and find a magical fish-dip covered banana desert/dessert to accompany the sandwich. Brilliant! I started reading the paragraphs that were interspersed with the large and colourful photographs of the sandwich and its team of alternative lunchtime snacks. Apparently it could be purchased from the ferry terminal on Vancouver Island, which is on the west coast of Canada. Ideal. I like ferries, and ferry terminals are places of ever-growing anticipation for ferry-traveller enthusiasts, so it seemed to be the *perfect* location for a light, reasonably priced, pre-crossing snack.

Now, time for a few important details; it was a "Ham and Swiss" sandwich, which I presume is "ham and cheese" in ferry-terminal speak, and it was $5! That *is* reasonable! Although to be honest I had no idea what the Sterling to Canadian Dollar exchange rate was. It was too late for minor technicalities though, I was sold on this mission. This was the sandwich that would hopefully renew my faith in the sandwich industry. Speaking of which, was I alone in my quest for reasonably priced sandwiches? Or perhaps there were others who also shared an interest in the economic provision of lunchtime food? Possibly, given the time and effort that had been dedicated to *this* website.

I returned to *Google*, and soon I had entered another search based upon sandwich appreciation. The little green bar slowly made its way across the bottom corner of the computer screen window as the results page loaded. I clicked a link at random, and soon I was being given a cheeky insight into the latest edition of Sandwich and Snack magazine! *The* Sandwich and Snack magazine! I couldn't believe it, there's *actually* a magazine that focuses on the creation, location and quality of sandwiches! It's not even a magazine really – it's a journal. A journal! That's even *more* official and important!

I suddenly felt like such an amateur. I had *no idea* that I had been dabbling in an industry with so much heritage and discussion. It didn't stop at a publication either, there was an organisation too! "The British Sandwich Association". Wow, this was too much! They had a whole *association* dedicated to sandwiches! They *even* had a mission statement, which involves "promoting innovation and excellence" in sandwich making, and "providing a collective voice" for the sandwich industry. This was excellent. I've always liked the taste of innovation in my sandwiches, and I'm sure sandwiches are very deserving of a collective voice. They even held award ceremonies with awards! I imagine these involved people in dinner jackets handing out gold-plated sandwiches. Maybe they even called them "The Hammies". And even if they didn't (then maybe they should!) at least I now knew that I wasn't alone in my quest for good sandwich standards.

It was then that I noticed a little advertisement in the top right-hand corner of the interweb page that said it was British Sandwich Week from the 18th to 24th of May.

Well that was it. I knew where I had to go, and now I knew *when* I had to go. I grabbed my coat and headed down to the flight shop.

17

Now I know it said "British" sandwich week, and I know that Vancouver Island is in Canada, which is therefore not in Britain, but the ferry travels between destinations in *British* Columbia, and so I reckon that still counts. It was also my lunch break by the way, I don't just up and leave the office every time I find a long distance lunch trip to arrange.

I walked speedily down the high street with this exciting mission buzzing around in my head. I turned off into the shopping centre, and then weaved through the lunchtime crowds and into the travel shop, where I was immediately greeted by a man with a headset on. He was smiling wildly, and he straight away told me that it was all booked and that I should get a confirmation email thorough any minute. That was quick, I hadn't even opened my mouth! This really was an efficient service. I *then* realised that he was actually speaking to someone *on* his headset, and that he was just *looking* at me while he did it. How very confusing. So to counter this bizarre socially interactive triangle I had inadvertently become entangled in, I turned around to face the wall so I couldn't get further confused and say something stupid.

On the wall was a large map of the world. I quickly found Canada (partly because I am a geographical whizz kid, and partly down to the fact that Canada is the second largest country in the world and therefore bloody hard to miss) and then I found Vancouver, and the nearby Vancouver Island. It was quite a long way from England, and also quite small in the grand scheme of Canada. Suddenly flying all that way for lunch seemed slightly...I don't know...silly? No, that's too strong a word. *Inefficient.* Yes, flying to Vancouver for lunch and then flying back home again would be inefficient. So maybe I could make more of this opportunity...

'Hi there, sorry about the wait! How can I help?'

I turned back around abruptly, and peered cautiously at the man. He returned my stare with a bemused look that confirmed to me that he had indeed finished on the phone and *was* in fact now talking to me. I swiftly ended the now slightly inappropriate eye contact that had gone on for a few seconds, and took a seat opposite him at the desk.

'I'd like flights to Canada please.' I said, with a confident nod as I glanced back at the relevant part of the world map on the wall - as if to demonstrate my immense geographical knowledge and to confirm my intended destination in case the travel agent hadn't heard of Canada.

'Okay, and when would you like to go?'

British Sandwich Week, *obviously*. 'Mid-May.'

It was as if he hadn't foreseen the rush that would surely happen following my discovery of the timing of British Sandwich Week and the nice photograph of the sandwich on the website...

'And that's flying into Toronto?' He spoke with a hint of presumption in his voice.

No, *of course* it isn't! Who the hell flies to Toronto for British Sandwich Week?! Toronto is in Ontario – on the *other side* of Cana...oh. Toronto. Yes it is on the other side of Canada isn't it? I once again glanced over to the map on the wall. Hmmm, maybe I *should* make more of this. As Canada is the second largest country in the world there must be nice things there to see and do. In fact, other than Niagara Falls - which it shares with the US, and *isn't* even the largest or highest waterfall in the world, and the CN Tower – which is *no longer* the world's tallest building, I don't really know *what* is in Canada. This suddenly seemed like the perfect opportunity to find out.

'Errr, yes. Flying to Toronto, then flying back from Vancouver a few weeks later.'

Yes, that's what I said. "A few weeks later". That well-known and specific booking slot that all the major airlines offer.

'Okay, that will be £584.'

Obviously my vague timescale wasn't such an issue.

'Excellent.' I replied.

'Would you like me to book that for you?' he said, as his fingers headed purposefully over to his keyboard and then hovered the cursor over the "purchase tickets" button.

'No thanks!' And with that, I got up and left.

Now you might be thinking that I bottled the mission. Maybe you're thinking that it suddenly occurred to me that making a quite significant life choice – axing in a stable (if a little dull) job and jumping on a plane and travelling halfway around the world to hunt down a sandwich I saw a nice picture of on the interweb after conducting a compulsive and arguably *slightly odd Google* search was...well, a little...risky. Well you know what? You're wrong. I know a brilliant plan when I see one – mid-way down a sporadic list of unaccountable websites on a slightly advert-biased search engine. It was flawless. But that didn't mean I had to sign up there and then. Now *that* would have been risky. No, I wanted to procrastinate a little. The travel agent also seemed far too keen to wrap up the deal there and then to make a nice healthy bit of commission from what I considered to be relatively little work on his part. I just couldn't let that happen. He'd have to fight for it. Or at least offer me a lower price. And a go on his headset.

* * *

A brief interlude of irrelevance

Once I was out of the flight shop I strolled through the shopping centre in all its mirror and polished, tiled-floor blandness until I arrived at hell. Otherwise known as the card shop.

Masses of blindingly bright white lights glazed the racks of overly-specific and unnecessary cards that cater for more occasions than there are days in your life. Conversely, the lighting may sound quite heaven-like, but there is certainly nothing spurring you on to be good in life to therefore deserve to go through *this* entrance. I definitely saw it as more of a punishment. But it had to be done. Next Sunday was Mothers Day, and so being the kind and grateful son I am, I had to bite the bullet and step into this world of recycled paper and irritating novelty keyrings.

Somehow there always seems to be some event or occasion that the card industry feels warrants the supplying of cards for. With it being Mothers Day though, half the shop was dedicated to this occasion, and so it wasn't long before I had negotiated myself past the "Congratulations on having your in-growing toe nail removed" and "Sorry for running-over your hamster with my lawnmower" card ranges, and I was soon flicking through the appropriate section.

Despite providing three separate racks of mother-related cards, I found it incredibly difficult to find anything that would fit the relationship I had with my mum. It's not an unusual relationship; she is my mother, and I am her son. Simple. Surely this was one of the main inter-family bonds that Mothers Day is intended for? I mean, as far as I can work out, you'll either be a daughter giving your mother a card, or, as in my case, you'll be a *son* giving your mother a card. So *why the hell* couldn't I find a *single sodding card* that fitted this?! Oh there were plenty of cards *there*; "For you, Aunty, on Mothers Day" (no offence to aunts, but that link is a little tenuous), or "Happy Mothers Day, from all of us" (which is either a lazy offering from a multi-child family, or the card company trying to cheekily sneak in on the happiness offering). There were even a few cards with "You're like a mother to me" written on them, which could probably be deeply offensive - although I was tempted to buy it and add "...because you are" on the inside. There was *even* an incredibly sinister card featuring the tag line "Happy Mothers Day from the bump". How eerie is that?! It also seems unfair to assume the unborn child would want to be signed into such an agreement before it even potentially has a gender. And also, given what that bump would inevitably be putting its mother through in the coming weeks during birth, it might seem just a little two-faced. I also disapprove that every card seems to either have a bear on the front (often clutching flowers) or it has a poem written inside, that even with the most heartfelt family bond at stake, would probably make the mother open the envelope, read the inside of the card, and instantly throw up.

In the end I had to settle for "Happy Mothers Day from the cat". It was a little demeaning admittedly, as I then had to add "...and from your son" at the bottom, thus promoting the cat (who was oblivious to its offer of gratitude) above myself, but I suppose at least it wasn't directly implying a paternal bond between them.

I appreciate this rant has very little to do with Canada...or even sandwiches, but I wanted to get it off my chest. And no, I wouldn't be silly enough to embark on an international mission in search of an acceptable and relevant occasions card outlet.

Although...

No. For now I will just sit down, and calmly count to ten...

Chapter 4

Filling the Gap - next stop (but one): Canada!

I returned from my lunch break satisfied with what I had achieved. I now had a rough idea of the cost of flights to Canada, and I had emerged from the card purchasing ordeal with a reasonable amount of my dignity still intact. It was also still sunny outside, and that *always* makes things seem better. Hopefully they have sun in Canada too.

I decided to have a look at a few websites to see if I could find any cheaper flights than the man in the flight shop had found. Not that I doubted him of course – I mean *everyone* knows that people who spend their day wearing headsets and smiling will get you the best deals available – but I wanted to check anyway. Plus I didn't have any scanning or filing to do. A few skilful clicks later and I had found a flight that fitted in neatly with my complex itinerary; Canada: May. And after negotiating my way through a few option screens I was told that the price was a mere £1792! That must be an absolute bargain, because they phrased it as "*Only* £1792!", and the exclamation mark emphasised this amazing value-for money offer further, suggesting that even the flight operator *themselves* were stunned by how cheap it was! I then noticed that this was a business class fare. That made a little more sense, but to honest I wasn't really interested in flying business class. Aside from the extra expense, I feel that flying business class would go against the 'reasonable pricing' ethic that was leading me on this trip. I also found on my only previous experience of business class (a cheeky free upgrade a few years back) that the seats in this section have far too many adjustable positions to choose from, and as a result you're never completely convinced that you have chosen the most comfortable one, and it therefore ruins your flight while you make constant adjustments. I also remember being served the in-flight meal on a ceramic plate. A plate for god's sake! I have *all my other* meals off a bloody plate! As far as I'm concerned the whole novelty of mid-air dining is the clever plastic food trays! I moved on...

A few more interweb pages later and I found another option. This one offered a flight from London to Toronto for £149! And this time that's *me* adding the exclamation mark, because even *I* realise how cheap that is! That couldn't be right could it? It *must* be subject to additional fees. Maybe it didn't include airport taxes, or maybe you had to pay a luggage supplement if you're check-in bag weighed over seven grams. Perhaps the flight had standing room only, or it was heavily discounted because they would be using a learner pilot. If that was the case then I would be the *perfect* passenger, as I knew my phonetic alphabet and so if the trainee pilot got into difficulty then I could help out...with clear and precise spelling.

It soon became apparent that the fare was that cheap because it was a one-way ticket. If you wanted to fly back again then the return trip was almost triple the price. Cheeky. It would be fine if you were moving out there permanently, but despite the glorious photograph I had found on the internet I just couldn't rely on this sandwich having a life-changing effect on me, so for now I needed to book a return ticket.

Eventually the good people at STA Travel managed to sort me out with a flight that was *very* reasonably priced, and I had their assurances that the plane would be flown by a fully qualified pilot and that I would get my own seat, firmly wedged in the economy section where I belong. I even managed to get the ticket at an extra good price because of my lethal combination of charm and wit. Or because I was wearing hyper-fashionable socks. I can't be sure of their exact reasons or wording.

So I was all set! I had a mission, and I had a plane ticket. Sorted. Time to kick back and relax until the end of April.

Well...no. There were still some other bits and pieces to sort out. Number one being the need to tell the people at work that I would be leaving. This could be tricky. I was always liable to up and leave if a more suitable employment opportunity arose, but giving up my job in a time of economic strife and in a struggling employment sector to track down a sandwich overseas may initiate a few raised eyebrows. Maybe I'd keep that quiet, and instead I'd just say that I needed a break and wanted to go to Canada for...oh, I don't know...the scenery, perhaps? Yes, that sounded plausible. My 'official' reason for going to Canada would be that I was going for the scenery. Classic tourism.

So I did just that, and I think they bought it. Job done. (Well...in four weeks it would be!) And as an added bonus I found out that I had been accruing holiday time (which I was previously unaware of) and so I could add this on to the end of my work pay-sheet, meaning that I *might* now even be able to afford the trip! A definite bonus.

* * *

It was a few days later, and I was casually sipping tea in the bar that stood overlooking Hertfordshire's finest alpine slope.

In another attempt at livening up my current, reasonably dull existence I had taken up snowboarding in the past couple of months. This was partly because I had been hooked on watching the recent Winter Olympics in Vancouver (home of the reasonably priced sandwich!), and partly because everyone knows that snowboarders are cool.

Once a week I would head over to the new indoor snow facilities in Hemel Hempstead and I'd hit the slope in my hyper-fashionable boarding trousers, warm finger-disabling gloves, and an exciting brightly coloured belt, that when combined made me look totally radical. These afternoon bookings also included free tea and coffee after the slope session, and so not being a regular or especially proficient tea or coffee drinker, I used this freebie as an opportunity to get some practice.

While I was progressing quite quickly through the different snowboarding levels (via a few tumbles and bruised limbs) my hot beverage consumption was proving less successful. On this particular occasion I had deployed a tea bag into an empty mug, and then attempted to poor hot water over it. Sounds simple, right? Wrong. I thought it was going well, but then I noticed that the water was turning into tea before it hit the tea bag. That seemed very clever. Maybe this was some form of highly advanced pre-emptive tea bag, or *maybe* I was some sort of trainee Jesus – because turning water into tea was *surely* only a couple of steps away from turning water into wine – but then I realised that I was actually pouring *coffee* onto the tea bag.

A man who had been pouring his own drink beside me saw what I'd done, smirked, and then took a deep, judgemental intake of breathe.

'Yeah I've done that before,' he said whilst shaking his head sympathetically. He was clearly a level 2 tea drinker, while I was only a level 1. I didn't like the idea of losing face, especially to one of those sympathetic-head-shaker types.

'No, it's how I like it.' I replied sharply, picking up my *cofftea* and moving away from the self-service table, raising my eyebrows in a cocky 'so-there' kind of fashion, whilst simultaneously trying to take a victory sip of my drink.

This didn't go well. The boiling hot liquid instantly singed my lips, causing me to flinch, which in turn triggered the spilling of my fresh cup of mix-caffeinated-disaster down my t-shirt. I sighed, and walked away; head down, face well and truly lost.

After a few moments of dignity restoration and frantic t-shirt mopping I took a seat at one of the nearby tables. Soon I was joined by a few other snow-goers, who had somehow read and understood the heavily coded labelling on the thermos jugs ('Coffee', 'Hot Water') and had therefore successfully arrived at the table with either tea, *or* coffee. No one had even spoken and yet I was already at the bottom of the social hierarchy.

Soon though, the usual small-talk had broken out, and we were all finding out where everyone was from. It quickly became apparent that some people had travelled a long way to be here; one person had undertaken a three-hour drive each way to enjoy the artificial-snowy delights of Hemel. I hadn't. I'd had a fifteen minute drive up the road (which would no doubt become a lot less on the way home after the amount of caffeine I was about to consume).

'Where have you come along from?' one woman enquired in my direction. She was eyeing my drink slightly suspiciously as she spoke.

'Watford,' I replied, quickly picking up my mug to shield the sludgy contents from her vision before she sussed me and my calamitous pouring error.

'Ah, that's a service station isn't it?'

No. No it isn't. And once again I was forced to explain the confusion that often greets a Watfordian when confronted by an inquisitive outsider.

Watford is a town in Hertfordshire, twenty miles northwest of central London, and home to approximately 78,000 people. Watford Gap is a service station between junctions 16 and 17 of the M1 motorway in Northamptonshire, and home to an ever-changing handful of road-tired caffeine addicts.

There are two common mistakes that people make when you tell them you are from Watford. They either believe that you are from the place where they film the television soap *EastEnders* (which is actually set in the *fictitious* East London borough of *Walford*), or they assume you live in a service station next to a motorway. I think this is largely down to the fact that Watford Gap comes up in many interweb searches for Watford, or because it is on a major road artery running through the country, and as a result lots of people have passed signs for it.

Anyway, this lady had gone down the service station route, and after explaining to her that I *wasn't* in fact born, bred and educated under the sales counter of *Burger King*, she went on to talk about how she had been to Watford Gap services and had eaten a very expensive meal. Fascinating.

Well actually...

Service stations *are* renowned for over-priced food. And drinks. And petrol. And everything else they sell while we're on the subject. They are monopolistic roadside enclosures that offer people on the move the things they want out of necessity at an *unreasonable* price. A true beneficiary of the free market. And you know what? I *bet* they sell sandwiches!

One thing that had been slightly bothering me since my sandwich incident in London was that I was worried that I didn't have enough perspective on what constituted unreasonable pricing in terms of sandwiches. I had no gauge to ascertain whether I had *actually* been held to ransom by the sandwich industry, or whether in fact I was just being out of touch with how much a slice of cheese stuffed into a piece of bread should cost. I know that *I* considered £3.55 to be too high a price, but that doesn't mean that the sandwich market as a whole agreed with this. Now I sensed an opportunity to get some perspective. And not only could I attempt to find out the real

28

boundaries of sandwich over-pricing, but I could also investigate this location that many of my fellow town-dwellers have had presumed as their home.

This meant one thing...

Road Trip!

Chapter 5

Sun, sea(ts), and sand(wiches): a whole lot of Watford

The next day I was back at work. I had finished my day's administrative duties and was once again looking for something to do to fill some time. This was restricted by the need for me to stay at my desk to answer any incoming calls that may come through, which I would inevitably do so in a pleasant and polite manner, but ultimately I would be of no help to the caller, and I would horrifically mislead them, or more likely I would just end up taking a message. I'm not suggesting that I haven't learnt anything in my time there, for instance I now know that under British building regulations; a staircase becomes a ladder at 55 degrees. One day that will get me out of a tricky situation, I'm *sure* of it.

So I was at my desk and I had the world at my fingertips in the form of the internet. Well...about 85 percent of the world. I didn't have access to the usual type of restricted sites; email accounts, auction websites, forums, gambling sites, pornography etc. But for the most part this wasn't too much of an issue.

I found my way back onto *Google*, and decided to do some research on Watford. Or Wat*fords* as it turned out. The endless source of semi-reliable information that forms *Wikipedia* seemed like a good starting point, so I found my way there, and typed in "Watford".

It brought up a page of information about Watford (shock, horror). It said it was in Hertfordshire, near London, and that it was next to the M25 and M1 motorways. Oh, and it said that there was a river or two running through it, and a canal. This was nice. I agreed with all of this. I scrolled to the bottom of the page to where it said *"other results for Watford"*. This sounded more exciting, so I clicked the link and was soon being told about Watford Gap services. To be honest I wasn't expecting to be told a lot about this. I mean, how much can you write about a few odd buildings next to a motorway? I was wrong though. Watford Gap services turns out to be massively significant. Well, in terms of motorway service stations at least...

Watford Gap services was the first service station in the UK, and also apparently the most notorious. That's a very intriguing word that conjures up all kinds of mental imagery, suggesting that it could be a place that has been witness to covert operations, dodgy dealings, and possibly murder!

This isn't the case though. It is in fact "notorious" for being the country's first service station (opened in November 1959), for confusing people who stop there (by being named the same as a large town further down the motorway) and for serving crap food. All very interesting I'm sure you'll agree, but not really worthy of a book. Not like sandwiches at any rate. There was a song written about it though, but it was quite derogatory about the place, and for various reasons it was banned from the album it was written for, and so is now apparently hard to get hold of. What also gives this service station significance (and its name) is its proximity to the neighbouring village of Watford, and as the motorway, railway, and canal all pass through the 'gap' in the hills here (make sense now?) it also made the perfect location for the first service station. It also sits more or less in the middle of England, and as a result has become an unofficial boundary between the north and the south of the country, and jokes have formed about things being "the best this

31

side of Watford Gap". This isn't helped by motorway signs having "Watford and the North" written on them, suggesting anything beyond Watford is "The North", although *that* sign refers to the more *southern* Watford. The Watford *I'm* from. So basically I'm starting to understand the confusion.

Despite the apparent complicated existence of this place, I was still sure that I should visit it. What set it in stone was the opening line on a motorway service station website that I found a link to, that read; "One of those services which everyone talks about, but you never use." Well, it was time to change that. But I decided that going on a road trip to a service station to eat a potentially overpriced and unpleasant sandwich could be a little dull, and so I whipped out my phone, and sent a text to a couple of my friends.

'Going to Watford Gap services for a sandwich. Coming?'

In all honesty I didn't hold out much hope of finding anyone to join me. It didn't hold much potential as a glamorous eating destination and I hardly put much effort into selling it. I was therefore pretty surprised when I quickly got two replies saying; 'Yeah, okay.'

Excellent.

* * *

It was a bright, sunny Sunday afternoon as I got in the car and pulled out onto the road to go and pick up my friends before setting off for the Midlands.

First stop was to collect Geoff, who was conveniently already in position when I pulled up outside his place. With him onboard, I pulled out of his road, and headed for Lewis' neck of the woods. This is a route I've done on numerous occasions, and as I was less than half a mile from home, it was quite a surprise that I went

32

straight on at the traffic lights instead of turning right. I'd gone the wrong way. That wasn't very clever. Three minutes into the trip and I'd already messed up. This wasn't a good start.

So after a brief diversion around by the station we were back on track, and soon we were all in the car and heading for the motorway! I put a CD on to get the road trip party rockin', and then slowed up as the traffic lights at the junction ahead turned red, meaning we had to stop. It was here that I realised that I had over-compensated with clothing layers given how warm and sunny it was, and so while we were stopped at the lights I attempted to remove my jumper. For most people this would be quite an easy task to carry out, but I quickly became entangled in my seat belt, and so in my haste to complete the mission before the lights turned green, I gave the top a fierce tug. Luckily the jumper came off, but then both Lewis and Geoff made loud exclamations of surprise and outrage. I didn't understand why, but now the lights were changing, so I quickly slipped the car into gear and pulled off. It was then that I looked down and realised that I was completely topless. The others were now laughing uncontrollably, and I also noticed a few strange looks from the passengers in the car that had been beside us at the lights. This was strange. I was sure I had put on a t-shirt this morning.

It turns out that I had, but in my over-energetic top-removal exercise, the t-shirt had come off with the top, so I was now driving along topless. In a car full of guys. I looked like a tw*t. Conveniently there was a bus stop ahead, and so I pulled in and managed to restore my outfit to a more acceptable format by swiftly pulling back on my t-shirt. It was just as well the bus stop was there, because we were then straight onto the M1 motorway – next stop Watford Gap!

I'll be honest; the journey up there wasn't massively exciting. After the initial excitement of going the wrong way and then my unexpected strip tease at the traffic lights, the motorway just stretched out before us as we meandered north along it. Unfortunately the M1 isn't really Britain's answer to Route 66, and where *that* iconic road cuts through the heart of the US, passing through spectacular scenery and evocatively named places such as Tucson, and Sante Fe, the M1 has Luton, and Newport Pagnell.

We cruised along for around an hour and a half as we were put through numerous contra-flow systems and speed restrictions as a result of ongoing 'motorway improvement' works, every so often passing a sign telling us the distance until the next services. They always seemed to be thirteen miles away, and I'd get my hopes up that the next one would be the right one, but then they would be dashed as we got to the exit turning and it would be the wrong name. It was important to get the right one, as it would have been a *disaster* to go all that way and eat an expensive sandwich in a service station that everyone doesn't talk about.

We eventually made it to junction 16 of the M1. I remember the map saying that the services were between junctions 16 and 17, so that must make it close! I eagerly kept my eyes peeled to the banking at the edge of the hard shoulder as I awaited the all important signpost and distance marker. It turns out that the distance between junctions 16 and 17 is bloody long, and so I had to take the occasional glance back at the road ahead of me – just as a precaution - to avoid other vehicles/cows/fellow-expensive-food-researchers.

And then there it was! Watford Gap Services! The place of dreams! (...or of refreshment and light bladder relief.) I grabbed the steering-wheel and swerved (carefully) across two lanes and into the entrance slip way, where I became momentarily confused by the vast selection of arrows directing different sized vehicles in wildly conflicting directions, before pulling up into a strangely coach-shaped parking bay. We had arrived!

We got out of the car, and made our way over to the bridge that spanned the motorway below. I didn't want to rush into the sandwich buying event, so I thought a spot of deafening traffic noise and a light touch of bracing air pollution would help ready me. We crossed over the bridge and went down to the south-side services. These seemed a little nicer than the north-side area where we had parked. There was a large open green picnic seating area – presumably where they held the live music that accompanied the 50th anniversary celebrations that took place here last November. Oh yes, I had done my research! It was a magnificent place. You could really sense the heritage.

Actually it wasn't, and you couldn't. You could just sense miserable, weary travellers and smell exhaust fumes. Maybe it was the inhalation of these fumes that clouded my initial judgement. They were almost *certainly* responsible for causing me to want to have my picture taken by the "Watford Gap" signpost.

Anyway, once we had seen the glamorous side of the Gap, we walked back over the bridge and into the north-side complex. Here we went to the main food counter, and I began to eye-up the options. One particular sandwich stood out. It was a ham and cheese baguette. The overpriced London baguette had a cheese-based filling, and the reasonably priced Canadian sandwich had ham and cheese in it, so it seemed like the right choice. I checked the price. It was £3.99! That *did* sound unreasonable! Brilliant! I picked it up and took it over to the till, where a friendly lady took it from me and scanned the barcode.

'Would you like chips with that?' she enquired cheerily.

Ha! You're *really* gonna try it are you? You wanna try and further rinse my wallet? You think you can lure me in with a series of money-making add-on offers like the rest of them, is that your game? Well I know how it works young lady! So no, I *don't* want your "chips", so why don't you take your "chips" and shove them up your—

35

'I *said, would you like any chips with that?*' she firmly repeated. Presumably my in-head rant had left a long period of silence that suggested I hadn't heard her the first time.

'Oh. No thank you.' I said sheepishly, before picking up my sandwich and walking away.

I walked over to the newsagent-type shop to have a look through the magazines while I waited for the others to get their refreshments. As I flicked through the latest edition of *Heat* magazi— errr, I mean *Top Gear* magazine, I noticed out of the corner of my eye that this shop *also* had some sandwiches. And *then* I noticed it had the ham and cheese sandwich that I had just bought. More intriguing still, was that here it was £4.25! That's *even more* expensive than the one I had bought from the shop twelve metres away! The *same sandwich* was twenty-six pence more expensive within the *same* building! That's the most ridiculous thing I've ever seen! And the fact that this one was overpriced goes without saying.

I walked over to the seating area where I was joined by the others, and I unwrapped the sandwich. It *did* have a scrawny piece of ham in it, *and* a few slithers of plastic cheese - but that was it. No salad or condiments. What irritated me more was the fact that they had cut both ends off. Why?! The ends of the baguette consist of perfectly good bread!

I ate it. It was bland, dull, dry and tasteless. This was undoubtedly an *unreasonably priced sandwich.* I think I had found the upper limit.

As we sat that on the uncomfortable plastic seating finishing off our selection of overpriced roadside disappointments, I looked around and noticed the wide variety of people that were at the service station; there were suited business men and women, a scout troop, a spattering of bus drivers, a man with dreadlocks, a group of full leathered-up bikers, elderly couples and even a posse of people wearing sunglasses indoors!

It crossed my mind that these places – service stations – were one of the few places where you find such a fantastic mix of different social groups in the same building. All of these different people were from different walks of life, and were here, briefly united by the same location, but all of whom will have recently been, or will soon be, in completely different places and doing completely different things. They may all have a shared meaning within their groups; such as the scouts maybe heading off on a scout camp, or the bikers off to a biking rally, or the indoor sunglass wearers off to a vanity/ego posing competition, and yet they don't bat an eyelid that these other groups are around them. It really is...erm...a cultural melting pot. Urgh! I *hate* that phrase! It's a travel guidebook cliché, and basically just a polite way of saying that a place is a mish-mash of people and cultures and therefore has no real identity of its own. But it's kind of appropriate, so I'll let it go. Anyway, enough of that, we had a village to explore! I was reaching out to collect up the sandwich packaging to throw it away when I noticed the sticker on the front. It read; "Freshly made by PAULINA". I don't think this is something that Paulina should be bragging about. The sandwich certainly hadn't been good enough to warrant the full capitalisation of her name.

We made our way back out through the automatic doors of the front entrance and walked over to the car. During our pre-snack excursion over the bridge to the south-side of the services we had spied a little service road that led out from the north-side services and onto a road bridge that crossed the motorway. We had walked along it and found that it had "No Entry" signs at either end of the road. So it was a road that could not be entered from either end. Some would call that a pointless road, but as the only other way of getting over that bridge would be a five mile detour; involving re-joining the motorway and heading on up to the next junction and looping back down on the main road - we called it a cheeky short cut.

37

And so, with our heads ducked low to avoid the motorway police we had previously spotted in the car park, and whilst all simultaneously humming the theme tune from *Mission Impossible*...and *then* the theme from the *James Bond* films (the *Mission Impossible* theme is a little short and repetitive and it was taking us a while to weave around the car park) we headed out behind the lorry parking area, and dived up the narrow lane. I slammed it into third as we hit the main straight of the service road, and within seconds we reached the bridge. We'd made it!

I 'hung a right' (which I believe to be the cool, 'fashionable' term for turning right) and before we knew it we had crossed the bridge over the motorway and were passing a sign indicating we were now in Watford. This was it! The incidentally famous "Watford of the North"!

A gentle left-hand bend took us through a small collection of neat houses and cottages, and then I noticed a fenced-off gravel area in front of a small one-storey building, set back on the right hand side. I pulled into the parking area in front of the building, and after getting out of the car, we noticed the sign saying it was the village hall. There was also a board saying that there was a 'Bible Talk' happening there today. This *was* today, and so maybe that explained the small gathering of other vehicles that were in the parking area, and even more so the silhouettes of people we could see through the windows of the hall. I saw that the main door to the hall was ajar. I'm not sure if this is a personal thing, but I find something slightly sinister about a door that is 'ajar'. An open door is inviting, and encourages you to go through it. A closed door indicates the opposite – that you should leave it alone. But a door that is *ajar* is *intriguing,* and it somehow lures you towards it, suggesting that you *could* go through it, but that *if* you do, you do so at your own risk...and that you'll probably get bashed if you do. Maybe in this instance you'd get bashed with a bible given the talk that was going on today. Not that I'm implying that these villagers were bible-bashers – they could equally get you with a rolling pin.

Anyway, we swiftly made our way out of the car park and away from my own special episode of *Midsomer Murders*, and headed along the main road through the village. It struck me that there was a lot of modern housing in the village. It was also a very idyllic setting, with rolling sheep-filled hills stretching out behind the main street. Oh, and the motorway on the other side, providing the gentle soundtrack of rumbling traffic. Many of these properties had Aston Martins and BMWs parked up nearby in abundance. It definitely felt like a place that was growing in size thanks to urbanites trying to escape hectic city life. My geography teacher would be proud of that observation. We also counted in the region of twenty large white posters dotted around the village, all of them with "NO WIND FARMS HERE" written on them in large, bold, black lettering. The people of Watford were clearly intelligent folk, because wherever you looked, you could indeed *not* see any wind farms.

We turned off the main road at a T-junction, which indicated to us that we had reached the other end of the village. It had had taken us a good six-minutes. You definitely couldn't walk through *our southern* Watford on a Sunday afternoon in that time.

A left turn saw us loop back around past the parish church and then we found ourselves back at the village hall. This was disappointing. We had expected there to be a pub in the village, so that we could stroll in and look incredibly out of place because we imagined that it would be a very 'local' type of pub (full of locals) and then we would head to the bar and order a drink and the person behind the bar would eye us suspiciously and say; "You're not from round 'ere are you?" as they poured our drinks, and we'd reply; "No, we're from the *real* Watford" and then we would gulp down our drinks super-fast and run out of the door and back to the car, before being chased out of the village by a mass of angry villagers, who would all be hanging off the back of a truck and waving pitchforks.

But now this couldn't happen, and it was shame. In fact we didn't see any people anywhere, except for those silhouettes that were enclosed in the delights of the *New Testament* at the village hall. They should have put more posters up; "NO PUB HERE", "NO SHOP HERE", "NO SERVICES OR FACILITIES HERE WHATSOEVER". It was time to leave. So we got back in the car, accidently wheel-spun on the loose gravel in a "we're from out-of-town" rebellious fashion, and then sped off south down the A5 in the evening sunshine, for a slightly more pleasant rural routing back to *proper* Watford. It had been a successful trip, but it was time to stop procrastinating, and time to get on that plane!

…But first I feel I should briefly clarify what I constitute as a sandwich. After all, if I was going to do this mission properly then I couldn't risk getting caught up in descriptive controversies. This was a serious business.

A sandwich is a filling encased within two pieces of bread. This can include rolls, baguettes, bagels and subs. The filling can be varied and can be hot or cold. Having said this I do not consider a burger to be a sandwich, although I realise that they do fit my description and criteria for being one. Let's just call it a grey area and hope it doesn't crop up.

Chapter 6

Canada: the land up-over

Toronto, Ontario

So I was off! Well…*almost.* A final few uneventful days at work, a few trips into town to pick up a couple of bits and pieces (such as some Canadian Dollars, as it suddenly struck me two days before my departure that they may come in handy) and *then* I was off!

I soon found myself in Terminal 3 at Heathrow airport and being (quite literally) blown away by the astonishing ferocity and drying power of the *XLerator* hand dryers that they seem to only ever have in airport toilets. They're so powerful (and stylishly named!) that this one blew my watchstrap open, gave my arm hair a centre parting, and dried out my skin so much I felt I needed to drink some water to compensate. Phenomenal. Except I now had an empty water bottle, and so I had to go and refill it, and in the process of doing that at a neighbouring water fountain I spilt some water down the front of my t-shirt, and so I returned to the hand dryer to dry it out, which repeated everything…and so you can see how I passed my time in the departure lounge.

When I finally had my bottle and body water balance about right, it was time to head to the departure gate. Here we were told that the plane was slightly delayed, and so I got out my notebook and began scribbling a picture of Canada. Yes, it was that specific.

41

This drew the attention of a lady next to me, who, judging by her accent was herself Canadian. It all made sense really.

'Are you going home or visiting?' she asked while scrutinising my picture.

'Visiting. I'm spending a few weeks [hunting down a sandwich...] backpacking across the country.' I replied.

'Oh, good. Canada's nice.'

This was excellent news. The whole trip could have been in jeopardy had she said it was a crap place to visit but hearing these words from a native were reassuring. So now I could relax on the flight. Quite literally, as when we did finally board the plane I found I had a row of seats to myself. Result. Bring on seven and a half hours of mediocre films and oddly seasoned chicken.

* * *

Having flown up over the North Atlantic, and with about an hour to go before landing, the clouds cleared out of the window to reveal a vast land far below, interspersed with masses of frozen, snow-covered lakes that I took to be north-eastern Canada. It was very dramatic, and slowly, as we headed south, these frozen lakes became *less* frozen, until they were positively wet with water. Then, those with window seats were greeted to the sight of one particularly large lake, and suddenly a selection of isometric shapes could be seen jutting out of the land skywards from the shoreline. I concluded that this was Lake Ontario, and that the grey blocks on the horizon formed the skyline of Toronto!

The clear skies made our arrival pretty spectacular, and the only thing that momentarily disrupted the landing experience was when something struck my head as we made our descent. I found the offending object underneath the seat in front of me. It turned out to be the casing of the cabin light that was above me. It's good to know these planes are made of such sturdy materials.

Distraction over, I looked back out of the window where I could just about make out the distinctive needle shape of the CN Tower piercing up into the clear blue sky at the centre of it all, and before long we were bumping along the tarmac as we taxied towards the airport terminal building. We had arrived!

It was a smooth run through the terminal building and baggage collection (although I *obviously* didn't run – that would draw suspicion to the fact that I might have pinched the in-flight headset – which for the record I hadn't) and it even included a pleasant exchange with the lady on the passport control desk, who asked what I was doing in Canada, and when I replied saying that I was backpacking across the country, she said in a positive (and not remotely patronising) fashion; "Good for you."

This was nice of her. She even smiled when she said it. I like Canadians.

My next task was finding my way into the city because the airport was around thirty kilometres outside of the centre. I walked over to an information kiosk and asked how to get to the city centre. I got a blank look from the man behind the desk, and so I Canadiasized my question, and asked how to get "downtown".

This proved far more successful, and he proceeded to give me two options;

1: Get the airport shuttle bus for $18.

2: "Ride The Rocket" to Kipling then take the TTC
   to King Street for $3.

Well it was a no-brainer. The second option was far cheaper, it was more complicated and therefore interesting, and most importantly of all – it involved "Riding The Rocket" – which sounded *massively* exciting!

I followed the man's directions to 'Pillar R' outside the terminal building, and found "The Rocket" waiting for me. It was a bus. This was a little disappointing admittedly, but I got on it anyway, and then it pulled off at a slightly less-than-rocket-like rate of knots.

In my haste to get on the bus and whilst simultaneously trying to manoeuvre my two bags and the numerous leaflets and tickets the info-man had given me, I thought I had dropped my map, and so I set about peering under the bus seats to find it. A friendly Canadian lady in the seat behind straight away started helping in the search, and therefore I felt very guilty when I noticed the offending piece of paper sticking out of my pocket. So we were both on an eager hunt for something that wasn't missing. I decided not to tell her, and instead I suggested giving up the search and claimed that it wasn't important and thanked her for trying. Well I was new here, and I didn't want to look stupid.

A fifteen-minute journey took us to Kipling Station, where I got off and boarded a subway train heading east towards downtown Toronto. A swift change of subway lines and a couple of stops further on and I was in the heart of Toronto's financial district, and more importantly I was only a couple of blocks from my hostel. Once back above ground again, I took out the crudely scribbled map I had constructed before I left home, and I was stumbling through the narrow doorway that led into the hostel six minutes later, despite the airport man telling me it would be a twenty minute walk. Maybe he was a slow walker, or maybe he was just slow. Well after all, he didn't know what "city-centre" meant.

Now, normally when you arrive at a new place after a long journey, you relax, or maybe take a casual stroll around your new, surroundings. Not this time. When I had been reading up on Toronto and had booked a couple of nights in this hostel, I had discovered that a band I liked happened to be playing in the city the night I arrived, so I had bought a ticket. So, having ditched my bags in my dorm room on the seventh floor (which I chose to walk up to; not having grasped the fact that seven sets of stairs is quite a lot to walk up when you have seventeen kilograms of socks and batteries on

44

your back) and then headed out towards the docklands with the aid of another map I had thrown together before I had left.

As I made my way through the grid systems of the city's east end I noticed a sandwich shop on the other side of the road. I realised I hadn't really eaten in sixteen hours, and so I crossed over and went inside. I was greeted by *another* friendly Canadian from behind the counter. These 'friendly Canadians' were quickly becoming the standard type of Canadian, and it was nice. Soon I was eating a 'BLT' bagel – which cost a very reasonable $2.65. I felt this was a good transitional sandwich to start with on my trip, as a bagel was a very North American encasing, but a 'BLT' filling was very British. Maybe that sums up Canada; situated in North America, but as a country it is monarched by the Queen. That's probably very stupid, and I almost instantly regret writing it. And yes I *am* also aware that "monarched" probably isn't a word.

Sandwich eaten, and after around half an hour of further weaving through the streets of Toronto I turned down one of the quays branching off the main dock road and found a queue of people. They looked like they were gig-goers, so joined the queue, gazing out across the water at the Toronto skyline as I waited. It was a very novel setting for a queue, so I was quite happy being part of it in the warm evening sun.

The venue itself was well laid out. It was a box-shaped room with a large open floor space in front of the stage, with a mezzanine level high up above, and vast arrays of lights across the roof rigging. The band themselves were pretty good too, although they did say how they think Canada has their best fan base, and *not* the UK as they said most people think, despite saying that the UK *is* their favourite place to play when I've seen them back home. Rock bands are fickle.

When the lights went up at the end of the show at around ten forty-five, everyone piled outside and most jumped into one of the many lingering taxis. I did not. It takes a lot to persuade me to get into a taxi - a gun to the head possibly being the only time I'd consider it (and even then I'd probably protest a little) – and so I set off back through the dark, deserted streets of the docklands towards my hostel. I was thinking that this may not have been the cleverest move, as I walked in the shadow of the Gardiner Expressway, crossing under the bypass and cutting through a couple of unlit parks, but where's the fun in playing it safe?

It was then that I was approached by two rather suspicious looking characters as I neared the home stretch and my hostel, but when they got close enough that I felt sure I was about to lose my wallet and designer shoelaces, they stepped aside to allow me space to pass. Even the undesirable Canadians are polite!

Soon I was back at the hostel, and after dragging myself up the seven flights of stairs (when will I learn...) I fell into bed, smacking my head on the upper bunk as I did so, just to guarantee a swift loss of consciousness after a busy twenty-three hours of awakeness.

* * *

I got up early the next day with the exciting prospect of a city to explore ahead of me. I grabbed some clothes, my map, and my camera (wearing the clothes as a more practical way of transporting them) and set off in the bright sunshine towards the harbour front. I walked through the shadows of the towering office blocks that surround this part of the city, noticing how clean and surprisingly quiet the streets were, even on a weekday morning.

Ten minutes later (having now firmly got to grips with the road crossing customs of Canada thanks to endless crossroad junctions) I was right where I intended to be; at the base of the Canada National Tower! I like tall buildings. And tall towers. In fact I just pretty much like being anywhere *high up*, and so at 553.5 metres tall, this is one of the highest buildings you *can* be up. It *was* the tallest tower in the world until recently, but it was beaten by the Burj Khalifa in

Dubai, although apparently the CN Tower is still the tallest 'tower' in the world, it's just no longer the tallest 'free-standing structure' in the world, even though a Chinese tower apparently beat it last year. The observation deck is also only about half way up the tower. Confused? Me too. It still claims to be the tallest free-standing structure in the Western Hemisphere though…but to be honest, the 'Western Hemisphere' is a pretty ridiculous and crap geographical sub-division to make. So essentially there are probably plenty of places where you can be higher, but the views were meant to be nice all the same, especially when it was sunny (which it definitely was) and so I was happy. Anyway, with my head already hurting before I even got in the lift to gain all that altitude, I purchased a discounted ticket for the tower thanks to my hostelling card, and boarded the glass lift for the ride up to the observation deck.

The views were predictably far-reaching and captivating. I find these tall buildings very useful homing beacons for when you are on the ground in a city you're not used to navigating around, as well as a good viewing point for recognising or spotting other places that you may wish to visit when back at ground level. There were clear views out across Lake Ontario, with the distant New York State coastline just about visible in the afternoon haze. Just off the Toronto harbour front were the Toronto Islands, which are home to some boat-owning Torontonians and a small airport. Off to the north-west of the city I could just about make out the main international airport where I had flown in to the previous day, as well as a few other urban centres, signified by small crops of tower blocks rising up awkwardly from the gridded suburban landscape below. Right underneath the tower, and through the glass floor that has been implemented to add to the tower's tourist experience, I could see the large white roof of the Rogers Centre, another significant landmark on the Toronto skyline, and another visitor draw. The stadium, which opened in 1989, was the first to have a fully retractably roof. Sadly it was closed at the moment, but after spending a good half hour enjoying the views from high above the city, I returned to earth and wandered around the stadium perimeter to see if anything was happening beneath its fancy roof in the coming days. My luck was in. The *Toronto Blue Jays* baseball team were playing that evening. And the next evening apparently. And again a couple of days after that. All of these games were against the *Oakland Athletics* too. This was strange; they must get pretty bored of playing each other all the time, but maybe as Oakland is near San Francisco in California they have to make the most of the two thousand mile round trip. Anyway, the point is that I had found a way to see inside the stadium *and* buff up on my baseball, and all for a mere $13. Sorted.

Once I was finished at the stadium ticket window I decided to grab something to eat from a local deli and head over to the harbour front. I picked up a few sandwich ingredients and went to pay for them. The man who was serving on the till smiled a lot and called me 'superman'. I didn't really understand why, but it was nice all the same.

I crossed over the road outside of the deli where a sign said that this new-look waterfront area had opened in June 2009. It showed. Architecturally innovative wooden and stone walkways led myself and a handful of suited lunchtime office-escapers around a small selection of moored boats and well-kept grass areas to a very neat artificial beach and a wooden promenade. Here I found a bench and put together a homemade sandwich ($1.30) and ate it while looking out over the island opposite, with the clean and modern harbour side development to my left, and an old and derelict looking factory to the right. The relative silence that I found myself in at the heart of this city was slightly disconcerting given the four and a half million residents that apparently live here, with only the gentle breeze coming off the lake and the occasional buzzing of plane engines as short-haul flights took off and landed at regular intervals from the little airport on the island daring to break the calm.

48

That evening I headed back through the streets of downtown Toronto among the herds of blue and white clothed *Blue Jays* fans. This was actually a little misleading, as when I had found my way up and around the endless concourses of this huge stadium to the nosebleed section, I found the stands relatively deserted. I pretty much had a whole block to myself as I sat down beneath the clear evening sky, with the roof now open. I suppose when you play the same team over and over again in the same week the significance and excitement of the matches start to decrease.

The game kicked-off (or batted-off) right on time; at 7:04 pm, as it said it would on my ticket. This seemed a strange time to start, but then again why should things start at neat time intervals. Good work *Blue Jays* for being different. Unfortunately this good work did not continue, as baseball is a pretty slow moving sport, and the two teams largely failed to entertain during the three and a half hour match. The *Blue Jays* did end up winning, but that was really down to just one of their players, who hit three homeruns in consecutive innings. Even the process of closing the roof as darkness set in was a lengthy and drawn out affair, with complete closure taking a little under forty minutes. I decided that I would skip tomorrow's rematch.

Chapter 7

Water, water, everywhere...
but then your heart will sink

Niagara Falls, Ontario

I made my way up through downtown Toronto the following morning, which may sound like an oxymoron, but I'm reasonably confident that it makes sense nonetheless.

I walked up one of the major streets that runs perpendicular to the harbour front, which led me to the City Hall complex. It's a large open concrete area with raised meandering walkways set around a rectangular water pool, which all sits in front of a grand looking building with a clock tower, and a modern pair of curved tower blocks to its side that make up the civic centre offices. I wandered up to an entrance way that was attached to a building that appeared to house a library, but after trying the door and failing to open it, I decided to move on. Call me a quitter if you like, I don't care.

I continued up Bay Street until I reached my intended destination; the bus terminal. Once inside I joined a short queue, and soon I had purchased a return bus ticket to Niagara, for a very reasonable $30. I then took a seat in the terminal building, and passed the time aiding numerous passing Canadians about where they had to stand in the bus station *in their own, home country* to catch various buses so that they could travel *within their own, home country.* I mean - c'mon guys.

It was a two-hour trip to the town of Niagara, passing through relatively unspectacular scenery along the way. Occasional glimpses of water sparkling in the sunshine were the only respite from small suburban developments and flat, open farmland as we made our way along the highways around the broad perimeter of Lake Ontario.

At around one-thirty we pulled up at the bus station in Niagara and everyone got tentatively off the bus. A few other bus-trippers asked me if we were in the right place for the waterfall, or which direction it was in. Maybe it was because I have one of those knowledgeable faces, but to be honest I didn't really have a clue where I was, or which way we should be going. Most people succumbed to the heat or caved in to the pressures of geographical ignorance and jumped into a taxi to be thoughtlessly chauffeured to the waterfall while they flapped about in their jewel-encrusted-buckle handbags for a bottle of the Alps' finest volcanic spring water. But I didn't, because I am an adventurer! And I was too poor. And I didn't have a handbag. So I did what all good adventurers do, and I put on my sunglasses to shield the confusion that would have no doubt been glistening in my eyes. I figured that where there is a waterfall, there is inevitably a river, and so if I found this I knew I had a fifty-fifty chance of turning along it in the right direction and finding the falls.

So. The river. I was looking around my surroundings in a thoughtful 'hold-on-a-sec-I'm-just-getting-my-bearings-and-then-I'll-be-straight-off-in-the-right-direction' kind of way (don't deny it – you know *exactly* what I mean) when I heard the unmistakable whirring of helicopter rotors overhead. I reasoned that that they were probably rotating above a helicopter, which in turn would probably be transporting some of the champagne-sipping tourist types with their designer flip-flops and genuine *Armarchi* leather camera holsters on an aerial tour of one of North America's leading tourist attractions. So I figured if I followed this sound then I would be on course. Unfortunately ground-level navigation by skyward helicopter is a little tricky – especially when you don't actually ever catch sight of the helicopter in question, but I worked out its rough direction based upon the rapidly fading sound of it's rotors, and after a nice ten minute stroll through suburban Niagara in the ever-increasing Ontario heat, I heard the unmistakable sound of flowing water. Someone was washing their car by the sidewalk. *But beyond that* I could see a ravine that soon revealed itself to be the towering banks of the Niagara River! Now, left or right? Well, judging by the fact that the water was flowing from right to left, and guestimating that the water level was around fifty metres below the top of the river bank, *and* knowing that Niagara Falls is around 50 metres high…I turned right.

My logic and reasoning proved correct, and after a further ten minutes of following the main road through the Niagara old town suburbs along the riverbank, I saw a large and architecturally impressive bridge appearing through the trees. This was the 'Peace Bridge' that links the Canadian side of the river to the US side, conveniently indicated by the pair of national flags that hang high above the centre of the bridge. Beyond the bridge I could faintly make out a white mist and the sound of gushing water. I was pretty confident I was in the right neck of the woods now.

As I passed under the arching form of the Peace Bridge the first part of the waterfalls became clear; this was Bridal Veil Falls, also know as the American Falls. This stretch of cascading water appears to run parallel to the river as it crashes down the side banking to the rocks below, but it actually joins the US side of the river to a series of small Islands (also on the US side of the border) at the point where the river bends around. It's a further five hundred metres upstream (south) along the Canadian side that brings you to the main event.

Despite only being the 50th highest waterfall in the world, Niagara Falls displaces more water over its top than any other, and most of this water goes over the edge at the awe-inspiring (and Canadian) Horseshoe Falls. This appropriately named (being very much horseshoe shaped in appearance) masterpiece of mother nature is certainly a spectacular sight, with masses of tourists flocking to the railings at the river edge from the adjacent quaintness of Queen Victoria Park to snap away at this giant natural water feature.

I joined them, and weaved my way through the obligatory tourist-poses being struck by groups of happy holiday makers to mark their visit, until I found a break in the view-obstructing people chain where I could take a few of my own photos. I did this quickly and efficiently, partly because I have a cheap and uncomplicated camera, and partly because the spray from the waterfall was misting up the lens. Oh, and because I'm not very adept at striking authentic and original tourist poses under the time pressures of concise public photography.

I had read that throughout history people had tried to go over the falls (with varying success rates) in barrels, but I had also read that if you do this you get a hefty fine. So with this in mind, and realising that I had carelessly left my human-sized barrel back at the hostel, I opted against giving it a go.

I hung around for a few minutes to (literally) soak up some more of the free-falling water, and to watch the rabble of matching blue-waterproofed tourists being projected into the mist from a sightseeing boat on the river below, before turning around to head up Clifton Hill that overlooks the falls.

And here is where it all goes horribly wrong.

As I crossed over the park towards the new town area, I temporarily got caught up behind a group of what appeared to be blues brothers. A group of around eight men in suit jackets and trilby hats were spread out across the path (preventing any chance of a smooth overtake) and so I was forced to adopt their slow pace. Maybe these were the blues brothers plus extended family; the blues cousins, or the blues brothers and sisters (as I now spotted a small cluster of unusually dressed women trailing to one side of the men). Perhaps they were all heading to a blues brothers party, or maybe there was a blues brothers convention happening in town today. *Maybe* I should stop saying "blues brothers" and consider that they might be part of a religious group. In light of this I decided that it might not be appropriate to take a photo of them. They must have been struggling enough in all that heavy black gear on this hot day without being singled out as a novelty feature by frustrated tourists who were stuck following them.

When I finally found a gap between the jail-house rockers I made a break for a street that led up the hill. Here I passed a rather fancy twenty-odd-storey high hotel and a casino, an observation tower, and even a Hard Rock Café. These were certainly not your usual riverside establishments. I carried on up the street, and soon found myself at the heart of Niagara new town. It was grim. Every building was a games arcade, an expensive fast food outlet, or an overpriced and gimmicky tourist attraction. Giant plastic models and overly colourful shop fascias masked a world of tackiness and adolescent depravity that you would expect to find at some of Britain's seaside resorts, and *not* at one of the great natural wonders of the world. The waterfall that brought all this candy-floss-coated mayhem was now well out of sight thanks to 'horror-show' billboards and buzzing neon signposting. Novelty sirens and ear-piercing shrieks filled the air as I stood despairingly by the roadside while I waited for the street vendors to manoeuvre their cart-hoards of souvenir crap from corner to corner in front of me.

54

I had planned on grabbing a bite to eat up here, but there was no way in hell I was going to find a reasonably priced sandwich (let alone one of any quality) in this synthetic dump. Despite my love of being up tall buildings I didn't even want to go up the observation tower, as I didn't want to concede to the greed-driven industries that led to the moral and physical destruction of this place. It was then that I bumped into a couple of people who had been staying at the same hostel as me in Toronto, and so we had a moan about how on earth this eye-sore could have been allowed to happen, before escaping quickly back down the hill to the park and river. Then, after a few final glimpses at what we (and everyone else) had come all this way to see in the first place, we began to amble along the pavements back towards the old town and the bus and train station so that we could get out of Niagara. This place had been badly damaged.

As I got on the bus an hour or so later, I noticed the numerous shopping bags filled with cheap, plastic waterfall memorabilia and "I Love Niagara" t-shirts that many of the others on board seemed to be clutching. These were no doubt the same people who had panicked when the bus hadn't delivered them directly to the waterfall viewing platform, and who had jumped brainlessly into a taxi at the first sign of a road junction.

I took my seat and put my mp3 player in my ears to mask the sound of rustling as my fellow passengers dove to the bottom of their plastic bags to see who had bought the largest novelty key ring. Actually I put the earphones in my ears. This place had been a let-down but I wasn't ready to shove large chunks of plastic into my brain just yet.

I pressed play and sat back to reflect on my four hours in Niagara, and was relieved that I had only made the day visit as I had been advised to do by other hostellers, instead of staying in the overpriced tourist hotspot any longer as I had originally intended. I considered how Niagara was as a place not unlike the water that draws people to it. It starts off high up; with the fantastic spectacle of the falls leaving you gazing in fascination…and then it plummets wildly as you move on towards the town and all of its deplorable exploits.

Then I realised that I'm not very good at similes, and so I turned up my music, and went back to looking out of the window.

Chapter 8

Definitely not home from home

London, Ontario

*It is illegal in Canada to pretend to practise witchcraft.

The bus that took us back from Niagara was handily equipped with onboard televisions. However, instead of offering us a film to pass the journey, or even a bit of information about Canada and its potential offerings to visitors, it instead filled our vision with adverts for DIY shops and hi-fi components. So if I ever get round to furnishing a house while I'm here then at least I will be ahead of the game.

It did throw a few 'useful' insights into the world of travelling though. Every so often a helpful tip would suddenly appear on the screen. One said that it was important to "always ensure you have money with you". Brilliant. But these advertisements and so-called 'tips' were also interspersed with random facts about Canada. Now, I can't verify these facts beyond my understanding that this is a reputable coach company, but if accurate, then they are undoubtedly vital to know for any visitor to Canada. I was going to list them here for you, but I felt that this wouldn't give them the emphasis they deserve, so instead I have opted to begin all future chapters with a different one. This particular one intrigues me greatly, and makes me wonder whether the actual practise of witchcraft is acceptable. I shall keep you posted if there are any further developments on that front.

I was pretty tired once I made it back to my hostel that evening. It had been a busy day, and the unexpected Spring heat and urban-trekking had taken its toll. This was further aided by my journey up the seven flights of stairs to my room, where I arrived to realise that I was thirsty and so I had to trudge down *eight* flights of stairs to the basement kitchen to fill up my water bottle, and here I got chatting with some fellow travellers and we ended up playing cards until one in the morning. I then had to return up the eight flights of stairs back to my room. A bash on the head from the bed frame was therefore surplus to requirements tonight, but I got one anyway. I suppose it's good to be consistent.

The next morning I had to check out of the hostel. This meant one final trip down that sodding staircase and I would be free of seventh floor residency. As it happened I forgot to bring down my pillowcase, so it was in fact my final *three* trips up and down that sodding staircase.

Once free of the hostels complicated bedding returns system, I zig-zagged my way back through downtown Toronto for what was meant to be my final time, stopping briefly to have a sandwich before my next trip. I found what I believed to be a chain 'coffee shop' type place that was comparable to the type of place that I bought the original sandwich from in London that had caused this trip. Big city/chain coffee shop – it was going to be a good test.

I had a roast beef sandwich that came with cucumber, peppers, cheese and even leeks! It cost $5.69. This wasn't a bargain, but it was imaginatively filled *and* they didn't charge me extra to have it grilled *or* to eat in! Take that London! I was also now also getting used to the tax system over here. Unfortunately Canada has a similar system to the U.S. in that the price on the label is the pre-tax amount, and so you arrive at the counter to pay and they whack on extra amounts for the numerous and complicated taxes they have out here that vary between provinces. It's very annoying, and means it's tricky to have the correct money ready. You don't pay tax on bread and other "necessities" though, which is nice. Well that's how it works in Ontario anyway – god knows what will happen later on when I venture off into new provinces.

Sandwich session over, I made my way once again to the bus station. A brisk walk (well, as brisk as you can be with a full stomach and seventeen kilograms of clothing, shower gel and electronic chargers on your back) and I was soon pushing my way awkwardly through the large glass doors of the terminal building to the enclosed forecourt, where I found the bus I needed, slumped my backpack on the ground for under-bus stowing, and then got on board. I was off for the next part of my quest; I was heading for London…London in Canada!

* * *

When I was back in England I had been looking at a map of Canada and I had spotted a city not too far from Toronto (in Canadian terms at any rate) called London. Now I know that it is a common occurrence for colonies of the UK to share place names with those back home, but when I had read up on London, Ontario, I had discovered that they had tried to imitate London, England, seemingly wherever possible. They had named many major roads and places to replicate those made famous by English London (Oxford Street, Covent Garden, etc.) and they even had a park called…(you guessed it) Hyde Park. I thought that I should therefore see if they replicated the unreasonable sandwich pricing structure adopted by the English capital, and so I had booked a bus ticket there, along with a couple of nights accommodation so that I could investigate.

Further more, when I had been searching for "Watford" on *wikipedia*, it had actually turned out three results. I mentioned my home town (Watford, Hertfordshire) and the 'iconic' Watford of the North, but there had also been a *third* Watford that I didn't mention. This was Watford in *Ontario* – in *Canada*! And you know what? It just happened to be a few miles outside of *London*, Ontario – just like Watford, Hertfordshire. Coincidence? No. Probably not. We've established their fondness for imitation out here, but it was certainly worth investigating if possible. So here I was on a two-hour bus journey heading out west from Toronto. It was time to sandwich up in other-London, and complete my triangulation of Watfords!

* * *

London is a city of around three hundred and fifty thousand people (a good amount of these are students) and it lies about halfway along the highway between Toronto and Detroit, Michigan (in the U.S.).

We arrived at three o'clock in the afternoon, and once again the sun was blisteringly hot as I plodded along the wide and desolate York Street pavement through a pretty run-down and not all that enticing looking area.

After half a mile or so I turned right down Wellington Street, where I dropped down through an underpass, re-appearing in the sunshine beside a collection of quite unfriendly and scruffy looking people. Not that I'm making a fuss, because I was pretty scruffy looking too, and trawling around with my backpack and day bag slung in various configurations across my back and front as I hunted down my new residence was hardly giving me the most approachable facial expression.

After another half a mile I decided to check my map and discovered that I had probably walked past the hostel, and so I stopped at the next crossroads and waited for the lights to change.

I'd had no formal briefing on how the lights work in Canada in relation to when vehicles can go, and when pedestrians can go, but it seems very much like a system orientated to favour the pedestrian. From what I have encountered so far, vehicles can turn across the pedestrians' path, but will (almost) always give way to pedestrians, who in turn seem to be very obedient and wait for the lights to change to allow them to cross. So with this in mind (and being as I am a conscientious traveller) I decided to be patient, and although there was very little traffic about I waited for the white lights of the 'crossing person' signal to light up. I waited, and I waited. I waited for a good three minutes before the aching in my shoulders reminded me of the weight of my backpack, and so I decided that enough was enough and I made a break for the other side of the road.

When I finally reached what was apparently the hostel (based on the street number) I did a double take, because it didn't really look like a hostel. It looked like a run-down house. Some would say it had character, but I felt it had an air of desertion about it. I wandered up to the door (there was no sign saying it was a hostel, just a couple of initials on a board outside that I recognised from the internet description of the place) and here I found a hand-scribbled note stuck on the wall. It said not to ring the bell or bang on the door if it was not open, but to ring a mobile phone number that was written below. There was no sign of life from within the rotting wooden walls, and all the windows were shut up and had net curtains or shutters blocking any view inside. Luckily I had a Canadian "cell" phone, and so without too much bother I managed to sift through my day bag and draw it out and switch it on. I dialled the number that was written on the note, and after a brief pause a computerised woman told me that the call "could not be connected". This was highly inconvenient. I tried again in case I had dialled the wrong number. The same thing happened; the call "could not be connected". Hmmm. I tried one more time; just on the off chance I had accidentally misread the number on the scruffy note and had dialled the number for the soulless, bad news hotline.

I hadn't. This was not good. I then threw caution to the note and tried ringing the bell (yes, things were getting serious) but the bell didn't work. So I contravened the only other instruction on the crappy note and banged several times on the door. Still nothing. This was not the greatest welcome I had ever experienced while hostelling. I walked around to the back of the building where I found a gravel courtyard, a few piles of rubbish, and a deserted terrace. Things weren't improving. I went back around to the front of the house and gave a few more despairing bangs on the old wooden door, and then tried a couple more times with the phone number. It was all to no avail though, so I pulled out my map to assess my options. There was supposed to be an overpriced motel about seven kilometres north of the city. This was far from ideal, but that was it. There were no other hostels or even any other real accommodation alternatives at all. I had one last fruitless attempt at the phone number, cursed, and then I picked up my backpack and headed back out onto the street in the direction I had come from. As far as I could tell there was no life at this hostel, and I couldn't afford to hang about on the off chance someone would show up to let me in.

I slowly trudged up the road, keeping a keen eye out for any passing vans that may suddenly stop at the sight of me, and then from within its plain exterior hoards of wildly cheering hostel staff and travellers would jump out and scream and shout and hold banners that read; "Nearly had you! Welcome to London!" and then I'd jump in the van with them all and we'd drive past the crumbling old wreck of a building I'd just been standing forlornly outside of and we'd turn a corner and be at the *real* hostel that was actually a stunningly picturesque gothic castle by a lake and we would all have a barbeque in the sunny well-maintained gardens of the castle and eat, drink and dance until the early hours and they'd tell me how they had been playing this trick on backpackers for years and we'd all laugh and start face-painting or something. But that didn't happen. None of it. There wasn't even any indication that this was the type of town you could *buy* face-paints from!

As I approached the underpass I once again saw the group of undesirable looking people that made me decide to walk up the other side of the street. This time however, I saw the faded sign that was hanging from the building they were all lingering outside of. It read; "The Hope Centre", and there was something else below it about "second chances". Oh god. I upped my pace. I then noticed a shoe in the middle of the main road. A single shoe for god sake! Is there anything more terrifying?! I was out of here.

As I hurried through the underpass I got caught at the crossing. I stood there desperate to cross, but at no point did the fazing allow for pedestrians to walk. I looked back and saw some of the 'second chancers' starting to dissipate from their urban cluster, and some of them began to head in my direction. *Still* no opportunity to cross. By now a queue of traffic had formed in the lane beside me, and behind the wheel of one of the cars was a man staring menacingly at me. I could almost see the hate seeping from his eyes as he angrily revved his engine. To hell with this – I'm going.

I took a couple of rapid glances down each of the roads and then bolted for the other side. At least with my main backpack on my back and my day bag to the front if I was going to get hit I would be reasonably well padded.

Thankfully they were not needed, and I made it to the kerb intact. I headed back along York Street towards the bus station, praying the various twisted faces of new hope London were not in pursuit. Suddenly I noticed a big sign to my right. It was the railway station. I turned off sharply, leapt elegantly (stumbled scrappily) across the parking area, and piled through the entrance. The stark contrast hit me with a bang. Or maybe that was the door slamming against my backpack knocking me forward. The outside heat and humidity mixed with my frenetic escape antics had been dramatically replaced by a serene station lobby with soothing music and potted plants. I dragged myself over to the ticket desk and asked if there were any trains. Just any trains. I didn't care where they went.

'There's one leaving for Toronto right now' the man replied, nervously checking his watch. 'Do you want a ticket? You need to make a decision right now.'

As if I hadn't had enough pressure in the last half an hour!

'Errr…' I gave it a split second thought. 'Does it go on to Ottawa?'

I suddenly thought that I could jump ahead in my schedule and this was my next intended destination. The ticket man looked less than impressed with my questions.

'Errrm…yes.' He replied indecisively. 'But it stops at Toronto.'

This didn't make sense. Did it go or not? Anyway, there was clearly no time to explore the details. I wanted to leave as there were no more trains from London that day and so it had to be now, wherever it would take me.

'Okay! I'll go!' I burst out.

He grabbed his walkie-talkie and radioed in to a colleague to see if the train had left. It hadn't. He quickly printed me a ticket, I threw thousands of dollars at him in exchange, and then he said, 'Run!'

So I did. I stuffed the ticket and change in my pocket, thrust my bags over my shoulder and ran up the concourse in the direction of another slightly exasperated looking train employee. He guided me up a ramp and then I dived through the carriage door. I was on.

I found an empty seat, and as I collapsed into it an announcement came over the carriage tannoy system apologising for the delay in departure. Did they mean because of me? That was rude; it was only forty seconds behind schedule.

Anyway, I was happily escaping back east. I had been in London for fifty-two minutes. My mission to sandwich-hunt and to triangulate my home town's namesakes had gone horribly wrong.

To be honest I didn't even know what triangulating towns really meant, and from what I saw I bet the sandwiches in London were crap and overpriced. But it didn't matter anymore, because at least my problems were over.

Or so I thought…

Chapter 9

Saturday night on the town

Toronto, Ontario *(Round 2)*

*It is illegal in Canada to make burgers from polar bear meat.

Conversely; polar bears are not always unduly punished for eating human meat.

As the train rumbled along I began to relax after my quick and efficient escape from London. I had found a comfortable seat (actually all the seats looked pretty similar, but I'm sure mine was all the nicer having been made to run for it after a last minute escape plan) and I could sit back and enjoy the South-Western Ontario landscape as it serenely slid by the window. I removed my shoes as is always the first step to settling in to an extended period of seatedness, in an attempt at easing the backpackers' problem of 'travellers' hot-foot'.

'Travellers' hot-foot' occurs from frequent moving around in thick trekking socks and unforgiving footwear. A lack of breathability causes an uncomfortable heat build up in the foot and therefore creates the need to air the foot at every opportunity, regardless of the frowns and strange looks you may get from nearby people.

So with my shoes neatly stowed under my seat, I sat back and switched on my mp3 player and gazed out of the window. The scenery wasn't hugely compelling, and it didn't help that we stopped at a far from foreign sounding place called Aldershot. I hadn't travelled across the Atlantic to find these places. I wanted to visit places like Ottawa! Actually that was a good point - I'd been so caught up in escaping London that I hadn't really confirmed *where* I was in fact travelling on this train *to*. I searched around in my pocket and pulled out the ticket I'd hastily bought. I'd been unsure what exactly the fast-acting man on the ticket desk had sold me in the end, and so I was slightly surprised when I saw that I had a ticket to Ottawa. I was even *more* surprised that somehow I had paid $120 for it. *One hundred and twenty dollars*?! How the hell had *that* happened?! I'm *sure* I didn't have that much money! I could have *flown business class* for that much! Why weren't the train staff constantly bringing me glasses of champagne and giving my hot feet massages? I'd *clearly* paid enough! This was bad news indeed. I *thought* I was heading back to Toronto. Now I was in a predicament.

While in my dazed state of confusion and heat exhaustion I had enquired about going straight on to Ottawa, I had soon realised that this may not have been the best idea given that it would be a five hour trip through Ontario to the nation's capital, and therefore I wouldn't arrive there until close to midnight, and the station was quite a way from the city centre and so without a hostel reservation or a means of getting to the city I may encounter some problems.

Now I had a decision to make. I asked one of the train employees, and he confirmed we stopped at Toronto. So I could either get off and find somewhere to stay back in Canada's largest city – a city I knew quite well and that had plenty of accommodation options but where I would waste most of my ticket value, or I could board another train at Toronto and carry on to Ottawa, utilising my rash ticket purchase but risk being stranded on the city's outskirts.

I looked around me, hoping that my neighbouring passengers would step in and say something inspiring that would make my decision easier…or maybe if I stared hard out of the window I'd see something that would sway me towards one of the two destinations.

Nothing. *Useless*. It looked like it was all on me.

The clouds began to move in over Lake Ontario as we neared Toronto. I hope this wasn't a sign pre-empting the possible outcome of the decision that I would have to be making in the next twenty minutes. I starred at my ticket that sat on my lap before me, as if my focusing in on the printed information may cause it to change and offer up a solution.

No such luck. Stupid London. Look at the mess it's got me in.

I took a deep intake of breathe as a semi-audible indication to those around me that I was about to make an important decision, and also to maintain consciousness as I had realised that with all this complicated thinking I had forgotten to breathe for the best part of a minute. Well I'm male so I can't multitask…

Toronto. Yes. Despite the immense pain I felt at wasting a ticket I was sure that getting off in Toronto at a reasonable hour with its greater accommodation options and the station's central location was the sensible option. Done.

Well as I'm male I'm also decisive...

As the train doors opened I allowed the other passengers to "de-train" first (as is the phrasing they use here – much to my amusement) so that I had some clear aisle space in which to haul out my backpack from the luggage rack. I then ambled along the platform and up to the main station forecourt, where I once again took out my half-used ticket and had a glance at the back. It *did* say refunds were possible, but given that I had only bought the ticket two hours earlier and having used it to get to Toronto, *and* with the Ottawa train leaving in a few minutes it seemed highly unlikely I would gain anything. But I looked up to see that there wasn't a queue at the ticket window and so with nothing more to lose I made a timid enquiry.

'Yep, I can do that for you,' the man replied cheerily.

I was amazed. I honestly wasn't expecting to get anything other than a wildly flapping hand ushering me away and an instruction to stop wasting the ticket sales person's time.

This was brilliant! God I love the Canadian train network. Not only that but beside me was a lady getting hugely aggravated over a ticket she had bought, and she clearly wasn't getting her way as she kept swearing. I found this absolutely hilarious as I find it very difficult to take a swearing Canadian seriously – they just don't suit it. The ticket lady clearly didn't share this sentiment though, as she called station security, and so I left the ticket area before I got further entangled in this situation that was apparently "fucking retarded".

So here I was in a far more suitable location in which to find sleep after a hurriedly re-arranged plan, *and* I had just been handed eighty dollars! Things were on the up. Now I just had the small task of finding a bed for the night...

* * *

I was feeling a little weary as I made my way out of the grand hall of Toronto's Central Station, despite sporting an eighty-dollar smile. It was just after six o'clock in the evening, but it was still pretty hot and humid as I set off in the direction of a hostel I had heard about from a few other travellers I'd met a couple of days earlier. I fancied a change from the hostel I'd been at before (plus I didn't feel like another seven storey stair climb after the day I'd had) and so I headed north-west through the downtown streets of the city, as the buzz of an impending Saturday night out began to build in the bars and restaurants around the towering office blocks that lined my route.

After a fifteen minute walk and a couple of wrong turns thanks to the comedy stylings of the tourist map I unfortunately had to rely on, I arrived at the hostel I was looking for. It looked pretty busy as people made there way around the lobby area while they arranged their evening plans. I walked up to reception and waited patiently as the man ahead of me made his enquiry to the lady on the desk. I was certainly looking forward to ditching my bags and then going off in search of a cold beverage that I could slowly consume in the evening sunshine and reflect upon the day's ups and downs.

Soon the man was finished and I stepped up to the desk.

'Could I have a bed for the night please' I said, mustering up as much cheerfulness as I was capable of given how tired I felt.

'I'm afraid we're full tonight' the lady replied, scrunching up her face in an attempt at portraying as much sympathy as someone can when delivering bad news regarding an issue they really couldn't give a sh*t about.

It did little to soften the blow. What did she mean they were full? It was the *off* season. Toronto had no major draws in Spring – that was another reason for being here at this time of year. Was there a sandwich convention going on that I had inexcusably not heard about?

I stood slightly bewildered at the desk for a few seconds before lying to the lady.

'Okay, thank you.'

But I wasn't remotely thankful. This was highly inconvenient. I picked up my bags and shuffled out of the narrow entrance way and back on to the street.

As I made my way out the lady had slightly redeemed herself by saying that there was another hostel a couple of blocks away, and so I checked my map and set off once again on my quest for a bed for the night.

A few minutes later, and after another standard brief misdirection thanks to the map, I was in the reception area at the hostel. It had only been a couple of blocks away but you could have been fooled by the fact that everyone in here was Irish. I'd not met any Irish people up until now (in Canada that is), but here was an Irishman getting directions to a nearby bar (shocking), another group of Irish girls on the computers to my right, and even the guy that greeted me on reception was from the *Emerald Isle*.

They talk about the "luck of the Irish", and I could have done with a bit right there and then, but it wasn't to be.

'Hi, do you have any beds available for tonight?' I asked with a slightly less confident tone creeping into my voice.

And then came the response I wasn't really expecting, but I was nevertheless fearing.

'Sorry, we're all booked up tonight.'

Shit.

'We have some female beds available - for girls' he hastily added on the end - just in case I wasn't aware of what constituted a female in this country.

Fantastic. Can I leave my bags here while I go and get a gender-switch operation?

'I don't think that's going be of much use.' I replied. Trying my best to suppress both my disappointment and frustration, as well as the sarcastic undertones that had appeared in my speech.

'We've got space tomorrow night though.' He chipped in, clearly trying to redeem himself.

'Great. Can I check in early? As in today?'

'Errr…'

'Don't worry.' I sighed. 'Do you know of any hostels that will have space tonight?'

And with that he took my map from me, and far from confidently circled a seemingly random point in China Town.

And so once again I made my way out of the door, having at least secured a bed for tomorrow night, but still with little progress on finding accommodation for *this* night.

What the hell was going on? Why were these hostels full? There was nothing special about today or this weekend. I trudged along the lively Dundas Street and then made the right hand turn up the wide Spadina Street, with its tram lines and groups of weekend party goers. I was getting very hot now, and increasingly bothered while I'm skirting around that common word-pair phrase.

It was a tiring fifteen minutes of fighting my way through the crowds as I made my way into the heart of China Town. The strong smell of spices drifting out from neighbouring restaurants and eateries, reminded me that I was getting increasingly hungry. A bed was the priority now though, everything else had to wait. I turned left into a slightly quieter side street, and I began eagerly assessing each of the buildings I passed as I was now in the area where this latest hostel was supposedly in. There was no sign of a backpackers' haven down here though. Tiny shop fronts held little promise of supplying low-cost accommodation to the tired and needy. It didn't strike me as the nicest part of town either, or though in retrospect this was probably largely down to the girl that came charging down the pavement towards me with the most horrific look upon her face and a truly frightening sound emanating from her mouth. It was like something from *The Omen*. Could *this* be a *bad* omen? It certainly wasn't a *positive* occurrence.

A few more streets gave little indication that I was getting any closer to a good nights sleep, and I was beginning to despair and get increasing angry with the man from the previous hostel for his crap directions. I soon found myself in a grubby back street market where I decided to ask someone if they were aware of any hostel in the nearby area.

A very enthusiastic Chinese couple stepped up to the plate, and after calling together what appeared to be a family conference, they were soon gabbling on in what I have to assume was Chinese while they decided what it was I needed and where I needed to go.

72

After what seemed like several minutes of frantic discussion, they turned to me to announce their findings.

'Washing?' the man tentatively asked.

I sighed deeply. Unfortunately this was far from high on my list of priorities, but given the effort that they had gone to in order to help me, I duly took some rather peculiar and conflicting directions from the group, thanked them as sincerely as I could given the circumstances, and then I headed off again. It was no use. This hostel did not appear to exist. It was now getting on for seven thirty, and I conceded I was running out of time, energy and spirit. I had one last throw of the dice.

I was out of options. I had to lug my bags back down through the bustling streets of China town, through the financial district and over to the city's east side where I had been based for my previous nights in Toronto. It took a good forty minutes to retrace my steps along the now all too familiar main streets that ran in perpendicular directions across the city, and by the time I finally arrived on Church Street I had a nice greasy coating across my forehead. I pushed my way awkwardly through the glass door of the hostel, and once again slumped my bags down by the wall opposite reception and stood in line. It had only been that morning that I had checked out of this hostel, but it seemed so long ago now, and it certainly hadn't been my plan to return so quickly.

When the lady in front had finished purchasing an internet token I stepped up and made the all too familiar enquiry, but no sooner had I finished my favourite opening line of the evening than the lady screwed up her face in that again all too familiar fashion, and my hopes were crushed once more. I starred despairingly at my map while the lady sifted through some papers in a draw and found a list of alternative accommodation in the city. She kindly offered to phone a few of them, some of which I'd already visited, and others that drifted dangerously into the 'hotel' category that my wallet would not have thanked me for visiting. Apparently there was a single room available in a hostel, but when I asked her where it was she was a little unsure and pointed to a vague collection of side streets in China Town. I let out an ironic laugh and told her not too worry. The only other option was a hotel a couple of blocks north from where we were. She said the person who ran it wasn't very nice, and after phoning the place it was confirmed that he was indeed a miserably sod, but that they did have rooms available. I thanked her and wandered back out onto the street for this last desperate attempt.

I meandered along Church Street and before too long I found myself outside of a slightly dodgy looking hotel. It wasn't the one I had been heading for, but it looked pretty rundown which could only make life easier on my finances. I walked up the rapidly deteriorating concrete staircase, but no sooner had I stumbled through the doorway then I was heading back out again. They were fully booked. Great.

I carried on up the road, my back aching relentlessly from carrying around all my belongings for the past three hours. I found the place that I had been heading for originally, and after the usual patient wait in the lobby, I stepped up in my role as the tired homeless traveller in the nativity.

Nothing. No rooms, no beds. Not even a stable out the back. I couldn't believe it. Even Mary and Joseph didn't have to put up with this crap. How had they had space ten minutes ago when the hostel had phoned through but now they hadn't? In my tired state I was starting to get a bit paranoid and I began to wonder weather it was my far from presentable appearance as a weary dishevelled backpacker that was not appealing to reception staff. Was I getting rejected because of this?

I semi-stormed out of the hotel, hoping to rub mud into the smart carpets that lined the entrance way, but in actual fact my shoes were very clean so it just caused me to scuff my foot on the floor which merely served to make my exit far from slick.

A couple more blocks later and a couple more instantaneous rejections from hotels and things were getting seriously desperate. I was *really* starting to go off this city, and I was *really* starting to hate my backpack. The worst part was that I didn't even *want* to stay at a hotel. There was no way I could feasibly afford their expensive rates, and what's more I liked hostel life, so it was really a no win situation, and yet somehow I was still losing badly.

I was now basing my search around crudely illuminated signs that hung on tall buildings to give an indication of possible accommodation. In one last attempt I found my way onto one of the cities liveliest streets, where I was bombarded by hyped-up revellers that I had to fight my way around with a backpack that was seemingly ever increasing in weight with every rejection I was dealt. Nothing. I was out of options. Every bed in Toronto was booked out tonight for some inexplicable reason. Unless you were a girl of course. I never expected my gender to hold me back so much on this trip.

I was pretty exasperated by now as I escaped from the neon lit haze of Toronto's party district and headed back to what I later found out was the part of the city that should be avoided. I should have realised at the time given the number of people who approached me and asked for money, but to be honest they only ever looked as scruffy as me. There was a nice irony to it too, as these street folk, with their hands cupped, eyes hopeful of a late night monetary offering, were greeted by me; someone who was himself homeless on this hot North American night.

It was time to take serious action. I had to face the fact that I wasn't going to find 'normal' accommodation for the night, and so I had to consider other alternatives. I stopped on a street corner (steady, that wasn't one of my options) while I thought through a couple of ideas in my head. I *could* go to the beach area. It had a clean artificial beach *and* sun beds, although how nice it would be in the dark, and more significantly how warm it would be in the early hours of the morning was debateable. I could head over to the station. I wasn't sure how late it was open to, but it may provide a bit of shelter for a couple more hours. Maybe I could head back to the hostel on Church Street and stay around in the seating area until they kicked me out. None of these were ideal, but I had to do something. I thought for a few more tiring seconds, and then I decided on a plan. I would head back to the hostel where I had been last night.

On my way I stopped off at a late night corner shop and picked up some refreshments. I was by now very tired, very hungry, very sore, and in great need of a toilet. I dumped my bag outside the shop as I attempted to cram my purchases into my day bag. Unfortunately the day's frustrations led to some rather over-zealous cramming, which in turn led to one of the zips on my bag breaking. This was massively annoying, but luckily the bag featured a double zip design, which left one functional zip left on the main pocket. Things had not gone well today.

I dragged my body and bags down Church Street once again, and piled through the door of the hostel. I went over to the lady I had dealt with previously at reception and politely explained to her how everyone had screwed me over in the past twelve hours. I then asked if I could utilise one of the large lockers that sat opposite the desk. She said yes. Finally, a positive answer. And so I dropped my bags to the floor, pulled out my wash kit and a couple of warm sweatshirts from my main backpack and stuffed it into a locker. I was now free of most of my gear, which was quite literally a weight off my shoulders. Job one; done.I then picked up my remaining belongings and headed out of the hostel. I had ridden "The Rocket" into the city just a few days before, and that had given me an idea. I set off towards King Street metro station.

I was going back to the airport.

Chapter 10

A short lesson in negotiating armrests

Toronto Airport, Ontario

It is illegal in Canada to change gear in a public vehicle while crossing a railroad.

So keep an eye out when you're on the bus...

I was off again, but this time I was more confident of finding a base for the night – albeit a slightly less comfortable one than I had planned. I had decided that having walked across the city for over four hours my best option was to head to the airport. I wasn't going to fly home, and nor was I going to attempt to sneak into a suitcase and sleep in amongst someone's neatly folded clothing while I was seamlessly delivered to another exciting destination. Although that does sound quite fun. No, my aim was far less exciting (but arguably slightly more practical).

If there's one thing I've learnt from travelling (which isn't actually the case. For instance; did you know that Air Canada is Canada's largest airline? Shocking, isn't it?) it's that I know airports are usually safe havens for homeless backpackers.

On numerous occasions I have found myself with time to waste at airports due to flight delays/early arrivals/love of airport architecture/secret desire to ride along an empty baggage reclaim belt to see what's on the other side…etc. and so I was confident that the terminal building would provide me with shelter for the night, as well as the all important 'Three W's'; warmth, washrooms, and water fountains. They are also normally pretty clean places – not that this was hugely important, and it might even have been a little hypocritical to require this given my current state. I found the subway entrance on King Street and descended into the dark depths of Toronto's subway system. It was actually very light and airy down there, and *not that* far below street level at all, but I thought that an alliterative cliché would add drama to the event.

I boarded the next train west, and sat down as I considered the night ahead of me. It wasn't a hugely inviting prospect though, and so I quickly turned my attention to the adverts that stretched out along the side of the carriage. Sorry, I mean "car" (that's Canadian for "carriage").

The deep concentration that I had been applying to find out the quickest and cheapest way to lose all that excess pregnancy weight I had been carrying around with me needlessly (brightly coloured pills are apparently the answer) was irritatingly disrupted by a noisy bunch of girls who had invaded my car a couple of stops after I'd got on, and who were all now sprawled out across the seats beside and opposite me. They were obviously in high spirits having completed another hard week of not learning anything, as the seven of them collectively hadn't known that Washington D.C. was not actually in Washington State. Luckily I was on hand to hand out a handy handful of insight into the layout of the U.S., for which they were all massively grateful. They might have been a bit short on their place-name knowledge, but they were certainly well trained at faking enthusiasm for it in the far from educational setting of the Toronto metro at quarter past ten on a Saturday night.

Another fifteen minutes and an uneventful second trip on 'The Rocket' bus and I was back outside the airport terminal building. It was going to be strange to go into an airport knowing that I wasn't flying off anywhere, but I decided that only spending four days in the second largest county in the world might not be doing it justice. I also had only had *one* real sandwich! It would never do. I gathered up my bags from the forecourt and made my way through the highly polished glass doors that led onto the vast and minimalist setting of the terminal check-in area. Home sweet home!

There was a strange sense of satisfaction and relief at being here. I was pleased that I had thought of this alterative to a night on the streets (and it had the added bonus of being free!), and I was also glad that I could finally use the toilet, as I was finding it increasingly difficult to stand fully upright after thirteen hours of holding it in.

At home we call the rooms that house toilets "toilets", but in Canada they call them "washrooms", which is probably one of the craziest things in the world ever, but as I was looking pretty grubby I did what its name suggested I should do, and I washed, much to the amusement of a couple of late night airport employees who happened to pass through. I had come prepared though; I had my travel towel and my toothbrush, and so I came out a few minutes later positively sparkling. Some would say I looked fit for a royal ball. Well, if you excuse the fact that I wasn't wearing any shoes anyway.

Having got cleaned up, I found an inviting row of seats near the window, and soon I had made myself at home, with my shoes neatly placed underneath the seats, and my jacket folded carefully beside them. I was all set.

* * *

I'll be honest with you - the night was long. Fair enough I was warm, and despite an underlying fear that I could be escorted from the terminal building by a heavily armed group of security personnel at any moment I was actually left unhassled for the whole duration of my time there. I'm not going to go as far as saying that I could relax and catch up on some much needed sleep though. The seats that I had found may have been plentiful in number (and strangely unoccupied at 3am) but unfortunately they all had armrests. This is great if you want to rest your arm, but bloody inconvenient if you want to rest any other part of your body. The triangular shape of the armrests meant that there was an awkward gap between the diagonal of the plastic and the seat underneath, making a relaxing horizontal lying position far from possible. I considered unscrewing the armrests to rectify this issue, but I quickly released that I had left my penknife with its trusty fold out crosshead screwdriver attachment back in the hostel locker. I then also noticed that the armrests were metal and welded into position, and therefore lacking in any screws that could have been unscrewed. So basically *I* was screwed. I'm not one to give up though, and within a few minutes I had managed to adopt a hugely unnatural position where by I was spread across three seats with my body wedged under the two divisional armrests at the hip and ankle positions. I then used my jacket and fleece as a pillow, and soon I was passing the time in relative discomfort and with the constant fear that I may fall off at any moment. I also had the added distraction of the intermittent beeping from the floor cleaner as it did its half-hourly rounds through the building. Maybe I could have adopted a more glamorous airport lifestyle like Tom Hanks in *The Terminal* if I had of had more ingenuity, but in all honesty I wasn't intending on making a habit of living in airports on this trip, despite the obvious financial benefits.

During the night I employed regular positional rotations as various parts of my body began to ache unforgivingly or go numb. I also did some light reading (which meant I wasn't really paying attention to, or absorbing what I was reading) and I occasionally scribbled in my notebook, every so often treating myself to a sock-glide over to the water fountain to suppress the dehydration caused by the days antics. It was a fun night all round really.

Eventually morning came, or rather the sun came bursting through the large expanse of glass that lined the front of the terminal and ended any hope of sleep, and so I got up and went about my morning routine of getting changed and washed up. I did this in the washroom you'll understand; I didn't just start removing my clothes in the presence of the queue of passengers waiting to check-in for the 6.40 to Frankfurt.

* * *

It was a little later, and I was playing an enthralling game of solitaire with myself using the pack of cards I always carried around with me while I was travelling. I was having a positively thrilling game when I was given an awful shock by my Canadian phone as it started ringing. I'd only had the phone a couple of days and there weren't many people who knew I had it. As a result I normally had it switched off, but I must have turned it on out of boredom last night, and now here it was making strange polyphonic noises at me. I quickly dug it out of my pocket and looked at the screen. This gave no indication of who might be calling, and so I started pressing at the button that I assumed would allow me to speak with the person on the other end, and ultimately find out who they were, and what they wanted.

No such luck. Despite pressing several buttons that looked likely as being the one that would facilitate conversation, the phone just continued to ring, with no voice to greet me at the other end. I started to panic as I began mashing wildly at the keypad in an increasingly desperate attempt to connect with my mystery caller. Who could it be? It might be someone telling me important news; such as an anonymous tip-off that I was being hunted down by airport administration for the excessive and literal use of the washrooms! Or *maybe* someone was trying to contact me to tell me that I had just won the Canadian lottery and that I had to claim the prize within the next thirty minutes or the vast some of money would be given to the nearest motorway service station sandwich chef! I couldn't let this happen. C'mon dammit! Speak to me!

It was no use. I pressed every button *at least* twice and I *even shook* the handset a few times, but it was all to no avail. I'd used phones before, but this one had got the beating of me. In the end I just placed the ringing handset on the seat opposite me, and put my head in my hands in an act of utter despair.

I'm sure the people around me must have thought I was trying to avoid a difficult situation that answering the call would trigger. Perhaps they thought that I was at the airport to fly off and escape a problem back home. Oh, if only they knew. If only they knew that I was in fact embroiled in an international quest to track down a sandwich, and that I hadn't just got of a plane, and that I had *no intention* of flying *anywhere*. If only they knew how much I wanted to answer that damn phone but I just couldn't work out how to. If only I hadn't been so sleep deprived…

Eventually the phone stopped ringing. It was all over - I'd missed my chance. I then decided that as it was 9.30am and as I had now been camped out at the airport for eleven hours I should probably leave. So I picked up my useless uncommunicative phone, packed up my cards, and went back to 'Pillar R' and got back on "The Rocket".

Chapter 11

There's no such thing as a free boat trip

Toronto, Ontario (Yup, I'm still here)

*It is illegal in Canada to publicly remove bandages.

Well it would be terrible if your arm fell off while you were out in the park one afternoon…

I arrived back in the city drained and tired, but I knew I wouldn't be able to check in to the new hostel until the afternoon and so I continued to stroll around downtown Toronto. I found a "shopping mall" (that's a shopping centre in Canadian) where I wandered around the shops with limited interest. I used the washrooms where I was surprised to find the *XLerator* hand dryers that I thought only existed in airports. As you can probably tell, I was having a slow morning.

A little later on and I was walking in a dazed state down by the harbour front when a man suddenly appeared in front of me.
  'Hi! Where are you from?' the very smiley person burst out enthusiastically – like a man who had gotten at least eight hours sleep last night.

'Errr…the airport.' I muttered under my breath, while trying to shield my eyes from the sun and work out who this silhouetted figure was and why he was blocking my path.

'What? Are you English? Great! Do you wanna go on a free boat trip?'

After twenty-eight hours without sleep this was a difficult situation to take in, especially as he seemed to have progressed through several stages of the conversation without my input. I also had the sun in my eyes. That never helps.

'Erm…' I literarily wasn't sure how to respond to all this, and the wildly smiling man clearly sensed I had my doubts and so he filled my stuttering pause with more sales talk – all whilst maintaining his smile of course.

'It's a completely free forty minute sail around the harbour. No catch. No obligation. It leaves in thirty minutes!'

He just wouldn't stop smiling.

Now, normally I'm suspicious of these offers, especially when they say "no catch", and "no obligation", as that usually implies the *exact opposite* in the oxymoronic world of sales and marketing speak. Also, when you travel in certain parts of the world you are often bombarded with great offers that usually involve you winding up with significantly less in your wallet than you started with, and usually nothing to show for it other than a novelty straw hat. Don't ask – it's just always the way.

Anyway, Canada didn't strike me as a novelty straw hat wearing country, and so I let this man convince me that this boat trip really was the offer I had been waiting for – the moment that my fortunes changed after twenty-four hours of bad luck and cock-ups. Could this be a sign…?

I was still waiting for the catch though, and eventually I managed to divert him away from the small talk and I discovered that if I really enjoyed my free boat trip I could sign up for sailing lessons.

Hmmm, that sounded a plausible reason; a free trial in which you fall in love with sailing, and then you return to shore and decide to give up your nine to five office job for a life of boom mast ducking and starboard anchor drops – all neatly provided under the costly supervision of *Wacky Smiles Sailing Club*. Everyone's a winner.

'Okay' I finally said, resignedly.

'Great! See you back here at one!'

And with that the man and his smile were gone.

I continued to walk along the harbour front with my spirits lifted by the fine weather, the pleasant surroundings, and now this opportunity to fill some of the time before I could check in to the new hostel with a trip out onto the water to get a new viewing perspective of the city. Maybe things really *were* starting to pick up.

I stopped by a clean, white stone wall that ran along the promenade and undid my bag to get out my water bottle. As I did this though, the zip on my bag – the *one remaining* zip on my bag – broke off. For the second time in four hours I dropped my face into my hands - which initially sounds like a terribly unpleasant event that would require urgent medial assistance - but actually if you act it out I'm sure you'll realise that it is simply a turn of phrase, and more significantly an action that pretty accurately summed up how I felt at that moment.

Could *this* be a sign? Maybe things hadn't picked up. It certainly didn't feel like it now that my bag was wide open and all my belongings were quickly distributing themselves across the footpath.

I sighed. I sighed heavily.

I grudgingly collected up my various travel documents and tourist paraphernalia and stuffed them back into the bag. Luckily it had a waterproof attachment that looped over the main body of the bag to protect it from rain/snow/bears, and this provided a temporary seal. It wasn't ideal though, and I knew this now meant I had to buy a new bag.

85

By the time I had finished with the zip-breaking episode and I had consumed some faith-restoring water from my water bottle, it was time to head back to the harbour to go on the free boat trip.

I arrived from a different direction to the one in which I had left so that I could demonstrate my unpredictable nature. It was also more convenient. Within seconds I was ambushed by the smiley man, and he guided me into a small wooden cabin where he instructed me to put on a lifejacket. I did so with all the professionalism of an experienced sea captain, and then he led me outside again and pointed at a boat just off the shoreline, telling me that this was the one we would be sailing on at one o'clock. He then said to wait over by a wooden bench where the boat would arrive, before he scuttled off, presumably to tempt other passer-bys with the delightful offer of a free sailing excursion.

As I stood there in my bright orange lifejacket I studied the boat that was to be our vessel at one o'clock. It was now three minutes *past* one, and the boat had now changed direction and was heading off along the harbour front and away from the jetty where we were supposed to be boarding. This was odd. It was then that I turned around to see a wooden fold-out sign that I hadn't noticed before. It was advertising a free forty-minute boat ride around the harbour. That sounded familiar. Maybe the sign was having a competition with the man. I'm not sure it was being as proactive as the man. It certainly wasn't smiling as much. Anyway, I was about to look away again to see where the boat that we would be boarding three minutes ago had got to, when I saw a sentence at the bottom of the sign that caught my eye. It read;

"SUGGESTED MINIMUM DONATION: $15"

I was stunned. *Surely* you can't have a suggested minimum *anything*? That *must* be an oxymoron. And "*suggested* donation"? Those two words don't fit together either. This was ridiculous.

Those three words formed a triple contradiction. But more importantly – the smiley man had lied to me. He had *specifically* and on numerous occasions *clearly stated* that this trip was *free*. I don't know if different people have varying levels as to what constitutes "free", but mine was definitely less than $15. About $15 less to be precise.

I was suddenly very angry. I was heavily sleep deprived, my bag was now broken and required replacing (which was extra hassle and an expense I hadn't planned for – not to mention the constant risk I faced of losing all of its contents across the stylish wooden promenade with every weary step I undertook) our supposed boat had gone awol, and now I had been *lied to* as well. This was the final straw.

So you know what I did? No. You're wrong. I *didn't* stand for it. I *didn't* purse my lips, fake a smile and continue with the boat trip and then get fleeced on my return to dry land. I *didn't* politely explain my predicament and try to wiggle out of it. No. I snuck off. That's right – I took a couple of quick glances around me to check the coast was clear of the smiley man and his crew of scamming pirates, and I dived into the wooden cabin where I dispensed hurriedly of my lung-restricting beacon of a lifejacket. I then took one more sweeping glance out through the doorway to scope the best escape route, before running off down the promenade and behind the harbour information kiosk. I had done it! I had avoided the wrath of the rogue sailing club! It felt good. I also wasn't aware that I was still capable of 'sneaking' anymore. I thought it was something you could only do up to the age of nine. Well, I proved that wrong!

Now I was free of that tourist trap I could continue with my day. Unfortunately this meant leaving behind the exciting world of covert operations and replacing it with the mundane business of finding and purchasing a new bag.

I guess it was convenient that I had been in a shopping centre only a few hours before, as I now knew where I should head to find a new bag. It was another hot day in South-Western Ontario, and I was getting pretty sticky by the time I walked through the automatic doors of the *Eaton Centre*, briefly receiving a pleasant cooling blast from the air conditioning system above. I scoured the passing outlets in search of somewhere that may sell bags, spending an irritatingly long time negotiating my way around the massive *Sears* department store without success. Eventually I gave up and found an information desk, where an information lady kindly gave me the information and directions to a relevant shop. Soon I was surrounded by bags, and being given a detailed demonstration of how all the bags worked by an enthusiastic Australian. He showed me a whole variety of different models that suited different activities and size requirements. I did a lot of authoritative nodding, which if you've never done before can be a daunting skill to master, but it is well worth learning. It paid off for me, because by seeing my no nonsense approach to bag shopping he didn't mess around trying to sell me the most expensive bags with all the unnecessary features such as endless secret zip pockets. You'll be familiar by now with my feeling towards zips. Instead he let me play around with the various strap clips and prod the bags in a highly sophisticated manner at my leisure.

A few minutes later and I was leaving the shop with my new flashy yellow and grey backpack on my back. I had successfully found a replacement that fitted my needs and I had transferred all my belongings into it having ditched my old bag. All in all it was a pretty satisfactory shopping trip, although it cost me the equivalent of two nights accommodation, and thus ruined the good work I'd done by saving a night's accommodation by staying at the airport last night.

By the time I had done all this it was mid-afternoon, and so I reckoned I could check into the hostel. I made my way back across to the east side of the city, collected my main backpack, and then set off back west through the city to the Irish sub-continent hostel. I checked in, got cleaned up, and then took a walk around the neighbouring streets before heading to bed after thirty-seven hours of being awake.

* * *

The next morning I was excited to discover that breakfast was included, and so I found my way through to the bar area where a man was sitting on a stool cooking pancakes. He asked how many I wanted, and I said two. He seemed pretty miserable. He told me he was from Aylesbury. I'm not suggesting the two were linked.

After a pretty basic but nonetheless enjoyable breakfast I packed up my stuff and went to check out. Having done this, I was about to walk out the door when someone called out behind me.

'Is your name Chris?'

I stopped, looked down at the details on my baggage tag. It was!

I turned around to the guy who I presumed to be the one who had spoken and replied 'Yes!'

'I thought it was!' he retuned cheerily.

'Is your name Jack?'

Now it was my turn.

'Yeah, it is!'

We were good at this game.

We quickly realised that we both knew each other from school back home. It *really is* a cliché, but it *really is* a small world.

And so after a few minutes of lively chat about our trips and what brought us to Canada, we said goodbye and I strode out of the hostel entrance towards the station. It was time to leave Toronto, and this time I didn't plan on coming back…for *at least*…a *while*.

Chapter 12

Beware of the leaf-puncher!

Ottawa, Ontario

*It is illegal in Canada to pay more than fifty cents in pennies.

Which can be pretty annoying, as you end up with a lot of pennies clogging up your wallet space thanks to the odd pricing of goods resulting from tax additions.

Boarding a train in Canada is not like boarding a train in England. In England you buy a ticket from either an electronic ticket machine, or from someone behind the ticket window (or if you're fancy you can book it online and have it posted to you). Once you have your ticket, you scan it through the turnstile before making your way onto the platform, and then the train pulls up and you get on. All these exciting processes can happen within a period of *literally* minutes.

This is *not* how it works in Canada. In Canada you generally pre-book your ticket (in the case of my special rail pass it must be at least three days prior to your intended day of travel) and it comes in the form of a large airline style boarding pass. You then arrive a good half an hour before the 'boarding time' that is displayed on the large departure board that hangs from the roof of the grander stations, locate the queue that has formed at the designated gate (the number of which is printed on your ticket), and then you wait as the smartly dressed train employees scrutinise your ticket before guiding you to your specific "car". They'll even hold your hand for you if you like.

Throughout your journey there is at least one attendant providing assistance in each car, who will also give the "chosen ones" a detailed guide on how to break the windows in an emergency. All this takes a lot of time, especially when the trains only move at twelve kilometres an hour. They are *seriously* slow. From all this I quickly got the impression that the train was not the predominant form of getting around the country, which was more or less confirmed by the number of Canadians who turned to me for assistance on how each part of the ticket purchasing and boarding process worked.

Despite my gripes over the excessive grandeur that is part and parcel of Canadian train travel, the journey was pleasant, with large comfortable seats, plenty of leg room, spacious luggage racks, and even power sockets for laptops by each seat. They also provided a free wi-fi connection service. The train attendants were also all very pleasant.

I passed the three-hour journey to the Canadian capital by listening to music and watching the flat scenery as it slowly trickled past the window, utilising the large under seat space to store my shoes. It was a hot day - travellers' hot-foot strikes again.

* * *

It was mid-afternoon when we finally came to a stop at Ottawa station. I re-attached my shoes, dragged my backpack out of the luggage racks, and made by way across the station forecourt to the bus stop. A short wait and I was soon bouncing along inside the number 91 bus heading downtown, with the sun beating down on my shoulders through the window as I studied the map I had open on my lap as I tried to get my bearings.

Soon a lady spoke up having seen my touristy appearance, saying 'Are you looking for the hostel?'

I was! She had me sussed good. She went on to tell me exactly where I needed to "de-bus", pointing out the hostel as we arrived at the stop on top of a bridge.

I thanked her, collected my bags, and got off – hanging around on the bridge just long enough for the bus to pull away again so that the lady would be out of sight when I walked away from the hostel, as it wasn't the one that I was booked to stay at but I didn't want to hurt her feelings or make her think I was stupid. I should have guessed there would have been more than one hostel.

As I made my way through the streets of Ottawa I was finding it increasingly difficult to see where I was going. The sun was hovering in the clear afternoon sky and shining directly into my eyes. This resulted in me getting ever closer to being run over at each road junction I crossed. To tackle this problem I dropped my bags to the pavement and began hunting about in them for my sunglasses.

I had been rummaging around for a good minute or two with limited success when I was interrupted by a voice beside me.

'Hi! Where are you from?' a chirpy female Canadian accent enquired.

Oh god. There weren't seriously any boats around here, were there?

'England...' I cautiously responded, as I stood up to face a small excitable girl with a clipboard.

'Cool! Let's sit on the wall and have a chat!'

And we did. I was in no hurry, and the fruitless search for my sunglasses had worn me out considerably, so I saw no harm in letting her babble on for a few minutes about whatever it was she was trying to get me to sign up to until I had caught my breath and found my sunglasses.

Surprisingly she didn't try and inflict anything on me though. She seemed happy just chatting about travelling and how she thought people in Western Canada were nicer than those in the east – except in Halifax (on the east coast) where she was from - they were apparently the nicest people of all.

She carried on with her enthusiastic assessment of all things Canada when she was suddenly interrupted by a smartly dressed woman who had stopped on the pavement in front of us. She was Parisian, and she wanted to know which bus stop she needed to be at to get to...somewhere. Maybe Paris, I'm not sure, but bizarrely, the girl who had been so keen to chat to me about seemingly nothing in particular suddenly jumped up and walked off with the lady, leaving me sitting on a wall on a busy street in the city. This was most peculiar, but I shrugged it off, and presumed I was now free to continue with my walk to the hostel, realising that having just loaded up my bags I still hadn't gotten out my sunglasses.

I found the hostel in a nice leafy suburban street. It was a tidy looking wooden house with a terrace out the front. I walked through the door and was greeted by racks of shoes. I instantly assumed that this was a shoe swap rack, much like the book swap shelves that many hostels provide. This was excellent, because I was pretty fed up of my shoes and there appeared to be some pretty nice ones on offer here. Unfortunately, just as I was eyeing up a swanky looking pair of *Merrill* trail shoes I noticed the sign by the stairs that asked all guests to remove their shoes upon entry. Damn. It was just a rack for residents to store their shoes. It looked like I would be stuck with these grubby sole-destroyers for a bit longer.

I did what it asked and then moved on into the house. There was a large lounge with a television on the right, and at the end of the hall was a kitchen. From seemingly out of nowhere a man, who turned out to be Mexican started asking me lots of questions. He was very friendly, but after the day's journeying I wasn't quite up for the Hispanic inquisition that he was submitting me to. Anyway, soon he shuffled off, and having checked in I was told that they were having a barbeque this evening, so I should pick up some meat and join in. I didn't need asking twice. I dropped my bags in my appointed dorm room and headed out for a stroll around the city.

I walked along a few nearby streets that were lined with lively bars and cafes, with people sitting outside in extended seating areas that spilt out onto the road. My map informed me that this was the area known as Byward Market. Beyond this I found myself in a very pleasant park, with winding tarmac pathways leading through well-kept and colourful flowerbeds and grass patches. Ornate buildings stood next to park, and having reached the other side I could see down to a canal below, and then looking up and across I could see the parliament building standing dramatically on the aptly named 'Parliament Hill' opposite. From here I continued along a raised peninsula, where I took silhouetted photographs of a statue in the slow-setting evening sun. I then walked over the large iron-built Alexandra Bridge that ran across the river, which I later discovered formed the border with the province of Quebec. There seemed to be little to distinguish the transition between provinces, but there was a subtle switch between signs written in English and *then* French in Ontario, to the French translation taking precedence once you crossed over into the French speaking Quebec.

I checked my watch and realised that it was nearly half seven and that I was hungry. To be honest it was less of my watch telling me that I was hungry, and more of the frequent rumblings that were making my stomach reverberate. I made my way back towards the supermarket that was conveniently only a block away from the hostel, taking a different route from the one I had come from because I am exciting and adventurous.

I was walking down the busy Rideau Street through the centre of town when I began to notice a large array of homeless people shuffling about. Most were appealing to passer-bys for money, but one particularly dishevelled man was simply bashing a decorative metal fence with the back of a small wooden brush. This was odd, and more importantly it was a complete waste of energy. It's a sad day when someone who was old enough to have a long, thick, grey beard doesn't know the correct operational procedure for a brush.

Further down the street I encountered an *even more* outrageous scene of street-abuse than that provided by the brush-basher - I saw a leaf puncher! Oh yes, you heard me right - a *genuine leaf-puncher*! Here was a man drifting irrationality all over the sidewalk ahead of me, punching leaves on the trees that overhung the pavement. It was truly terrifying. I upped my pace, and after a slightly nervy overtaking manoeuvre I was thankfully soon diving through the revolving doors of the supermarket to safety.

* * *

That evening the hostel's various guests and employees all gathered in the rear courtyard where an appetising selection of steak accompanied by pasta salad was prepared and cooked on the barbeque, before being duly consumed in the warm evening air in between swigs of frosty beer from the neighbouring bottle shop.

After we had finished eating I found a pack of cards on a bookshelf in the lounge, and soon it was decided that we would have a poker match. Now I'm not going to claim that I'm a hugely proficient poker player, and it was quite daunting when I learnt that we were playing for such high steaks. No, not *actual* steaks - they had all been eaten, but we would each be putting in two dollars! *Two dollars*! That's a day's eating budget or a seat reservation on a short domestic flight! Scary stuff. This was real pressure. I felt more nerves in the early rounds of this game than if you'd thrown me into a windowless room with only the brush-basher and the leaf-puncher for company.

The game quickly got going, and it turned out to be a lot of fun. The game had a nice International vibe to it too, being as it was contested by three Germans, a Mexican, a Dutchman, and a Brit. Luckily my combination of beer-induced focus and utter bewilderment manifested itself as a stunning poker face, which led me to win several hands.

Sadly by 2 a.m. my poker face had somewhat fallen off, and it was being rapidly replaced by tiredness. This affected my game, and after a few duff cards I went out, with one of the German contingent – Marvin, collecting the giant twelve dollar pot. He requested that I told you that.

Chapter 14

And that's how you make a wrench...

(More) Ottawa, Ontario

Cats can jump three times their height!

Erm... I guess the coach company must have run out of facts about Canada...

I awoke on a Tuesday morning, which was much to be expected as I had fallen asleep on Monday night. I got up and set off for another exploratory wander around the capital, having of course showered and clothed myself first. My wanderings led me to the parliament building, where I was promptly stopped by a sign saying that all the public galleries were closed. This somewhat disrupted my plans for the day, seeing as this was the main attraction for visiting the city. I stood outside in deep thought for over a minute while I formed a contingency plan. I decided that I would go and find a sandwich. It had been a while since I had thought about sandwiches (heaven forbid!), probably because I had been distracted by my recent encounter of impending homelessness, from being chased by 'rehabilitated' murderers, and the ever-present threat of being mistakenly leaf punched. But hopefully these issues were behind me (not literally or I'd never sleep at night) so I could focus on my original mission.

I had noticed a large deli counter in the supermarket when I had been picking up meat for the barbeque last night, and so I made by way back there to see if there were any sandwich based offerings that took my fancy. As I scanned the chilled racks of freshly made food (it's been a while since I've done any scanning...) I found a selection of plastic-boxed sandwiches. They all seemed to be stuffed full of the same thing – shredded colourfulness. Even on close inspection it was hard to distinguish exactly what was inside, and with the unhelpful label merely stating the filling was "mixed" I was left with no further option than to buy one and find out for myself.

I took my purchase back over to the park by the river, and chose a bench overlooking Parliament Hill as my eating destination. The sun was blazing away as I was becoming accustomed to, and all together the sandwich eating was an enjoyable time. I'm still not sure exactly what was in it, but I'm pretty sure that cheese and lettuce were the prominent ingredients. Importantly though, the sandwich had been incredibly good value, as for only seven dollars you got four half rolls, which is *two full* rolls! *And* they were big ones at that. Luckily I hadn't had any breakfast or I might have collapsed after all that lettuce.

This got me thinking; here I was in Canada on a sandwich mission, and yet I had no real scheme in place for assessing the sandwiches I ate. This suddenly seemed crazy, and that *definitely* needed to change! I needed a system that rated sandwiches to ascertain whether they were reasonably priced or not. I would have to judge each one I had, taking into account various aspects of the sandwich. Hmmm, yes this needed some thought. Some s*erious* thought. And probably a beer. Some *serious* beer.

* * *

I returned to the hostel to find Peter, the Dutch poker participant from last night, slumped in the lounge. He was bored, and so we decided we'd have another attempt at visiting parliament, because we both felt we had a few laws that we could put forward that would improve the country. Peter's were based around the inconvenient way that shops add on the tax at the till so you never know in advance how much you'll be paying, and mine were based around outlawing leaf-punching.

I made the brave decision that it was hot enough to warrant shorts. This was exciting as it would be the first 'short' outing of the season. Unfortunately this did not go to plan, and as I unzipped the zip attachments that turned my trousers seamlessly into shorts (which did actually still have seams), one of the zips broke off. I really was having a torrid time with zips. I sighed, completed the unzipping with the aid of a strategically bent paperclip, and then we set off.

We got as far as the entrance foyer of the parliament building before a woman with a clipboard stopped us. What is it about people with clipboards that make your heart sink? She did indeed deliver bad news. The only tour of the day was full. *However*, she then must have caught sight of the neat stitching on my newly transformed shorts, or maybe it was the imaginative lace configuration on Peter's shoes, but suddenly she twisted her face into a state of intense deliberation, before smiling and saying that she could slip us in as "1 visitor plus a guest". How that is any different from "2 visitors" I have no idea, but we weren't about to question it now.

So we got to go on a short tour around a corridor. It was quite a nice corridor though, and the guide was very informative and used lots of enthusiastic hand gestures to add to the event. We were told how Canada was formed in 1867, and that the parliament building (based on London's Houses of Parliament) contains the House of Commons and the Senate. We then got to leave the corridor, and have a quick look in the library that is used by Members of Parliament to research laws and other relevant information, such as the damaging effect of successive fist blows to a leaf. We were then ushered back into the corridor, before being allowed into the viewing gallery above the House of Commons. Once inside we were lucky enough to witness a live session, where MPs were taking it in turns to debate issues including the navy, abortion, and taxes. Peter was pleased. Much to my disappointment leaves were not discussed.

Nevertheless it had been an insightful and enjoyable visit to the engine room of Canada's government, and while I'm reasonably sure that is a pretty poor attempt at a metaphor, Peter and I *were* sure that it was time to pick up some more meat and beers for another barbeque back at the hostel. And so for the second consecutive night we passed the evening prodding steaks on the barbeque while drinking beers and chatting. We were in fact in mid-chat when a man appeared in the rear courtyard. He was probably in his fifties, and although we suspected he was also staying at the hostel, he had a weird habit of appearing from peculiar directions and not speaking. This evening we were in for a treat though, he broke his silence!

'You know the three words you should always say to a woman?' he suddenly said out of nowhere, speaking slowly and precisely, and with a tone that suggested that if we got the answer wrong then he would click his fingers and a swarm of killer-bees would fly in from nowhere and carry us away and make slaves of us in a bee cave up on a distant mountain where it always rained.

There was an awkward silence as we took in this bizarre interruption.

'Errr…I love you?' Peter offered cautiously.

Ah Peter, it was brave of you to try, but that answer was clearly too simple and obvious. It was what he wanted us to say. He had tricked us. Bring on the bees…

'No.' He shook his head slowly yet arrogantly, 'You say, "You are right".' And with that he raised his eyebrows and smiled evilly.

I didn't want to be the one who pointed out that in speech terms it would be far more logical to use an apostrophe, thus making it a two-letter sentence. Otherwise it sounds too formal and computerised. I mean, c'mon psycho man - I thought you were a pro!

He went on to tell us how he had been to a lot of places, and that he travels around "leaving women hanging".

At this point I couldn't help interrupting with my rare form of social tourettes that occurs in awkward situations, by trying to break the uneasy tension that this conversation had created by jokingly throwing in 'you mean literally?' which *had* he been a serial killer (which I still maintain is highly possible) would probably bump me quite high up on his list of targets.

Thankfully he soon slipped away as suddenly as he had appeared – probably to check on the bodies he had stowed in the boot of his car, and so the rest of us could continue with our meaningless but friendly discussions about shoe polish and other such important issues.

A little later as I headed through to the lounge, a woman sitting at the kitchen table spoke to me (the cheek!). Well when I say woman, you might be imagining a slim, friendly-faced woman with sophisticated black-rimmed glasses and wavy hair. Sadly this was not what I was confronted with. This woman was a beast, and to be honest that's doing her a descriptive favour. She was absolutely *massive* (and American...) and she was stuffing her face with a coleslaw sandwich. This was far from a pleasant sight, but what made it *so* much worse was the sheer amount of coleslaw that was dripping down her multi-chinned face as she spoke. It was horrible, and I actually felt physically sick being in the same room as her. What made this whole event worse was that she was tarnishing the appealing nature of sandwiches! I couldn't be put off sandwiches! That was the *whole reason* I'd come to Canada!

Thankfully, and just as I was about to lose the ability to ever comfortably look at a sandwich again, someone else arrived in the kitchen, and (no doubt grudgingly) took over the conversation. I still have no idea what it was she had been talking about. As I rapidly escaped the kitchen however, I overheard the end of a conversation her latest victim was having to endure about rubbish jobs. It ended with an intriguing and arguably quite poetic final offering from the coleslaw-covered fatty.

'I worked for a while in Jasper [a town in the Rocky Mountains]. It's the best place to hate your job.'

Later on I was sitting in the lounge with a beer, trying desperately to recover from two hugely bizarre moments of social interaction, and while also attempting to figure out my sandwich-rating system. However, I was soon distracted by the television that was on in the background. There was a programme on the *Discovery Channel* called *How It's Made*. This was evidently a series that looked at the process of…well, how things are made, and tonight we were being treated to a detailed twenty-minute break down of how a wrench is made. Fascinating. I *literally* had no idea that there were so many stages in wrench production! I think that the polished steel glazing of the outer handle of the wrench was probably my favourite stage. Yes, that one was good. I was a little gutted that I couldn't guarantee I'd be able to watch tomorrow night's episode though, where viewers would be treated to the captivating manufacturing processes of golf-buggy production. Travelling always involves sacrifice.

So I got as far as writing down the word "sandwich" followed by a semi-colon. This sandwich business was proving hard work. I needed another beer. And would you believe it, on my way back from the fridge I bumped into Peter, who requested my presence on the front terrace. Actually he probably phrased it less like we were in a period drama, but you get the gist. And so I reconvened on the terrace to play cards with Peter, a German and an Australian. You'll have noticed here that I struggle to remember more than one name per day, and for that I apologise to those who I have callously referred to by nothing more specific than their nationality. It is convenient though.

We played *hearts*, which I regularly didn't win, but others did, and we all laughed, joked and drank and it was fun. At one point the sinister man from earlier appeared just beside the terrace, where he took a couple of puffs on a cigarette before vanishing again. Weird. It was also here that I learnt that this hostel was situated just round the corner from a rehab centre. This was very quickly confirmed by the live theatre that we were then unexpectedly subjected to, as various oddly dressed individuals appeared at the hostel's terrace fencing asking for money, or in the case of one member of the cast; simply running around the empty street in front of us inexplicably screaming, with intermittent bursts of rolling around on the floor.

We decided to call it a night.

* * *

I slept surprisingly well, despite the various occurrences of the previous evening that could have easily prevented me from doing so.

As I lay in bed the following morning, staring at my watch while I selected the most desirable minute past eight in which to get up and head for the shower, I noticed the numbers on the digital display begin to fade. No! I was losing time! So I quickly chose that the nineteenth minute past eight would be my designated getting up time, but it soon became apparent that time may not hold out for the seven minutes that it would take for that to arrive, and so I had to bring forward my schedule. Inexplicably, this new getting up time of 8:12 seemed to coincide precisely with about five other peoples' getting up time, and so all the bathrooms were full and I had to wait. By the time I finally got a slot in a one of the much-coveted wash spaces and had showered and returned, my watch was blank. I was

103

out of time. I had lost time. Time was up. Erm, it was time to move on...

So I did – to Montreal!

Chapter 15

Where things get un petit français

Montreal, Quebec

*Cats have one hundred vocal sounds, but dogs only have ten.

And if you tread on their tales you get to hear a wide selection of these...

I'm not sure what time I arrived in Montreal, and nor do I know exactly how long the train journey was, but I would guess it was around three hours. Despite my watch now having completely failed I still chose to have it strapped to my wrist. I think this was a force of habit and I would have felt something was missing without it. It also neatly covered up my watch tan mark too, but then that's not really surprising given that it was the cause of it.

Montreal station was a little confusing. As with Toronto station it was a large, ornately decorated hall, but when you tried to exit the building it proved far from straightforward. Once beyond the perimeter of the hall I found myself in a maze of underground walkways that were lined with endless food outlets. They all served wide selections of pastries, cakes and other bakery products, as well as the original train-travellers' number one choice of refreshment – coffee.

It took a few minutes and a few wrong turns before I managed to fight my way through the crowds of coffee-sippers and food display cabinets to an escalator that would lead me up and out into fresh uncaffeinated air. Once I'd pushed myself through the doors to freedom I found myself on Boulevard René Lévesque, and it was then just a few blocks down to the Auberge de Jeunesse. Oui, mon français est très bien, merci.

I found the hostel, checked in, and then went out for a look around the nearby area, picking up some food to cook for dinner on the way back.

That evening, having cooked an exciting pasta based meal in the well-equipped basement kitchen I sat in the neighbouring seating area and watched the hockey on the television screen on the far wall. I'd heard a sneaky rumour that ice hockey was big in Canada, and this was evident from the recent Winter Olympic gold medal match that they contested and narrowly won against the U.S.A. in Vancouver. It was now the playoffs in the NHL, which I soon learnt consisted of the top eight teams from the league going into a cup style competition, each round of which involved a best of seven head to head series. That's right – *seven*. And they say it's about the money…

Tonight we were watching the Vancouver Canucks play the Chicago Black Hawks in game three of the series. Having recently attended a baseball game I was used to a slow pace of sport, where during play you could happily fold your ticket stub into a paper aeroplane, throw it inaccurately at a pigeon as it sat on one of the floodlight stands eyeing up an abandoned piece of hot dog bread that lay unattended on a seat down below, walk over to reclaim the useless piece of origami, discover that the pigeon was a magic talking pigeon, be on the receiving end of a torrent of abuse from the pigeon for trying to dislodge it with a crudely made paper-based weapon, apologise to it, buy it a hotdog as a form of an apology, suggest going on a world tour to promote the novelty of the talking pigeon, complete the world tour, return to the baseball match and look back up at the scoreboard and *still* nothing would have changed. In hockey, however, I barely caught sight of the puck as it was moving around so fast, and most of the time I just had to assume the camera was pointing in the rough direction of where it was currently being hit rapidly across the ice. Luckily the lady behind the bar then spoke, which was a timely break from watching the hockey as I was feeling physically drained from trying to keep up with the on-screen ice antics.

'Does anyone want any cake? It needs using.'

It was safe to say that pretty much everyone in earshot did. Free cake was not something to dismiss lightly, so the few of us that were in the near vicinity were each treated to a free chunk of black forest gateaux. Maybe *this* was the sign that things were picking up! It certainly tasted good.

* * *

The next day began with a little bit of shower-based complication. I went to turn on the taps when I noticed that both of them were marked with a "C". This was confusing, especially this early in the morning. Perhaps they were bi-lingual taps; using the first letter of the English for "cold" and the first letter of the French word for "hot", which is "chaud". After a good few minutes of exasperated tap-twiddling I eventually got the water to a temperature that was showerable in. This had been a taxing start to the day.

Thankfully I was soon well away from taps as I was outside, but annoyingly the taps in the sky had been left on. It was *absolutely hammering* it down. I ran between bus stops and skyscraper forecourts dodging the bullet like raindrops that were intent on making their way through all the various layers of my clothing.

After ten minutes of darting about I found myself heading down an escalator, and soon I was in another of Montreal's secret underground worlds. This one appeared to be a shopping centre, and judging by the number of people scurrying in and out of its various outlets it was far from secret. I took opportunistically to my surroundings, and after a few enquiries I had my 'time' issue resolved in the form of a now fully functional watch.

So, with time back on my side I went back up the escalator to see what the weather was doing. To my utter astonishment I emerged from the underground mall to be greeted by a clear blue sky. How long had I been down there? It had been so dark and the rain so heavy, I just couldn't understand where it had all gone in the ten minutes I'd been beneath the streets. I kept eyeing the sky suspiciously as I walked through the pleasant cobbled streets of the old town, just in case it tried the same trick again in reverse.

The rain didn't return. It was another nice sunny day, which worked out very well because I ended up walking for nearly three hours along the docks and through the eastern suburbs of Montreal as I made my way towards the Olympic Park, guided not by a map, but by the strangely angled tower that protrudes from one end of the Olympic stadium.

Montreal hosted the 1976 summer Olympic games, and apparently only finished paying for it this year (so good luck with that Vancouver) and as I am a sucker for a tall building (*especially* a slanty one!) I was soon ascending its heights via a cable car that runs up its spine. From the top I was treated to good views back towards downtown Montreal and over to the islands in the river opposite, as well as being provided with a birds-eye view of the Olympic park below.

Once a few obligatory photos had been taken, I descended back down the cable car and went on a tour of the adjacent enclosed stadium, as this was the only way to see inside. With the exception of the guide there were only three of us on the tour, where we were shown the swimming complex and then the inside of the seventy thousand capacity stadium itself, which no matter how hard we puffed out our cheeks, we just couldn't make it look full between the four of us. The tour guide told us that the tower was "the highest inclined building in the world". This is probably the most ridiculous 'highest building' claim I have encountered on my various travels thus far. I can't imagine it has a lot of competition in that category, unless another tall building is built badly.

There was another hockey game on that night (actually they were on every night at the moment) but this time it was Montreal's own *Canadiens* (also know as "the Habs") playing the *Pittsburgh Penguins* at the Bell Centre, two blocks from my hostel. Evidently one of the guys on the tour was a fan, and had paid three hundred dollars for a ticket. As crazy as that sounds, he thought *I* was crazy when I said I didn't watch hockey back home in England. It's a little worrying how caught up in their own little world some people can be. I did plan on watching the game on television tonight though.

I decided not to walk back to the city, and instead I took the quick and efficient underground metro system. This cut my return journey down to twenty minutes, giving me plenty of time to cook before watching the match, which was another exciting game where I still failed to spot the puck. Montreal won though, so everyone was happy (except probably Pittsburgh and its fans).

After the excitement of the hockey I returned to my dorm. Over the past couple of days I had become slightly deflated. While I was really enjoying my time in Canada, I felt like my sandwich quest was running a bit short on…well, sandwiches. It had always been my plan to head across Canada, exploring the land as I made my way towards the reasonably priced sandwich on Vancouver Island, but I had wondered if there were any bread-filled delights that may be significant to my mission that I would find on the way.

109

Having arrived in Toronto I realised that a good few of Canada's major cities were east of Toronto, and so I had decided to head in that direction to find more sandwiches that may hold some valuable insight into Canadian sandwich culture. I was now in Montreal, one stop away from Quebec City, which I had decided was the furthest east I would head. So far I had not found anything of any major importance on the sandwich front, and I was getting a little frustrated. But all that changed when I got chatting to a couple of people in my dorm.

Tristan and Sophie were English and they were based at the hostel while they found somewhere to live so that they could work in Montreal for a couple of months. It turned out that we had all worked at the same chain of DIY store back home, and so we therefore instantly united by our collective dislike of bright green polo shirts.

We had been talking about our travels for a while when I chose to mention the story of how I had come to be in Canada. Up until this point I hadn't told many people about my quest, partly because it was a long story, but also because I felt it may be frowned upon by the classic traveller – traditionally guided by friends, family or tourist attractions – and not so much by sandwiches.

I was wrong. Not only did they seem intrigued by the tale, but Tristan also mentioned something that was of great interest. He said that he thought he remembered reading about a place in Montreal that was *known* for its sandwiches. This was *massively* exciting! And after a little research it was confirmed that there was indeed a sandwich shop in Montreal – *this very city that I was in* – that was famed for selling its famous 'Montreal Smoked-Meat' sandwich to those who were patient enough to queue up for it. This place had queues for its sandwiches? Amazing. It *must* be good. Not only that but apparently it was popular with celebrities! This was all too much to take in, and so it was suggested that the few of us who had now gathered in the dorm would go out for a drink.

Half an hour later and we were sitting in a small upstairs bar a few blocks up from our hostel. I had just sat down with an incredibly specialist beer, presumably brewed in-house as is apparently common in Montreal's many micro-breweries.

'Which beer did you get?' Earl, the Canadian representative of our group enquired.

'A *Moosehead*.' I proudly announced, sipping the beer in a highly sophisticated manner to confirm my highly developed 'connoisseur' status.

'Urreegghh!'

I believe that to be the accurate written representation of the sound that greeted my answer. This wasn't the gentle murmur of impressed noises that I had been expecting.

I was then enlightened to the fact that *Moosehead* was the cheap, common, low quality beer. The *Carling* of Canada if you like. Why the hell did they give it such an exciting name then? I had failed previously on the coffee and tea front back in England, and now I had failed on the beer front in Canada. God I needed tomorrow's sandwich to be a culinary success.

After a round of drinks and a short walk we found ourselves in another bar, or more precisely – *at* a bar, in the imaginatively named 'Brewtopia'.

It was crowded with post-hockey match revellers, which is why we found ourselves spread across stools next to the taps. This did however make getting served easier.

The others all chose their beers from the menu, but I had been thrown off by my last mess-up. In the end I went for the exciting option, that consisted of a selection of beers ranging from 'blonde' to 'dark' in mini pint glasses served in a rack. Now I could really demonstrate some careful taste and quality selection.

Actually I couldn't. I wasn't sure what I was drinking, but most of it was reasonably unpleasant. I think one of them may have tasted 'oaky', or is that a wine flavour judgement? Ah, I don't care anymore.

Aside from the taste, what can be slightly unpleasant in Canada is the tip culture. I have no problem tipping waiters for good food service, but here they expect you to tip them an extra dollar for *every* drink you get served. This isn't ideal when you're on a backpackers' budget, and especially when drinks already cost six dollars each. And *especially* when you're sitting at the bar and you have to move the drink a greater distance from where the barmaid has poured it to the space in front of you, than she has from the glass shelf to the tap. It's ludicrous!

It was definitely time for bed.

Chapter 16

Well if it's good enough for Celine...

(*Plus de*) Montréal, à Québec

*It is illegal in Switzerland to flush the toilet after 10pm.

Was? Das ist nitch gut!

Right, I was beginning to doubt the validity of some of the coach's facts, but this one really takes the p*ss. (Or not after 10pm in Switzerland...) I find this particular one hard to believe, and where the 'cat facts' bore little specific significance to Canada, this one certainly doesn't, and so I am withdrawing any future facts from the beginning of chapters. So there.

Today was a big day. I mean I got up and I could *literally* feel a larger day around me. *Everything* was bigger than yesterday. Except for my breakfast, for I had forgotten to replenish my bagel stocks and so mon petit déjeuner was a little smaller, but then that was probably a good thing as I had an important sandwich to attend to today. Yes! My sandwich adventure was back on track, with a *sub*-sandwich mission, although it probably wasn't going to involve a sub *style* sandwich. Who really knew though? Sandwich hunting can be an unpredictable business.

I set off into another hot sunny Montreal day, heading to the nearby metro station where I boarded a train under the Fleuve St Laurent (river) to the islands. One of these islands has a large dome frame containing an eco...olgy...nature... place. Hmmm, okay, so I didn't visit this, because the island *I* was interested in was the second one, which was over the bridge. *This* island was filled by the Circuit Gilles Villeneuve, the Formula One track that would be hosting the Canadian Grand Prix in four weeks time. I'm not really sure why I like passing time walking around tarmac, but it has become a recurring theme in recent travels, and I did enjoy it once again.

It was quite surreal to be on this virtually silent island that is actually a nature reserve, knowing that in four weeks there would be the deafening sound of V8 engines blasting around it at two hundred kilometres an hour, with one hundred thousand wildly cheering motor racing fans packed into the half-constructed grandstands that I was now walking past. I even saw a butterfly flutter by on the pit straight. I suggest it would not be here come the 13th June.

Track walk done, it was time to head back to the city. It was getting on for one o'clock – lunchtime! I got back on the metro and headed up to Sherbrooke Station, situated in the trendy Latin Quarter, where I had been told the famous sandwich shop was to be found.

Twenty minutes later and I was powering through the streets of the Latin Quarter, my eyes flicking eagerly between street name signs and the little fold out map in my hand. I was mentally ticking off each street I crossed as I headed west along Avenue des Pins until I hit Boulevard St Laurent. This was it! Another hundred metres up the road and I could see my destination – *Schwartz's*. No, I wasn't standing next to it, and neither had I spotted the shop sign, I was too far away for that. It was actually another block until I reached the shop, but the collection of people outside had alerted me to its location from quite a distance.

114

I'd read that this place always had a queue outside, but I had *assumed* that this was an exaggeration used to hype the place up, but no! There really *was* a queue outside! Or more accurately, a gathering. There wasn't a distinct beginning or end to the rabble of hungry people outside the small shop front, but soon a man appeared from within to enquire about the number of people in each group. I guessed he worked there, mainly because he was wearing an apron. Aprons always suggest positions of authority in such places. As I was a lone diner I was ushered almost secretively to the front of the outside gathering, and through the narrow entrance way and into the bustling café scene that lay within.

It was absolutely rammed. Long, narrow tables lined the floor, each one squeezing in as many lunchtime eaters as was possible. I was seated up at the counter, in full view of the sandwich production that was frantically taking place on the other side. A paper mat was quickly laid in front of me, that told of the heritage of the place (it said was celebrating its eightieth birthday!...although I worked out that was actually two years ago) and the famous clientele that frequented it. These included none other than *Celine Dion*! And other famous Canadians who I hadn't heard of, presumably because I'm not Canadian enough. It was then ordering time.

'Erm...a sandwich please.'

Suddenly I felt slightly overwhelmed by the significance of the place and I knew that there was a lot at steak. I mean a lot *of* steak. Big lumps of it.

There was no need to be more specific then that though, and soon I had the result in front of me.

It wasn't so much a sandwich as a paper plate with a massive pile of red meat on it. Oh, and with a couple of flimsy slices of rye bread resting on either side of the meat-mountain. Two more slices of bread were later discovered towards the bottom too.

I wondered why they had given me a knife and fork for a sandwich, and I'd briefly thought they had misheard my order and thought I had asked for the lobster with a side of caviar. It turns out this was not an option on the menu; the smoked meat sandwich was pretty much all they offered. But then this is what I had come for, and after working my way through some of the meat avec le cutlery, I collected the rest of the meat together within the meagre bits of bread and ate it up sandwich-style! It was meaty. It was good.

As I moved off from my stool having paid the $5.50 and left a worthy tip, I noticed they sold *Swartz's* memorabilia by the door. I couldn't resist. Finding out about this place had been a real fluke, and now having learnt more about it (there's even supposed to be a film about it called *"Chez Schwartz's"*!) I would have been absolutely gutted if I'd missed out on its renowned sandwich offerings given my reasons for being in Canada.

So I left *Schwartz's*, having been there, done that, *and* having bought the t-shirt. It was blue by the way. I then continued in a westerly direction towards Parc du Mont Royal – the 'mountain' that stood behind downtown Montreal. I say 'mountain', because it is actually just a large hill. It's still very nice though, and after winding up though the trees on the tidy wood steps and pathways I found myself at a large viewing area outside of a large stone pavilion. The view was impressive, looking out across downtown Montreal, the river and its islands on the other side, and then the rolling Quebecan hills and landscape beyond.

I spent the rest of the afternoon walking around the park's numerous pathways, stumbling across a large metal framed cross that lights up at night and shines out over the city, before returning down the hillside to the city. As I made my way along the busy shopping district of St Catherine Street I passed a grocery store and decided that I would liven up my third consecutive evening of pasta with a different vegetable. I chose a pepper. It was promising to be an exciting evening.

I took the pepper to the checkout, and began the process of paying for it.

'Hello.' The cheerful sales assistant said, possibly guessing I was English from my European eyebrow configuration.

'Bonjour!' I brightly responded, for I am a man of the world and an embracer of foreign languages.

'Voulez-vous un sac?' she continued, whilst weighing the pepper and now believing I was at one with the Quebecan mother tongue.

I paused for a second while I considered if I did in fact want a bag, but this was mistaken by the till lady for miscomprehension.

'Would you like a bag?' she repeated in English.

'Er...si.' I inexplicably switched to Spanish.

She looked puzzled, bagged my pepper regardless, and then continued. 'Un dollar cinquante, s'il vous plait.'

I now looked puzzled. It was a *green* pepper, not a *gold* pepper. Why was it so expensive? I had chosen a green pepper despite preferring the taste of red peppers because green peppers are cheaper. Oh, and because the green pepper would add more colour variation to my red-sauced pasta than a red pepper. That's right – I'm a vain pepper purchaser!

Anyway, I was surprised at the amount this was costing. Peppers were clearly going to have to be a luxury item from now on. Again this pause also did me no favours on the language battle that was now ensuing.

'One dollar fifty.' She repeated firmly, and in English. Slightly *angry* English.

I paid the lady, and collected my bag-avec-pepper, adding a swift 'merci beaucoup' as I left.

I had thoroughly confused the poor lady as to my nationality, and she looked physically relieved to be moving on to the more stable-tongued food purchaser who was next in the queue. This exchange had not put me off though, and having had a sandwich success in

Montreal I wanted to experience more French Canadian culture, and I would do this by travelling deeper into its clutches.

Next stop – Quebec City!

Chapter 17

Sackgasse!

Quebec City, Quebec

As the 'facts' fell through I have decided to replace them with proverbs. But instead of using traditional proverbs, I have taken the beginning parts and adjusted the endings to make them fit with situations I have encountered whilst travelling.

*"He who laughs last...*risks being frowned upon by those who have already ceased laughing."

The train pulled up in the station after another three-hour trip, with clouds having built up ominously as the journey progressed. It was late afternoon, and as I stood in the station building studying a map as I tried to work out a route to the hostel, I could hear the rain pounding down on the glass roof panels above. The thought of lugging my bags uphill through the rain to the hostel was not an inviting prospect, but as my chauffeured helicopter was nowhere to be found, I stepped out into the grim afternoon weather and battled through the rain and along the narrow hillside streets.

I found the hostel with surprising ease given that I hadn't checked the map since leaving the station, and although pretty wet, I was cheerful as I slumped by bags down at reception and kicked off the standard hostel introductory conversation.

'Bonjour! Je suis une reservation!' I spoke confidently and with a smile.

The lady behind the desk looked a little confused. But why? *Surely* a hostel was used to people having booked a bed for the night? I would have imagined that's the most common occurrence that a hostel reception would face – a backpacker who has booked a room. Then I listened back to my sentence in my head and realised that instead of telling her that I *had* a reservation, I actually told her that I *was* a reservation. This could be a factor in her confused response. I tried again.

'Ah, pardon. *J'ai* une reservation. Pour une chambre avec un lit.'

This was far more successful, and I'm sure the receptionist was extra grateful that I had told her that I had a reservation for "a room with a bed", because otherwise she may have wrongly assumed that I'd had a reservation for a Polish tap dance lesson.

I was soon in possession of a swipe entry key-card, and after climbing a couple of flights of stairs to a long and wide hotel-like corridor, I had found my way into my corner dorm room. It had six beds in it and they were all empty. This was a surprise, but it allowed me the space to sort out and hang up all my rain-sodden gear.

I was making my way back down the stairs to go in search of a supermarket when I was faced with a daunting sight. As I turned around on the halfway landing I was greeted by a herd of teenagers coming up the stairs. I was stuck there for a good couple of minutes as they poured passed me shouting and screaming while I took shelter beside a decorative pot plant until they had disappeared into the corridor. God I hoped they weren't in the same room as me.

The name "Québec" derives from a word meaning "where the river narrows", and Québec City does indeed lie on the western bank of the narrowest point of the Saint Lawrence River. It is also the only walled city in North America, and within these walls is Vieux

Québec (the old town) consisting of the upper town and the lower town. The large hostel is situated in the upper town, two blocks up from Rue Saint Jean, the main street running through the old town. Along this street there is a selection of interesting speciality shops, trendy bars, and smart restaurants. Even the *McDonald's* here looks deceptively smart, with a dignified green and black facia and an array of planting and decorated fencing outside.

I found a mini-market on a nearby street, and soon I had all the ingredients I needed for another 'exciting' evening meal, albeit at a rather high price thanks to the smart, exclusive surroundings. You could tell this city had an interesting and unconforming edge to it, if only by the fact that they sold pasta in a box.

I continued to explore the old town as the rain had now subsided, following the curving streets as a welcome break from the dull grid systems of modern cities. Another very noticeable feature of Québec City was the disappearance of English from all signs and other written material. This walled city is quite literally the strong hold of Canada's French heritage, and everything is seemingly done to preserve this. I liked this element. I think it adds a new and interesting dimension to a place from a visiting perspective, and although I had clearly demonstrated that my French was far from perfect, I enjoyed making the effort, and it added to the eclectic feel that distinguished Quebec from other Provinces across the country.

Later on I set to work cooking my pasta from a box, before heading out along Rue Saint Lawrence for a drink somewhere where I could watch the latest hockey match between Montreal and Pittsburgh. A large bar with a few low-key revellers was my eventual stopping point, but after an expensive pint and a chat with a man who gave me a bit more insight into ice hockey, I decided to head back to the hostel. I was still the only resident in the dorm (thankfully the school groups were in their own part of the hostel) and so I went down to the bar/lounge area with a pack of cards.

It was far from busy, but there was one other guy who sat near me as I shuffled the cards aimlessly. It's normal backpacking procedure to open up the offer of a card game to the floor, and normally I'd be only too keen to do this. On this occasion however, there was something about this person who was sat opposite me that made me hold back. He was wearing a hat. But not just *any* hat – he was wearing a *cowboy* hat.

Now, call me prejudice, but I don't like playing cards with people who wear cowboy hats, unless;

a) they are *actually* a cowboy

b) they are wearing the hat ironically

Unfortunately this person appeared to fit neither option, and so I gave up and read my book. This turned out to be an excellent decision, as a little later I overheard a strained conversation between the German barmaid and the cowboy hat wearer, where he took it upon himself to bore her with stories in his dull, monotone voice about Germans he had met, while insisting on showing her pictures of them in case she knew any of them. He really was a tw*t in a hat. I went to bed.

* * *

The next morning, having narrowly avoided the mass gathering that was the school trip breakfast time, I was heading out of the hostel when I saw a piece of paper with some names listed on it. I was immediately curious, and wondered if I too should add my name to the list on the off chance it was for some kind of resident lottery, where the winner would get a free champagne boat cruise down the river, or perhaps you could win the opportunity to tear up any ridiculous hats worn by fellow hostellers.

I was wrong about the lottery. It turned out to be a list of people signing up for an informal tour of the old town that was part of a weekly schedule of events ran by the hostel. This sounded like a reasonable alternative to hat-destroying, and more importantly it would be a good way of seeing the town and meeting a few people. I added my name.

So a couple of hours later I was sat by reception with a few others, eagerly awaiting the city tour. It was led by the German lady who had been subjected to the cowboy hat drone the previous night, but here she gave an insightful...insight into Québec City and it's culture and history. Yes, I'm sorry my travel writing vocabulary isn't more...good.

We walked through the pretty narrow streets to the main square, where we stood outside the city hall. She explained why it had "City Hall" written on it, where no other signs or building's names were translated. The reason is apparently because as the French term for "City Hall" is "Hotel de Ville", they kept getting Anglicised tourists coming inside with suitcases hoping to find a hotel room for the night. Bloody tourists.

There are many quaint cobbled streets throughout the old town, some of which have incredibly detailed murals painted all across the side of buildings depicting life in the city. We walked up to the iconic Château Frontenac that sits at the top of the old town. This is apparently the most photographed hotel in the world, and so we...well, added to that reputation, and we took photos. We also stepped inside to have a look in the grand, bell-boy filled lobby area, where we quickly realised that we were very out of place and so we left again. From here we followed a curving road before going down some steps onto Rue du Petit Champaign, which, if I was writing a cliché packed travel guide, I would probably describe as 'achingly pretty', with posh cafes and boutique shops lining this narrow stone road at the bottom of the Funiculaire du Vieux Québec – the cable car that spans the short distance from the harbour side to the hill top promenade beside the Château Frontenac. I even saw a horse and cart go by. The whole neat, clean and ornate presentation of the old

123

town made it seem slightly unreal. It was as if it was a carefully moulded theme town - with a sort of 'high culture' Disney World feel to it that was all in stark contrast to other Canadian cities I had visited.

So it was all very nice and lovely and pleasant and nice. The tour was good too, and significantly I met Anne and Suzan, who were also on the tour. They were both Dutch, but *even more* significantly they asked if I fancied hiring a car with them and going out to a National Park the following day. I did. I even knew where you could hire a car from because I had spotted a rental shop earlier. I'm good at spotting the important things in places with such interesting architecture and rich histories.

* * *

So the next day we met on the dot of twenty-four minutes past eight, and we headed over to the car rental place. Over the course of the evening we had acquired two other passengers, and so there were five of us crammed into the tiny Hyundai hatchback for the two-hour drive out to the Parc National du Mauricie. The clouds that had engulfed the sky in the earlier part of the day were beginning to part as we pulled up in the car park at the edge of the National Park. I think we arrived a little early, as when we pulled up at around eleven o'clock the information centre didn't look like it would open until at least mid-July judging by the building work that was going on. Luckily there were some park wardens/builders on hand to tell us which hiking trails were open, and so we set off into the woods.

Canada is known for having exiting wildlife; such as bears, elks and whales. We did see what we thought was a whale in one of the lakes, but then we realised it was a rock. We also decided that it was unlikely that we would see a whale in a lake. Other than the rock, the only wildlife we saw was a very tame fox and a butterfly. I

124

suppose it was only wise to have a gentle introduction to outdoor-Canada.

During the hike we stopped to have lunch at a wooden hut in the forest. Once I had eaten my homemade baguette (well, we were in the French region...) I attempted to make fire using a flint and some wood. Sadly my Ray Mears alto-ego was missing and so it didn't go to plan, and I just ended up tired and with a lot of splinters in my hand. So I gave up, and instead I used a wooden stick to engrave some recently shed birch bark with the word "bienvenue". I then hung this "welcome" sign on the door of the hut, because I am internationally-enlightened person, and a keen woodsman.

Having had a good trek through the leafy National Park, we returned to the car and headed back to the city, discussing issues such as taxation systems and income percentage rates, as well as the public sector - as is presumably the norm when you spend any more than seven hours with the same group of mixed nationality people.

That evening I was sitting in the dining area, having eaten some more pasta from a box whilst watching yet more ice hockey. Someone then sat down beside me, and I instantly recognised him. It took a few seconds to recall where I knew him from, but then it came to me. It was Marvin from Ottawa – the German who had won at poker that night. His winnings had obviously served him well, as he was now eating a plate of warm, cheese-covered nachos from the hostel bar. We got chatting, and he told me how he had come to travel, which was because when he had signed up for National Service they had told him that he was 'too thin' for the army, and so he took the otherwise compulsory year off travelling instead. This was a brilliant reason for going travelling. *Almost* as good as sandwiches in fact.

Soon a Swiss-German, a French girl, and the Dutch duo joined us, and we sat round the large round wooden table chatting away in English, German, Dutch and French. Discussions inevitably formed around the various languages that were on display, and one topic of conversation involved words and phrases that each language used but that was actually from another language. My example was "dead end road", for which us English use the French term "cul de sac" – literally translated as 'bottom of the bag'. Having explained this term to Marvin using some not always relevant German and some excellent hand actions, he said that the German term was "sackgasse". This made me laugh. A *lot*. Probably a little *too* much in retrospect as some people looked at me funny, but I *loved* this word. It was so German and satisfying to say. It also sounded like an expletive.

We carried on exploring the fascinating world of language until people began to drift off to bed, but not before it was decided that we should all get together tomorrow and hit Québec City's museums. Someone had discovered that on the second Tuesday of every month in the 'off-season' you could visit all the museums for free. And guess what? Tomorrow was the second Tuesday of May, and the last week of the 'off-season'. Result! We could now spend the whole day going around all the museums in the city! That's the *whole* day being voluntarily detained inside dark museums learning about history when it was going to be clear blue skies and twenty-five degrees outside…

Sackgasse!

Chapter 18

We took the ferry out to Lévis, (where) thank-ful-ly we stayed dry

(Je suis toujours à) Québec City, à Québec

*"All work and no play...*does wonders for your bank balance."

This chapter title is supposed to be a 'clever' lyrical adjustment to Don McLean's song *American Pie*. No? Nevermind.

As the weatherman had predicted, it was a lovely sunny morning in Québec, but thankfully I wasn't at all bitter that we would be spending the day inside looking at faded parchment and dusty manikins wearing mock-ups of 1800s fashion. I *couldn't wait...*

So the five of us set off – Marvin, Patrik, Suzan, Anne and myself. First stop; le Musée de l'Amérique française. Situated in the Latin Quarter, it is supposedly Canada's oldest museum. Given how clean and modern it looked I'd guess that all Canada's other museums must therefore have been built last autumn. Sorry, I mean "fall".

We arrived at the museum via the Basilica Notre-Dame-de-Québec, which was again very smart and shiny. It is claimed that it is one of the continents first cathedrals, which again leads me to believe that most of North America has been built since 2007. I then found some written information inside that suggested (or rather told me) that it was actually built in the 1600s, at the time of Québec's first bishop, Monseigneur de Laval, whose name we would be seeing a lot of in the next couple of hours.

From the cathedral we made our way through to the museum, which involved boarding a lift that had a very innovative feature where you could listen to your own chosen piece of music. Sadly I don't think this had been entirely thought through though, as the journey was only around seven seconds long, and so we didn't even have enough time to make a selection. Nice thought though.

The museum itself was a neat collection of displays based upon the Francophone history of Canada, depicting how the French migrated to Québec, and then how they wandered off and wound up in Western Canada and the United States. It was a well laid out collection of exhibitions, with lots of glass display cabinets and interactive buttons to press to give that authentic museum feel to it. I think we all enjoyed the learning experience, and we nearly got the opportunity to tell some of the important museum researchers this, as when the doors opened of the lift we were using to make our way out of the building, we found ourselves in a busy office full of people with beards and glasses who were all looking very serious and holding documents.

'Bonjour!' we all said politely, while frantically jabbing at the "close door" button.

Once back outside we had a quick bask in the sunshine before a group of school children started throwing rocks at us from a nearby balcony. Bloody kids. This city was plagued with them. We decided that this was the cue for us to move on to the next museum. Having said this, no one had actually really bothered to find out where the next museum was, and so we ended up just walking about for a while, enjoying the warm sunshine and the intricate architecture of the area. As we ambled along in the sun someone finally asked, 'does anyone actually know which way we're supposed to be going?' and no one really did, but that was all fine, because it was sunny. Yes, it *was* sunny. Had I mentioned that?

It wasn't long before people started saying that they were hungry, which may or may not have been linked to the sun, but everyone nevertheless agreed that it would be a good idea to eat something. It was at that same moment that I pulled out my city map to find out where we should have been going for the next museum, and on the top left corner were the words "eat here" written boldly in black biro, and an arrow pointing at a street. Was this a sign? Yes of course it was, and I quickly remembered writing it the previous evening. It had been Marvin who had told me about this place - a restaurant that was apparently the first place in Canada (and presumably the world) to sell 'poutine'.

'Poutine' is a popular cuisine in Canada, and many people had been going on about its wonders since I had been here and so I thought it was time I tried it. *Especially* as we were now just a few streets from its origin – *Chez Ashton.* I put together my compelling case for wanting to go there, and because I delivered it with such flare and passion, everyone thought it was a good idea. Or it could have been the incomprehensible blabbering and map waving I was doing that made them concede to my request. They probably just wanted to shut me up. Whatever it was, I put on a convincing show.

So we set off for *Chez Aston,* but we had gone but a few metres when Suzan shouted; "Tiny Bus!", which signalled a dramatic head turn followed by me running like all hell had been let loose down the street. I shall explain.

Earlier in the day I had noticed a box zipping past me while we were crossing a street. This happened again a few minutes later, but this time I caught sight of this mystic cuboid. It was a bus! A *tiny* bus! It *looked* like a normal bus, but one that had been shrunk...or at least shortened drastically. It was also very quiet, which is why I never heard it coming. This was because it was an "Écolobus", which either meant it was a bus rushing around giving out unhealthy bacteria, *or* it was delivering people around Vieux Québec for free and in an efficient and environmentally friendly fashion. Anyway, I had made it my mission to photograph this novelty source of public transportation, but due to their niftiness and quiet nature I kept missing the opportunities.

The *first time* I tried to capture it I pulled out my camera, lined it up, and then stupidly pressed the 'off' button instead of the 'take picture' button. Easily done...

The *second time*, I ran after the bus, came to an abrupt stop, pointed my camera, zoomed-in, and clicked. The bus pulled away, and I returned to team-museum with a big smile on my face. This promptly fell off when I looked at the picture and found I had overcompensated on the zoom, and all I had done was taken a close up image of a terrified looking woman on the bus, probably wondering why on earth I had come charging towards the window to photograph her. This was most irritating.

This was therefore my next opportunity. Third time lucky. The tiny bus had already past me, so off I went careering down the busy Rue Saint Jean. Luckily there were traffic lights ahead, and more importantly they were red. The bus stopped, I aimed the lens, and I took the photo. Perfect. Framed to perfection. It was mission complete. Now I could stop terrorising the bus-riding communities of Québec City. They *really are* small buses though.

Bus picture taken, we continued to the restaurant. Or rather the fast-food outlet. *Chez Ashton*'s was not a fancy dining alternative, but then 'poutine' was not a fancy food option. 'Poutine' is actually chips with cheese curds soaked in gravy. Mmmmm is the noise you're probably not making right now. I was also of this opinion, but I knew I should try it, and I knew this was the place, and so I did, and soon I was in possession of a shiny silver 'urine-sample tray' of mushy brown chip sludge.

It tasted about as good as my description of it suggests. It was soggy and chewy, and the cheese curds gave an unnerving squeak when prodded with a fork. Food should *never* squeak when prodded. This should be a rule. You've probably guessed by now that it wasn't very nice, but it was important I found that out, so in an odd sense I was pleased.

As we got up to leave, a seemingly endless line of teenagers began to push their way through the door. We just couldn't get away from these damn kids - Québec City seemed to be flooded with them, so we decided it was time to escape to the safety of another museum.

Le Musée de la Civilisation was our next stop. This is a very big museum with lots of large halls full of exhibits and life-size models of...history. There was a lot of information and displays relating to Québec's aboriginal people and the arrival of early settlers in Québec, and how that developed into Québec's modern day culture. This was all done with the aid of various-sized glass cabinets, but also with a wide variety of interactive features, including buttons, handles, wheels, videos, and even draws you could open and look inside of, which contained more bits of appropriate history. It was *all action*! One of the exhibitions was on the Egyptians, which I couldn't quite understand as I've never heard of a strong Egyptian influence in Canada, but as soon as we were presented with the opportunity to dress up like *real Egyptians* in one of the activity rooms, this was all politely forgotten. My only complaint was that there was no real guidance on how to put together the various pieces of cloth that were on the shelves, and even after careful cloth-attachment, I still looked predominantly like a tea-maid. *Maybe* that was actually the real Egyptian look. Marvin had pulled off a far more superior look though, so I conceded defeat and we moved on, especially as one of the million school groups that were saturating the city was now descending on this exhibit, no doubt to vandalise

131

any historical values that north-east Africa had granted to their Egypto-Canadian ancestors.

The final exhibition we went into was a new special limited time one. This *was* exciting! It was on 'The Seven Deadly Sins', and it had dark lighting (I still can't work out if that's a contradiction...) and strange noises coming from the walls too, which all made it extremely mysterious and creepy. As we entered we were given a headset, which also made it *even more* atmospheric! Actually it didn't. It just made it easier to follow the stories as otherwise it was just a collection of mock-up house scenes with no written material to explain them.

Having said the headsets made it easier, I'm not convinced they did. In fact I felt sorry for the rest of the group, who despite all having a very good grasp of English, must *surely* have been left baffled by the stories told at each of the seven displays, because I could honestly say I didn't have a clue what any of them were about. The characters just spoke in riddles that seemed to bare no relation to anything, and even the displays themselves made little sense, even when the occasional light would suddenly illuminate a chair, or a shoe. I didn't get it. The final straw was during the last of the seven sins, in which a person was described as being "as dead as a mackerel", which is a phrase I've *never* heard used before. I'm also pretty sure something would only be as "dead as a mackerel" if it was a dead mackerel that was being referred to, in which case any animal or living being that was no longer alive could be used.

It was a certainly a puzzler, and a good indication that it was time to leave the museum.

It was early evening as we headed back through the city streets towards the hostel, after what had been a successful and culturally-enlightening day. It had also been very good value, I mean where else can you open draws full of rusty coins and dress up as a tea-maid for free? It may have been quite hard work on the brain at

132

times, but it had done wonders for our travel budgets. Because of this we could justify living it up tonight, and so we thought we would go out for a hedonistic evening of wild debauchery. After I had eaten my eighth consecutive evening meal of pasta of course. From a box.

* * *

We reconvened at eight o'clock, and headed back over to the waterfront. As we walked through the streets we were surrounded by busy restaurant gardens where residents and the higher-class visitors were dining on exciting fish meals and bottles of delicately poured mid-price wine. I wasn't jealous though, because I had forked out on some exciting polystyrene wrapped green beans to accompany my boxed-pasta.

We passed the Château Frontenac, where a man stood serenading passer-bys with his tenor-sax rendition of *Celine Dion*'s *My heart Will Go On*. I was wondering how long it would be until I heard that song here. We then took a shortcut that I had found, that led us to a large stone wall overlooking yet more elegantly situated restaurants by the water. As nice as it was, it hadn't worked out as a viable shortcut, and as none of us thought jumping down from the thirty-metre wall would add any sophistication to the view being appreciated by the nearby diners, we turned around and went down the long way. This place was positively teaming with tiny buses – if only I'd known that they gathered like flocks of rebellious teenagers by the ferry terminal I could have saved myself a lot of running (and dignity).

We were at the ferry terminal because we wanted to catch the ferry, and so logic had told us this would be the ideal location to facilitate this. It was a wise decision, and soon we were on the large boat for the treacherous eight-minute journey from Québec City over to Lévis on the other side of the river. The views of Québec

City at night from the water were meant to be nice, so we took our positions on the blustery top deck to experience this. It was indeed very pleasant, and it provided us with the perfect opportunity to explore our various cameras' 'night modes'. However, my camera was insistent on utilising the 'auto-blur' function, and so I gave up and just used my eyes to enjoy it.

It was just as well that Lévis didn't have a lot to offer, as our return tickets didn't allow us to get off, and so we hung around on board while the crew ran a strangely-timed fire drill (that thankfully didn't involve us jumping off into the freezing river) until they deemed the vessel safe to return to Québec's waterside. As we disembarked the ferry a man appeared from behind me and then delivered an earth-shattering question.

'Did you enjoy the trip?' Okay, so I lied about it being earth-shattering.

'Yes, it was very nice, thank you.' As if *he* was responsible for that...

'Ooo, are you English?'

Dammit! I'd been caught *again*! He had suddenly got very excited. I guess we are pretty special.

'I am.' I replied, figuring it was probably too late to slip into my excellent Danish linguism.

'Oh, wow! *Coronation Street* is my favourite show! I watch it all the time!'

...Had he thought I'd *been in* it? This was a terrible way to impress me! What *was* he thinking? And how could he watch it all the time? Wait! *Why* would he *want to* watch it all the time?

'Greeaat...' I smiled through gritted teeth, before promptly demonstrating my swift English turn of pace as I caught up with the others. *Coronation Street.* I mean *really...*

It was then suggested that we went to a bar, so we walked *beyond* the walls of the old town and onto the main Grande Alleé Est street

134

– a very long and straight road that had a lot of bars on it. Coincidence? No.

In hardly any time at all we had found an exciting looking place. It had a blackboard outside, and a nicely painted railing on top of a small well built wall. That's essentially all I look for in a bar, so in we went! The inside was semi-sunk under ground, and although small in area, it was brimming with merriment. There were numerous small, round tables with lots of happy, smiling French-Canadians positioned around them, sipping away at various fancy looking cocktails or a beer. There was also a small stage, and on this were a couple of men with guitars playing music. I though this was excellent - live music was a *real* bonus.

We managed to pinch a few chairs from around the bar, and pack them in around a couple of spare tables in the corner. We then ordered a jug of beer from the table-service man. I think he was compensating for being very short by being muscley, and also by having a silly haircut. He didn't endear himself to us any further when he returned to the table with the smallest jug I've ever seen. It was pretty much just a pint glass with a handle. He also delivered it with the wonderful, customer friendly line, "The tip's not included." Nice.

Him aside, it was a nice atmosphere in the bar, and the music was good too. We were even treated to positively terrifying performance of *AC/DC*'s *Back in Black*, by a really fat, sweaty man with a ponytail and a horribly tight (and increasingly see-through) shirt. Who knew someone so large and ungainly looking could screech at such a high pitch? He put his all into it; I'll give him that.

It did however signal the end of our evening (we wanted to get out before *Celine Dion* made an unexpected guest appearance) and so we headed back to the safety of the walled city.

Chapter 19

There's no such thing as a free lunch… (but there's one hell of a good-value dessert on offer if you ask nicely)

Chute Montmorency et L'Astral, à Québec

*"Don't look a gift horse…*up in the *Argos* catalogue. They don't sell them."

I awoke to a full dorm on my last morning in Québec. This was quite the contrast from the empty room I was left alone and shivering in on my first night. Ah, okay I wasn't really cold and shivering – I have an excellent silk sleeping bag liner that works wonders on cold nights – but that's beside the point. The point is that I had one last thing to do in Québec City, and today I was completely focused upon this one important mission…

…That was until I went downstairs and through reception, where I passed another one of those fantastically alluring sign-up sheets. The hostel was running an informal trip to a nearby waterfall. It was…tall…and wet. Hmmm. The picture did look nice, but I was still a little sceptical after the disappointment of Niagara Falls (or at least the neighbouring town) and I also had a *really* important thing to get done today.

But in the end I was swayed by it. I just couldn't resist a list of names in a table formation – I wanted in, and as I stood by the sheet deliberating, Marvin and Patrik passed by, and they *too* were tempted, and so that was it. We were all sold on it. To Montmorency!

The newly assembled group set off on the trip later that morning. We had to catch a public bus for the hour journey out to the waterfall, meandering around numerous Québec City suburbs along the way. We got off the bus at what appeared to be the final stop, about seven kilometres from Québec City. It was then a short walk through a wooded area to the top of the waterfall.

Chute Montmorency is eighty-three metres high, which is over thirty metres higher than Niagara Falls. The waterfall is at the mouth of the Montmorency River, just as it joins up with the Saint Lawrence River. The first view we got of the falls was a dramatic one – from above the water as it plummeted over the edge courtesy of a suspension footbridge. I was glad I had come to see another waterfall, because I like the word 'plummet', and there aren't many other situations that are so appropriate for its use.

After crossing the bridge we headed into a large, open parkland area, with just a few pathways cutting through it. There was one small brick hut building, but this was all closed up. This was great to see after the disastrous touristic development of Niagara, as Montmorency was sympathetically recognised and left as an unspoilt piece of nature. We then cut back over to the riverside where we could now see the waterfall face on. It was a spectacular sight, with the water gushing violently over the rocky edge of the river, before…plummeting (I promise that's the last time I use that word) down into the mist below. There was more though. Those that were feeling energetic could go down the four hundred-odd wooden steps that make up a rather precarious looking staircase that juts out from the riverbank rock face. As part of the committed 'team-museum', we felt up to the challenge, and raced down to the bottom where we found ourselves on a long concrete promenade that runs parallel with the lower part of the river. Here, Marvin and myself decided it would be fun to run down towards the wall of water and up a few steps to a concrete viewing platform that was right in the shower mist at the base of the falls.

It *was* fun, but it was also increasingly difficult to stand up as we got blasted by water as we attempted to take a sneaky photograph. It was then a hasty retreat to the relative dryness at the foot of the staircase, before we made our way back up the stairs to meet up with the rest of the group in the sunshine where we could dry off. It was only once we had got our breath back that we realised that from our position on top of the north bank of the river that we could see the mount of Vieux Québec in the distant haze, spreading down from the distinctive silhouetted shape of the Château Frontenac at the top of the hill. It was a great sight from a fantastic setting.

From here we went back across the bridge and over to the other side of the river, where some of the group stopped at the smart restaurant on the south bank for refreshments, while most of us simply sat outside and enjoyed the sunshine and views out over the river, where we could also watch the cable car that was transporting people from the top of the falls down to the river mouth below.

It was then back to the bus stop for the return trip to the city, after a very enjoyable outing to an excellent waterfall. I'd thoroughly recommend it if you're in the area - I reckon it's better than Niagara.

The bus ride back was fun too. An elderly French-Canadian man who barely spoke a word of English was trying to talk to Marvin, Patrik and myself as we sat at the back of the bus. The other two didn't speak any French, and mine is pretty limited, and so it was an interesting exchange that was a little short on depth and understanding. The rest of the hostel tour group (who were all

French natives) found it hugely entertaining as we struggled to exchange sentences about…well, I'm still not entirely sure.

I think we worked out that he was a policeman who was going into the city to go to church. I in turn managed to tell him that we were staying at a nice hostel, where I had a reservation for a room with a bed. I hope he didn't think I was weird or that I was making inappropriate suggestions. I then ran out of 'useful' French, and so I filled the awkward silence by telling him 'J'ai un pantalon bleu'.

To be honest he probably knew that I had blue trousers on, as he could quite clearly *see* that I had blue trousers on. I also doubt that even if he *hadn't* noticed that I had blue trousers on that he would find this a particularly enlightening statement, but sometimes it's the little details in life that make the day worthwhile. They were jeans by the way; I don't want you imagining that I was parading around this elegant city wearing giant, bright blue clown trousers.

The man seemed nevertheless grateful for our chat, and he even managed to string together enough English to tell us that it was a pleasure talking to us. This was very kind of him, and it had been nice talking to him too. I'm sure he would go home and tell all his friends about us and my excellent blue trousers. I also firmly believe that Anglo-French-Canadian relations will be all the better for it.

We got off the bus and said goodbye to the French contingency, and then it was time for today's big mission - the one objective I had set for the day, before I had been rudely distracted by sign-up forms and pretty waterfalls. But no more! I was done with distractions. I was *motivated.* I was *focused.* I was *intent.* I had German *and* Swiss German allies. And most importantly of all - *I* had blue trousers!

I led the newly formed *Québec City Quest Alliance* (QCQA) in the direction I reckoned we needed to be heading in, and once we were clear of the tower blocks and had marched purposefully into open green space, we saw it - in all it's faded brown peculiarity – *L'Astral*.

L'Astral is a revolving restaurant set above the Loews Hotel, just off Grande Alleé Est. I had seen this place featured on a notice board in the hostel, and it had said that it was well worth a visit.

I had been having a great time in Québec City, but there was something I needed to do to 'sign it off' if you like, and so I to complete my visit I thought I had better have a sandwich. Having been developing an extensive set of criteria for sandwich assessment I thought that combining a sandwich with a tall-building visit would make for a great location-sandwich, and so here we were, three backpackers, traipsing through the lobby of a fancy hotel.

We found the lifts without being intercepted by hotel security, and soon we were inside the express elevator that we guessed went up to the restaurant. There were a few buttons on the control panel, but all of the letters engraved on them were in French and so we didn't know what they stood for, so we weren't sure what to press. After some careful consideration and a bit of well thought through logic we ended up guessing, and the lift ended up not moving. So we scrapped that plan, and just jabbed at all the buttons until it *did* move. Thankfully we went upwards, and within seconds we had stopped and the doors were opening.

We were immediately greeted by a very smartly dressed lady standing behind a small podium stand, such as those that important speakers stand behind when they are about to speak importantly about important things.

'Bonjour. Voulez-vous voir le menu?' She spoke quickly, and Frenchly.

'Oui,' I eagerly replied. This looked liked the type of place that would have nice menus that were certainly well worth a look.

She handed us a menu - which was indeed a lovely dark blue mottled folder, with excellent calligraphy and fine lamination. We studied it for a few seconds.

I think the lady saw the frowns grow across our faces, and she probably combined this facial response with our scruffy backpacker attire, because she then offered us the slightly lower-priced lunch menu. Sadly this 'lower-priced' factor was all relative, and we still found the prices written before us to be rather daunting given our economy travel ethics. They didn't even *offer* sandwiches! This was a predicament. I thought for a second, realised that at this increased altitude I was incapable of doing this effectively, and so I gave up and tentatively enquired about dessert. The notice board in the hostel had suggested visiting *L'Astral* - recommending the cakes at around ten dollars a slice - presumably because it was a cheaper option and the hostel knew their target market. So I figured it was worth a shot. The lady must have then accepted that we would not be boosting restaurant profit margins this afternoon, and as the place was pretty much empty, she told us that we could have the final remains of dessert for four dollars. Perfect. We were shown to a table next to one of the large curved glass windows where we all proceeded to order tap water. This probably really pissed them off. The only other guests were a sparse selection of stern-faced business types or smartly dressed parents with well-presented children who didn't scream or cry or cover their faces in the posh food they had in front of them. These other guests had tables with table cloths. We didn't. We clearly were not worthy. This was fine though – we weren't in it for little presentation details. We were here for food scraps and nice views.

We got up and walked over to the carts of left-over desserts. Left-over or not though, they were amazing. There was a fantastic selection of gelatine fruit slices, cakes and pastries. We weren't exactly sure what we were allowed to have, so we just took as much as we could and then rushed back to our table and ate it quickly, glancing around us in case we had misinterpreted what we were entitled to, worried that actually we should only have had a grape each. We seemed to be getting away with it though, and so we went back up for seconds and got completely stuffed on luxury puddings.

141

You may think that with all this covert eating we didn't get to enjoy the views. Not so. As we stuffed our faces we were slowly rotated around the restaurant as a three hundred and sixty degree view of the city was laid out before us. We could see right across Vieux Québec and the vast green expanse of the Plains of Abraham stretching up to it. We could see out across the river to Lévis, and further beyond to the inlet near Montmorency Falls. All of this was set in the glistening afternoon sunshine too. It was great. We didn't *even* have to walk as far when we came to leaving the restaurant, as by the time we had finished clearing the remaining dessert offerings into our stomachs, the outer seating area of the restaurant had rotated us round to the exit lifts. Given how fat we now were after eating this worked out nicely.

As far as my sandwich missions had gone up to this point, this one was arguably the best; good company, fine service, excellent food quality, large quantities, fantastic location and setting...and all for under seven dollars! (Once a bit of tax and tips had been added.) The only *slight* point of contention would be that it *didn't actually* involve a sandwich. I feel this is only a minor technicality though, and nothing a small administrative adjustment couldn't fix.

Chapter 20

A Taste of Canada
In search of a reasonably priced sandwich and/or dessert

Quebec to Nova Scotia

*"The early bird...*greatly disturbs the late starter"

The lift must have been significantly heavier as we descended to the ground floor after our lunchtime dessert raid, but we were all very satisfied with what we had achieved for such a reasonable price. Because it had been *terribly* reasonable, and that was clearly very important to my trip. We stepped out into the sunshine and headed up onto the Plains of Abraham – scene of the Battle of the Plains of Abraham between the British and the French that occurred on the 13th September 1759. The war lasted fifteen minutes. If only all wars were this decisive.

Fifteen minutes may seem brief, but it was still longer than the amount of time Marvin, Patrik and myself spent on the Plains, as no sooner had we stepped onto the grassy mounds of this riverside parkland than we spotted *our* modern day enemy; the school trip group. There were *literally hundreds* of them, and they were rapidly assembling in battle formation – pairing up and heading our way. We ran to the hills, and that's not because we're *Iron Maiden* fans, but because we figured that being on higher ground was the best defensive strategy. The Citadelle fort was just up ahead at the top of Vieux Québec, but before we reached that we leapt over a narrow bridge and began making our way along the high, precarious walls of the old town, where we could keep an eye on the herd of soul-destroying teenagers as they circled ominously below. After this swift detour around the old defensive ruins and walls, we dropped back down to solid ground and made our way back to the hostel.

It was soon time to leave Québec City, but I had time to kill until my next train journey and so I sat back in the lounge at the hostel with my pack of playing cards at the ready. I didn't get a chance to use them though, as soon I got chatting with Anita, an Irish girl who was looking to spend the year working in Canada. She seemed the tolerant type, and she was also very enthusiastic about travelling which was good, and so (especially after recent exciting sandwich and dessert missions) I was happy to explain my important sandwich quest to her. She seemed very interested in it, or at least she very convincingly *pretended* to be interested in it. Then she asked me if I'd had a 'Tayto sandwich'. I hadn't, and this seemed to shock her, which scared me a little, so I asked her to calm down and explain it, which she did.

The 'Tayto sandwich' is a sandwich consisting of crisps in bread. Simple, right? No. Well yes…but apparently there are lots of different flavour crisps you can use, and then you can add lots of other exciting ingredients or accompaniments as deemed necessary to make the perfect 'Tayto sandwich'.

This is apparently a massively popular sandwich snack in Ireland, and it must have been a combination of my lack of awareness of this piece of Irish snack heritage and my intrigue over all things 'sandwiches' that led her to put out a request to her friends and contacts back in Ireland for their thoughts and recipes for the perfect 'Tayto sandwich'. More information to follow then…

Soon it was time to leave, so I picked up my bags, said goodbye to the people I'd spent the last few days with, and then I set off down the hill to the station. I was a little sad to be leaving because I'd had a great time in Québec City, having met some really good people with whom I had visited some very interesting places, seen some great sights, and of course had some fantastic dessert.

I got to the station and walked up to the bus information desk. My ticket said that I needed a bus transfer to the train, so I walked over to the bus counter.

'No, that's a train ticket you've got there' said the lady behind the desk after I had showed her my ticket. 'You need to go through those doors behind you and over to the train counter'.

So I did. And I patiently waited until the man ahead of me had finished and then I stepped up.

'Er…no, you need to get a bus transfer. That's a ticket for the bus.' The man dismissively responded.

I sighed. This was all very unhelpful.

Then another lady from behind one of the neighbouring desks sparked up. 'There's usually a bus, but I think this evening they're sending taxis on behalf of the train company. They should be out the front in about twenty minutes.'

Ah, finally some progress.

I left the counter and found a seat by a television screen that was showing the latest ice hockey match between Montreal and Pittsburgh.

A line of taxis pulled up outside the station building at quarter past seven as I had been told they would. A smattering of passengers had gathered together by the front doors of the building to greet the convoy, and after a few moments of confusion as the taxi drivers scratched their heads while battling with the logistics of getting all of us passengers and our bags into the cars, we were all on our way. I was in a car with an elderly Australian couple, an English pair who

145

were on holiday visiting Eastern Canada, and a young Canadian woman who was conducting a research project on bumble bees.

It was a forty-five minute drive to Charny, which is a small station somewhere on the outskirts of Québec City. It's quite a small station, and once we had all moved ourselves and our luggage into the waiting area it was pretty crowded. Luckily it wasn't going to be a long wait, and we were soon heading out onto the platform to board the train that would take us on the nineteen-hour journey to Halifax, Nova Scotia.

The province of Nova Scotia is situated on the Eastern side of Canada. Halifax is the main city of the province, and it is also the furthest point east on the Canadian rail network, situated on the Atlantic coast.

It had occurred to me that although I was ultimately heading for a sandwich on the *west* coast, I should really try to get a fair comparison, and so I had decided I should head to the *east* coast for a sandwich, just to get a good balance, because I'm a professional, and I wanted this done right. Another reason for heading further east – the opposite direction to that of my original sandwich goal – was that I realised that I needed to do some laundry, and Halifax sounded like the type of place where I could get this done. So combining these two excellent reasons, logic prevailed, and I was left with no other option than to buy a ticket for the trip through *The Maritimes* aboard the train known as *The Ocean* to Halifax.

The man at the luggage check-in desk at Charny station had given me detailed instructions on how to board the train. Yes, I had imagined it would be a straight forward case of; train stops; doors open; get on. But no. This was the *Canadian* train network, and therefore it required far more formal procedure and complication than that.

146

As a 'comfort-class passenger' (economy/poverty-stricken 'slumming it' passenger), I, along with the other less glamorous or heavily financed travellers had to make my way along the platform, cross over the railway track siding, and continue up until I was next to a large white propane tank. Once here we would wait in the wilderness until the train showed up. We were then instructed that when it *did* arrive, it would stop at the platform – but whatever we did we mustn't board the train at this point! Oh No! The flashpackers who were in 'sleeper-class' and who were waiting in the more traditional setting of the actual the station building vicinity would get on at this point. The train would then close up its doors and move forward slightly, for some inexplicable reason, where it would stop again, and *then we* could finally get on. It all seemed very unorthodox and quite frankly a little unlikely. They really know how to drag out train travel here. But oddly enough it all happened exactly as the man had prophesised. The train arrived; it stopped; we remained on the platform in the ghostly mist - pierced only by the blinding headlights of the train; the train doors closed and then it moved forward slightly; the train stopped again; we got on the train. It all went like clockwork...if your clock is very old and needs a firm tap on the side every so often to keep it ticking properly.

The train itself was surprisingly plush given the economy status. Each row consisted of a pair of seats on one side of the aisle and a single seat on the other. The train had started in Montreal, and so all the double seats were taken, leaving us newbies with a single seat. These were very comfortable though, with low-reclining backs that slid forward at the front so as to not interfere with the space of the person in the seat behind you (unlike on an aeroplane). The seats were also on a raised platform, providing a large space under each seat for bags, as well as a netted compartment overheard for extra belongings. We also had individual window blinds and a drop down

147

table on the back of the seat in front. It was all very impressive, and with the addition of a pillow and blanket provided by the friendly train staff it was all quite comfortable and exciting as we set off into the night.

* * *

I didn't get a lot of sleep as the train rattled along, but thankfully the journey didn't seem to drag on too much. The train didn't really rattle either – that's just a stereotypical/cliché description of trains. I'd actually describe the motion as bumbling and sporadic, seeing as we stopped a lot for no apparent reason and seemingly in the middle of nowhere. This was a little disruptive and slightly worrying as sometimes all I could see out of the window at these random stops was a car stopped facing the train with its headlights on. I saw no sign of cowboys storming through the carriages though, so I presumed we weren't subjected to any modern day wild-west style hold-ups during the night. Infrequent station stops also slowed the journey and disrupted any sleep we may have been getting as some people got off the train, and others got on. During these stops we were sometimes allowed to step out for a cigarette break, or for those like me who don't smoke – a leg stretch.

The scenery throughout the trip was nothing hugely worthy of writing home about, which was just as well really, as I'd heard the Canadian postal system wasn't the best. The landscape was mostly dominated by woodland with the occasional small lake breaking up the banks of trees. In some areas there were signs of deforestation, whether natural or not it was hard to tell. I also wasn't exactly sure where we were at any point during the journey as there was little indication given by the surroundings as to our location. All I could go on was my understanding that the route took us along southern Quebec, through New Brunswick, and then across Nova Scotia to the coast.

* * *

The train pulled up in Halifax late afternoon, and although I hadn't slept much I spent the last half hour of the journey eagerly watching the slowly urbanising landscape out of the window as we drew closer to the city. I was also using loud music to kick my brain into gear through the provision of my mp3 player.

Whereas with other Canadian cities I'd had some idea of things I could do, with Halifax I didn't. All I knew is that I wanted to do some laundry, and eat a sandwich. Oh, and I wanted to touch the Atlantic Ocean - you know, for symbolic reasons, as then I could touch the Pacific Ocean when I made it out west and that would be kind of cool...probably. But whatever my reasons, these activities would not necessarily fully occupy the duration of my stay, as I had booked three nights in Halifax, partly because I thought I should spend at least a couple of days there as it was a day and a half's travel to get there and away, and partly because that fitted with the next available departure back westwards.

It was only a five-minute walk from the station to the hostel, and soon I was dumping my bags beside a creaky wooden bunk bed. Having sorted myself out I went off in search of a supermarket. Conveniently it turned out that there was one adjacent to the station, and soon I had been over to it and come back, and I was now in the very large and functional hostel kitchen cooking up a steak and a salad. Actually the salad took very little cooking as I've never been a fan of pan-fried lettuce, but the point is that I wasn't eating pasta for the first time in...well, quite a few days.

I was pretty tired from the train journey, and so after eating I had a brief wander around the neighbouring streets before I headed to bed at around ten o'clock. I was looking forward to lying horizontally and getting some good sleep before I went off in search of some east coast activities...and sandwiches! I sorted out my

149

belongings and climbed up the back of the bed before collapsing onto the top bunk. This was nice.

…And that's when I saw it. Caught in my narrow line of vision through the beach wood slats of the bed. Just sitting there on top of the post of the adjacent top bunk, in all its beige, creased up imitation glory. I stared at it for a second and blinked hard like they do in clichéd films. Nope, it was *still there*.

It was a cowboy hat.

It couldn't be…could it?

Chapter 21

"Erm...we sell haddock...?"

Halifax, Nova Scotia

*"Actions speak louder...*when accompanied by speech. Or cannon fire."

I rolled over to face the wall. Maybe it was just a coincidence. *Maybe* there were *other* cowboy hat wearers in Canada. Yes, I was over-reacting. It would be fine. I was just tired and needed to catch up on some sleep after the long train journey. I closed my eyes and quickly drifted off. I didn't see there being much that could disturb me for the next eight hours.

Thirty minutes later and I was rudely awoken by the sound of snoring. This was a night time interference I had thankfully somehow managed to avoid thus far on my trip, but I think the god of 'peaceful sleep' was taking revenge tonight, as the multi-toned rumblings emanating from this individual were making my bed vibrate. I turned back around to see the perpetrator of this *hideous* backpacker crime. And *guess what?* There, sprawled out across a *completely unmade* bed, and still semi-dressed (I guess I should be thankful for that) was captain cowboy – my enemy from Québec City. This wasn't fair! Was he following me? Oh how tempted I was to smother that un-housetrained s.o.b. with his own f***ing hat.

That would teach him to spend his evenings boring the hell out of hostellers and further disrupting the peace with this *horrific* snoring.

* * *

I woke up the next morning, which firmly suggested that I *had* in fact got some sleep, and for that I was reasonably grateful.

It was another nice sunny day on the east coast, and so I decided that today I would head out to explore the city. To be honest this had been my fantastically vague plan anyway, and so it was just a nice coincidence that the photos I would inevitably take on my wanders would be nicer as a result of the blue skies.

I talk of Halifax being a 'city', but I have since found out that as of April 1996 it is no longer the 'City of Halifax' as established in 1841, but it is now referred to as "an unincorporated provincial metropolitan area". However, I'm sure you will agree that this is a *far* less punchy 'trip off the tongue' term for it, and so for the purposes of writing-flow and readability of this highly factual insight in to Canada I shall continue to callously refer to Halifax as a 'city'.

My first stop was the Citadel, set on top of a large grassy hill in the middle of the city/"unincorporated provincial metropolitan area" (there, I'm easing you in gently). This was the first defence and warning station of any attack that may come in from the Atlantic. Thankfully (or not if you like your dramatic history) the fort never saw any action. As I walked up the stone pathway towards the outer walls of the fort, I was suddenly halted in my tracks by a voice speaking to me from behind. I *know* – the cheek!

'Hey, where did you get your shoes from? They're awesome!' the man who was probably a little older than myself said.

152

At first I assumed he was taking the mick as this was a strange comment to make to a stranger and because I'm English and I feel we have a tendency to think this way, but then I realised that *he* was *Canadian,* and so he was probably being genuine, as this was quite a Canadian thing to do.

'Thanks. Err...I'm from England...' I replied. Because I'm a genius and this is a default reply for the English when we are abroad and are unsure of how to deal with foreign requests.

I then realised how stupid this sounded, and so I said something else to justify what I had *actually* meant by my initial response.

'...so I bought them from a shop in England.'

There. That's that all cleared up. And with that he said "Ah" in a disappointed yet accepting way, and then I turned back around and continued walking.

And *then* I thought about it. That was actually *bloody rude* of me. Here was someone who had built up the courage to tell me - a complete stranger - that he liked my shoes, and who was also hoping to gain a little insight into how *he* could look as cool and fashionable as me, and then I, the cool and fashionable one, had just shot him down rather bluntly. This was *not on.*

I turned back around to face him.

'But they're made by an American company of musicians.'

And with that I told him the makers of the shoes and a few possible websites that may sell them.

He was very grateful, and we had a nice little chat about shoes and music. I think I was slowly starting to adjust to the Canadian way of things - which was good, because they have a very *good* way of things.

Having said this, I couldn't quite understand his enthusiasm for the shoes, as they were essentially just black plimsolls with a white block logo on the side. They were also starting to tear at the seam between the upper and the sole, *and* they were so thin I could feel every twig I stepped on. They were pretty much just a convenient pair of shoes to stuff in a backpack as an alternative to my more robust trail shoes.

Anyway, this didn't really matter, and it didn't change the fact that I urgently needed to send an email home to tell everyone back in England how fashionable I in fact am, and that if they cannot accept me for the fashion guru that I have *clearly* become, then maybe I should consider moving to Canada permanently, where I can distribute my hipness and keen eye for dress sense amongst the less enlightened.

* * *

The Citadel itself was…well, I don't like to sound too derogatory, but it was a little…lacking in…anything. It was (and presumably still is) essentially just a large gravel area with walls around it. There are a few buildings within the walls though – one houses a small museum that focuses on the important presence of the fort (that hasn't been involved in any battles), one has a lot of barrels in it (apparently filled with gunpowder – although I have my doubts) and one houses the gift shop. There is one exciting thing about it though, and this was the main reason I had come – the twelve noon firing of the cannon!

The helpful lady on the hostel reception desk had told me that at precisely twelve noon everyday they fired a cannon ceremoniously from the Citadel. This had seemed worth a visit, and so here I was, at ten minutes to noon, lining up with the rest of the tourists on the ramparts to witness it. What I had noticed upon my initial stroll around the fort was that there were hardly any visitors, and those that were ambling across the gravel were greatly outnumbered by military folk in period costume. Here however, a gathering of around twenty people had come together to witness the cannon firing.

The surrounding ramparts were sealed off as they prepared for this daily tradition. As the cannon was prepared, one of those in costume gave a short history of the fort and its presence in Halifax, an area that has a strong Scottish heritage. This was reflected in the outfits of the soldiers, and we were given a detailed explanation of the clothing, and every so often a joke was thrown in at the expense of the English. Everyone found this very funny. I just scowled at the man as I was the only Brit in the village. But of course another trait of the British is our fantastic sense of humour and our ability not to take ourselves too seriously, and so I wasn't really bothered. I actually appreciated the light-hearted nature of the talk, especially as military uniform discussions can be a little…well…boring.

Soon the hour was upon us, and the cannon had been loaded and checked, and the formal procedure had reached its climax. The guards stood to attention while the lead officer did some sharp barking of instructions in between receiving messages on his eighteenth century walkie-talkie. Some people took a tentative step back, a couple of mothers covered the ears of their young children, and a few faces winced as they prepared for the loud bang.

'Five!…Four!…Three!…Two! [sharp collective intake of breathe from the audience] One!…'

And that was it. Silence.

For a moment everyone stood still, wondering if it was all a big joke. I caught some people peering around at other people in case they themselves had been focusing so hard on limiting the impact of the 'bang' on their ears that they had inadvertently missed it.

But they hadn't. They had *advertently* missed it. Or possibly even *vertently* missed it – because it hadn't actually happened.

'Misfire!' the lead officer shouted, with just a hint of embarrassment in his voice.

'Ha!' I let out a small sigh of enjoyment.

155

After all the build-up about this being a *precise* tradition; "on the dot of twelve noon", *and* after mocking the English - I felt that they had got their comeuppance.

There were a few seconds of frantic (but of course disciplined) movement as the guards checked and prodded the cannon, and then at precisely thirty-six seconds past twelve...

'BANG!'

Job done.

As I made my way back across the gravel I bumped into the lady who worked on reception at the hostel. She had been the one who had told me about the cannon firing, and now she herself had finally made it down to watch it after meaning to for weeks. She asked me what I was going to do with the rest of my day, and when I said I wasn't really sure, she suggested I...no, she *instructed* me to go and have an "amazing east coast snack". This seemed an ideal way to pass some time. After all, I was in Canada on lunchtime-snack eating business, so I would be a *fool* to miss this opportunity. It was also lunchtime. Everything was working out neatly!

I set off towards the harbour front where she had told me in her thick Australian accent that I would find a selection of small wooden huts. It was apparently from one of these outlets that I could buy the snack from. On my way I passed through some pretty gardens, with lots of colourful flowerbeds and little ornaments, all set to a backing track of tinkling water. Lovely. Then it was onto the harbour front.

Now, although the Australian accent is by no means incomprehensible, I had not fully heard her word for word, but I was pretty sure she had said that the food item I was looking for was some kind of a 'battered fish tail'.

This sounded a little strange, but then it also sounded like a specialist item, and so I was sure it would be easy to find.

I spent twenty minutes walking up and down the smart, newly developed harbour front. It consisted of a series of immaculate wooden promenade walkways, interspersed with decorative features such as a massive stone whale dorsal fin that was curved over at the top (*Free Willy* style) and sticking out of the ground. There were also lots of boats, some of which offered boat-related tours, and there were also a selection of restaurants and cafes, which given the fine weather were full, with people spilling out onto their umbrella-covered terraces as they sipped pints and ate colourful seafood dishes.

I found a row of wooden huts selling various food types, and more specifically there was one that stood out as it was selling fish and chips. This definitely seemed like the place the Australian had spoken of, and yet I couldn't see anything on its menu board that suggested it sold a 'famous' battered fish tail. I walked around the quayside a little more, but I couldn't see any other huts, and there certainly weren't any more places that seemed likely to sell this cult cuisine.

In the end I headed back to the fish and chip hut, and tentatively enquired about the fish tail.

'Hi…erm…do you sell…erm…some kind of…*battered fish tail…*?' Yes. There was absolutely no conviction in my enquiry.

The lady behind the counter looked down on me (I mean she *literally* looked down on me – she wasn't being patronising - the counter was just very high up) 'Err…we sell haddock…?' came her reply.

'Erm…okay. No thanks.' And with that I turned and walked away. That clearly wasn't right, and now I had lost face too.

I continued to walk along the waterfront. I was frustrated that I couldn't find this important snack because it was a relevant mission that needed completing. I needed to know about these things – and try them!

I was mulling over how I could make my afternoon more successful when I spotted a newspaper article pinned in the window of a small building next to one of the wooden promenades. I saw in the headline; "Voted Best Ice Cream", and this instantly drew my attention. I read the article that described how the ice cream in this ice cream parlour was not only supposed to be *the best* in Canada, but that it had also been voted *the best* in the *world!* By no less than "an independent travel group"! Wow. Well this was quite the accolade! And as it was a hot, sunny day and I hadn't eaten because of my inability to find battered fish tails, this was *clearly* an indication that I should test to see if the ice cream sold in this shop called *Cows* was indeed the best in the world! I stepped inside and was instantly faced with a very long glass cooling cabinet filled with countless containers of multi-coloured ice cream. I looked up at the menu so I could select a flavour I fancied.

It could have been a coincidence, but all the flavours seemed to involve 'cow'. Whether this was a literal flavouring or not I wasn't sure, but I decided to play it safe anyway, and I went for mint. Mint doesn't go with cow; it goes with lamb, and so I reckoned I was safe with this choice. If I had been a fancy flashpacker I could have afforded two scoops! But I wasn't, so one would have to suffice.

My single (but generous) scoop came in my personal selection of a waffle-style cone, and cost $4.24 after the addition of tax. This seemed quite expensive, but I suppose if it was the world's greatest ice cream then it would be well worth it. It also came with a complimentary serviette. They know how to treat people here.

I took my ice cream out into the sunshine, and found a nice pile of rocks by the promenade to sit on while I ate it – looking out across the water as I did so. It was very nice (the view and the ice cream), but then I very rarely ever eat ice cream, and so it would be difficult for me to conclusively say whether it was the best in the world. It was certainly the best I'd had on this trip though, and once again the setting of my eating destination, plus the variety and status of the ice cream on offer made it a very reasonable and enjoyable snack. This was therefore very important to my research project, even if (again) it wasn't actually a sandwich. So I really ought to knuckle down at some point and find a more sandwich type sandwich here on the east coast to keep my mission on track…

As I sat on the rocks mopping up the drips of green, melted mint ice cream from my hand with my complimentary serviette, I spotted a small ferry pulling up beside a little terminal building just a bit further along the waterfront. A ferry! I was in Canada *because* of a ferry – or more precisely a ferry *terminal*, so maybe I should get some ferry terminal practise in!…whatever that means. So I jumped up and set off back down the promenade.

The ferry crossed over to Dartmouth, a town on the other side of the water. It was only a twelve-minute crossing, and an absolute bargain at $2.25. They required the exact change at the sales desk though, but luckily I sussed the nearby change machine and got the right coinage. This is more than could be said for the Canadian woman behind me in the queue, who needed my assistance in obtaining change. Money goes in the slot – coins fall out into the tray. I mean *really*.

The views back over Halifax harbour were nice, with its mix of industry and docks lining up beside the modern harbour front and glass tower blocks. Out on deck the blustery sea breeze provided a welcome cooling effect given the heat of the day, and so the journey was very pleasant.

As I sat on my plastic seat on the upper deck I considered what I would do once we arrived in Dartmouth. I realised that I had no idea as I didn't know what was there, but I had a brainwave of how to fix this. I pulled out my map of Halifax.

Now, in most places that I had visited so far in Canada I could get hold of a map. I like exploring unaided, but I found that maps were useful for attracting the attention of Canadians – *particularly* the *friendly* sort that I had found so abundant, and through this I would learn about a place, or at the very least have an interesting chat. The map I currently possessed of Halifax was the most touristy tourist map you could hope to find; it was *ridiculously* large, *very* colourful, and it had those disproportioned 'pop-out' city attractions, and therefore it was *perfect* for gaining attention. And sure enough, no sooner had I unfolded this giant, laminated paper extravagance than the gentleman beside me lit up. He didn't smoke or have neon contact lenses though, but he engaged me in tourist chat. It had worked like charm. He said that I could walk around Dartmouth Cove and follow the waterside along a pathway to Woodside, where there was another ferry that I could catch back to Halifax. This sounded ideal. I was sorted.

It was a very pleasant twenty-five minute walk along the shoreline, with the new-looking pathways winding around the cove and past one of the cities three universities. It was in one of these inlets that I took a brief diversion over the shingle beach and down to the water so I could touch the Atlantic Ocean. I even tasted the water by licking my fingers. It tasted salty and cold. Yep – it was definitely the Atlantic! This was a symbolic moment, as it signalled the furthest easterly point of my journey. My adventure was now going to be leading me west - right across the width of Canada, finishing on the west coast and the *Pacific* Ocean...and the reasonably priced sandwich! But of course first I needed to find an *east* coast sandwich, and I still had no idea where I was going to find a suitable offering...

Chapter 22

A sand-wich was unexpected

(Some more) Halifax, Nova Scotia

*"Fight fire...*with water. It will stop you burning your bridges."

So I began my epic journey west on the Woodside Ferry. This was not a particularly quick ferry, and so I decided this would not be my dominant form of cross-Canada travel. I also felt that the lack of water on the route would make this an inefficient mode of transport. However, it was perfect for this short water crossing, and soon I was back in Halifax walking along the harbour.

I headed in the opposite direction to that of which I had walked along before. This led me towards the industrial area and the docks. This is also where the nice promenade ran out, and so I was forced to cut in across a car park. It was here that I noticed a large building ahead with cannon logo on the front. It was one of Halifax's two local breweries. This evening they were putting on a barbeque at the hostel, and *everyone* knows that the perfect accompaniment to a barbeque is beer. *Especially* locally brewed beer. *Cold*, locally brewed beer.

I walked into the brewery where I was faced with a large warehouse full of giant vats and shiny beer making pipes and machinery. I also noticed a man, or more accurately – a friendly Canadian beer sample offering man. This *was* a lucky find.

The man told me a little about the history of the brewery, and then a little about each of the beers. As I have consistently proved, I am no expert on beer, so when he said I could have a mix 'n' match selection of the six different types of beers they brewed I couldn't really say no. So I didn't. He had himself a deal.

Back at the hostel the barbeque was in full swing. And by this I mean I was sitting in the kitchen at a table eating my tiny, thin, under-cooked cheap 'burger' and a few leaves of lettuce. Okay, so it wasn't the finest barbeque food I'd ever had, and nor was it the wildest party Canada had ever seen – but then the hostel was quite empty, and they hadn't asked for much money for the meal. This low-key evening was about to change though, because *guess who* walked through the door while I had a stringy piece of celery hanging out of my mouth! It was my cowboy dorm buddy! Crap. I needed a beer, *right now*!

He wasn't actually wearing his cowboy hat though. No, instead he was fully kitted out in a ridiculous pin-stripe suit. Dear god, what *was* he doing? I shouldn't have asked, although in my defence I only asked this question *in my head*, and so he had absolutely *no right* to sit at my table and answer it. But he did. Without me saying anything *or* inviting him to join me, he sat down opposite me and began telling me about how he was going around restaurants writing notes for reviews – despite not being a food critic. So essentially he was dressing up like a spanner and dining out alone for no financial reward. Genius. What was even *more* intriguing was that he went on to tell me a story that by all accounts was quite dramatic (if a little dubious in regards to its credibility) but what impressed me most was that despite this he delivered the story in the most drawn out and BORING way imaginable. His dull, *painfully* slow monotone speech left me dreaming of choking on the remainder of my celery that was becoming lodged uncomfortably in my throat. How could anyone *seriously* be this dull? It was amazing.

After around four minutes – the *longest* four minutes of my life – I couldn't physically take it anymore. I managed to choke down the celery, and then I got up and said I had to go and do some laundry. I grabbed another beer from the fridge and headed off to gather my clothes. Freedom!

One of my main reasons for coming to Halifax was to do laundry, and so I collected up my clothes to be laundered, and headed down to the basement to get it done. Luckily the machines were empty, and so I could throw my clothes in, add the washing powder, and away it went! I then returned upstairs and sat in the lounge with a beer. Thankfully this room was free of cowboys, and so I could sit back, relax, and watch some television.

While the beer and sit down were relaxing, the television was not. Unfortunately the news was on, and where I like to keep on top of current affairs and stories – the news did not allow for this. Sadly the news is presented in a 'sensationalist' fashion, and so only the most 'shocking' news is delivered, and this is delivered with as much drama as possible, and thus the in-depth content and facts are watered down or completely missing. A top story today is completely forgotten tomorrow.

I must have been on my third or fourth beer by this point, because I was clearly getting to a philosophical phase of thought after these observations. I also decided that I had enjoyed some of the beers a little more than the others, but by now I couldn't remember which. I think one of the nicer ones was 'Amber' and another was 'Raspberry'. But to be honest they all tasted 'oaky' to me. I therefore felt it was probably time to move my washing into the dryer.

I headed downstairs, narrowly avoiding bashing my head on the low entrance-way, and I made the switch with ease. I checked on the clothes during transfer, and although they didn't smell massively clean, they were at least not too wet and so I reckoned a short run in the dryer should do the trick. I piled in the clothes, shut the door, put in my two dollar coins, and pressed 'start'.

I was about to head back upstairs when I noticed the small orange light on the dryer. It was next to a box that read 'rinse'. Rinse? Why would it need to *rinse* them? The clothes have been washed, *this* machine should be *un*rinsing them...

Oh god.

And then, slowly, it dawned on me. For some *inexplicable* reason (and I can't even blame the alcohol for this) I had put my clothes into the *dryer*, and now I had just transferred them into the *washer*. This was *definitely* the wrong way around. How the *hell* had I managed that? I've used these *exact* types of machines hundreds of times before on my travels – what had caused me to do this now? What was worse was that I could do nothing to stop the washer, as it had now also occurred to me that having successfully dried my dry, dirty clothes, I was now washing my dirty clothes without washing powder! I went back over to the dryer, and sure enough the drum was full of the fine white powder. I picked up a handful and let it slip between my fingers. A perfect metaphor for how this situation had rapidly got out of hand. I had been defeated by the laundry service. One of the only reasons for coming to Halifax and I had well and truly f***ed it up.

I cleaned out the dryer of the powder remnants, and then returned upstairs, banging my head on the low ceiling (that up until this point I had thankfully managed to avoid) and upped my drinking rate accordingly. This evening had not gone well.

A bit later on I checked my email, where I found a message from home telling me that this week had been *British Sandwich Week* according to the radio. *What?* No it *wasn't*! *British Sandwich Week* was *next* week – when I would be triumphantly arriving in British Columbia for the all important west coast sandwich. I checked the website for the *British Sandwich Association* to confirm to myself that the radio was wrong. But it wasn't. On the *BSA* website it said;

British Sandwich Week – 9th – 15th May 2010. But how could this be?! I saw it myself and it had said it was the *18th 24th May 2010.* I did a quick interweb search and found conflicting dates on numerous websites. Bugger. I must have used a bad source. Why hadn't I checked with the *BSA* as the upstanding informant on all things sandwiches? I suppose I hadn't expected there to be so much controversy over the actual dates. This evening just got worse. I was in the wrong place. I'd screwed up *again*. This evening had *really* not gone well.

* * *

The next morning was dull. The weather was dull as the sun was hidden behind clouds, and there was a dull ache in my head from where I had bashed it on the basement doorframe. The wannabe-wild-west-wacko in the bed next to me was still present and snoring away too. I needed a boost. A mental one – *not* the chocolate bar.

I got up and showered and then made my way down to the kitchen to get a glass of water. Yes, I live on the edge – I'm sure you don't need reminding. I sat down at one of the tables having picked up a copy of *The Coast*, a Halifax newspaper that was on a rack by the door. It was predictably filled with local news, which I don't blame it for as it is a local newspaper. I glanced at the sport section that featured articles about the recent Stanley Cup hockey play-off matches, and then I flicked back through to the front of the paper, passing a column that was commenting on the state of news broadcasting, and specifically highlighting the exact same issues that I had observed from watching news broadcasts. This made me smile, but what made me smile even more was a paragraph expressing one journalist's views on the subject that sum it up very eloquently.

"If you want to gauge quality, tune in at 5pm and chug a beer for every crime, accident, fire or weather story; you'll be shit-faced by 5.15."

I closed the paper, returning it to the front page, as I was just about to get up and replace it back in the rack when I noticed a banner-style headline at the top of the page. "Halifax 2010 Food Survey Results". Now normally this wouldn't especially interest me, but then I turned to the relevant page and saw that this survey was announcing the winners of the best food in Halifax, broken down into specific categories. I think you know what I was thinking. I flicked through the numerous pages that had been dedicated to this special feature, past the "Best Cake", "Best Coffee" and even the "Best Poutine" (now *that's* a bit oxymoronic – I can't imagine anything other than *unpleasant poutine*), until there, half-way down a column on one of the inner pages was exactly what I was hoping to find; the "Best Sandwich" category. This was *brilliant*! What were the chances that the food survey results came out *today*? Of *all* days! *And* of course *this* was now *British Sandwich Week*! I honestly couldn't believe my luck. After the irritations of yesterday evening, fate was repaying me. Now I knew which sandwich I had to have as my east coast and my *British Sandwich Week* celebratory offering. All I had to do now was find out where to get it from.

I finished up my exciting glass of water and ran up stairs to grab my map. I was very excited. (The exciting water must have helped.) Luckily the newspaper article had the addresses of the winning food outlets, and so I had cleverly tracked it down on my super-touristy tourist map and marked it with an X! Actually I circled it, I was just trying to add to the sense of occasion.

I left the hostel and set off for the sandwich, weaving through the millions of students that flood the streets of Halifax until I was stopped abruptly by a girl with a clipboard who ambushed me while I was paused for a sneaky map check.

It was amateurish of me to stop in such a vulnerable place – out in the open and surrounded by students – but I was getting so carried away with this latest sandwich hunt that I wasn't thinking straight, and I was pounced upon before I knew what had hit me. For the record she didn't actually hit me – it's just a phrase – this would also have been very un-Canadian of her as a nice Canadian.

After my slightly bizarre chat with the clipboard girl in Ottawa, I wasn't initially too bothered about this interruption. My experiences so far had suggested that Canadian clipboarders weren't too fussed about signing you up to things, and preferred just having a chat. Sadly this clipboarder was different – she was far more focused than the others, but that wasn't really what was bothering me.

She went off into a speech about why I should give her my bank details and how giving her money would be fantastic, but I stopped paying attention very quickly as I suddenly got distracted by trying to work out who she looked like.

'It's a great project, you can really—' she set off on her scripted speech.

She was very slight, with straggly reddish hair and a weird upper-body shifting/swaying movement.

'—and then we all meet up—'

Who was it that she reminded me of? It was the face too, *and* her tone of voice.

'—so you just have to give me your account number—'

I was looking at her with a high level of concentration and intrigue that may have looked like I was thoroughly absorbed by her preachings, but I was simply trying my hardest to pinpoint where I recognised her from. Was it someone I knew from university?

'—ten or twenty dollars a month—'

Maybe it was someone who worked on reception at the gym?

'—very rewarding—'

A celebrity?

167

'—sign you up now—'

I've got it!

'—bank number—'

She looked like one of the characters from the film *Chicken Run*!

'—name—'

Haha! Yes! *That's* who you look like! Oh, what's her name...hmmm...*Ginger*! That's it! I suddenly smiled widely.

'So what do you think?'

Huh? Oh crap. I'd been so distracted thinking about who she reminded me of that I had completely missed everything she had just said, and *now* she was looking for a response from me!

She stared at me expectantly – still resembling a plasticine chicken as far as I was concerned (I think it was the nose) – but that didn't change the fact that I needed to say something. Something that made me seem nice but that would equally preserve the limited contents of my bank account. I also needed to say something *quickly*, because there's only so long I could keep smiling at her without speaking.

'Yes! I *am* enjoying my time in Canada. It was great speaking with you!' and with that I walked away.

Yes, it was an *excellent* retort. That was a potentially tricky situation that I defused well. I handled the situation with a level of dignity and professionalism befitting of a true sandwich hunter. She looked a little confused, but ultimately disappointed that I hadn't signed up to whatever it was she wanted me to, but she was clucky ...I mean *plucky*, so I'm sure she'd soon find someone else who would be seduced by her awkward stance and funky perspex clipboard.

Distractions over, I could now proceed to the pinnacle of Halifax's sandwich industry.

Pete's Frootique didn't *sound* like the type of place where you would purchase a great sandwich, but that's where the article had said it was. It was actually a deli counter called *Pete's To Go Go* inside a supermarket complex on one of the main streets in Halifax.

I stepped up to the counter as I assessed the options. It was quite simple in the end; they offered ham and cheese, and with that being the default filling for these important sandwiches - ham and cheese it would have to be.

'Can I have a ham and cheese sandwich please.'

I suppose there was no real need to write out that line.

The sandwich cost $5.62 with tax, which initially seemed expensive, especially seeing as I was only given *half* a sandwich. That's right, I only got *half* a sandwich. This worried me, partly because I was hungry after all the unexpected thinking I had done with the clipboard girl, and also because I'm not sure if *half* a sandwich qualified as a sandwich. What did impress me though was that I was given a choice of bread (I chose a multi-grain variety) and the ham was freshly carved in front of my eyes from a large...ham. I also was offered a choice of lettuce and sauces, so this showed good quality contents and variety options. This was pleasing. I then asked to 'take-out' and so I got it presented on a paper plate wrapped in cling film. I also asked for a carrier bag; because I didn't want to be that guy who walks through cities holding half a sandwich, cling film wrapped to a paper plate.

Back at the hostel I ate the sandwich. After studying it closely for quality assessment purposes of course. My celebratory *British Sandwich Week* sandwich was pretty nice, and the large, fresh slices of ham had a very good texture and flavour to them, although it was a little short-lived, as after all it was only *half* a sandwich.

Half a sandwich indeed. What *is* the world coming to?

Chapter 23

(Go West) There's a sandwich there
(Go West) I the hope the price is fair
(Go West) They say the skies are blue
(Go West) It's what I've got to do

Nova Scotia *(back)* to Quebec

*"Every cloud...*has the potential to get you wet. So always bring a jacket."

Firstly I'd like to apologise for bringing *The Village People* into this. It was wholly unnecessary, so I'm sorry for that.

Despite my disbelief at being sold *half* a sandwich, I was very pleased. I was pleased because I had successfully completed two of my three east coast objectives; I had touched the Atlantic Ocean, and I had found *not just* a sandwich for comparison, but a sandwich that was considered the *finest* in Halifax, which was undoubtedly the most suitable one to have tried.

The only area that hadn't gone quite to plan was on the laundry front, which I had undoubtedly messed up with some real dim-witted splendour. Still, I had enjoyed my time in Halifax, and despite mixed reviews from people I'd spoken to before arriving in

Eastern Canada, it was a fun, lively place, with plenty of interesting things to see around the city and harbour front. Speaking of which, there was something I still needed to do at the harbour front. After my laundry incident I had come clean (excuse the pun) to the reception lady (actually don't – I'm quite pleased with it) by means of shaming myself and admitting to my idiocy, as I feel I had to do this in order to move on from this moment of utter stupidity. Unsurprisingly she found it hilarious, which was fine, but then she asked if I'd enjoyed the *Beaver Tail.*

'What's a *"beaver tail"*?' I asked her, hoping she wouldn't go on to describe it literally. I was also twisting my face into the kind of expression that I'm sure you'd deem appropriate for accompanying such a bizarre question.

'You know – the snack I said you should try down by the harbour front!' she replied, looking at me as if I was being ridiculous – like the type of person who dries their laundry before washing it during their travels across a country in order to eat lunchtime snacks.

'Ooohhh'.

Then it slowly dawned on me. I must've *misheard* her yesterday. It wasn't a *battered fish tail* I was supposed to have been looking for – it was a *Beaver Tail!*

Suddenly it all made *sense*! ...Except it didn't. Why the hell would you eat a *Beaver Tail*? That sounded horrible! It also seemed like something that may not be whole-heartedly approved by the *RSPCA.*

'The place is called *"Beaver Tails"* and it's a wooden hut. I think it's next to a *fish and chip* hut,' she continued.

'Ooohhh,' I said once again.

Dammit! I had been *right next* to it! I lost unnecessary face asking about *battered fish tails* when all I needed to do was step three feet over and I would have been sorted, and sorted out with a *'Beaver Tail'*.

171

In all honestly it still sounded slightly wrong, but I wasn't on this trip to question which speciality food snacks I did and did not have, however ethically unsound they appeared – I must try them! So I set off once again for the harbour front.

Ten minutes later and I was back by the row of huts next to the water. There was the *fish and chip* hut I had been to yesterday, and sure enough, right next to it was a hut called *"Beaver Tails"*. There was a board beside the service window displaying the different toppings they sold on the 'beaver tail' shaped pastries.

'Ooohhh,' I said for the third (and hopefully final) time. She had said 'batter' but she must've meant 'pastry'. Those crazy Australians.

I scanned the options, none of which sounded hugely pleasant, but eventually I settled on an "Avalanche", as it had the most dramatic name. I placed my order with the girl at the window, and then stepped back while the beaver tail was freshly cut off and topped with sprinkles. It cost $5.50. That's a sandwich amount of money. This had better be good.

As I waited I found myself looking up at the sky. It was getting ominously dark and threatening, and here was me parading around in just a t-shirt. Well, I had a few other items of clothing on as well, but nothing that would withstand a thunderstorm…or light drizzle.

Soon I was summoned to the 'collection window'. This was one fancy little hut! Another girl handed me my *Avalanche Beaver Tail*, accompanied by a serviette and bit of paper wrapping. These east coast vendors really do know how to treat visitors. Either that or they rightly assumed that I'd be messy.

I sat on a bench on the promenade and was just taking my first tail bite when the sky finally let loose. I got thoroughly drizzled on.

The *Beaver Tail* itself was impressive. Impressive in the sense that they had managed to put so many health-disrupting ingredients in such a thin snack. I guess the fact that they called it an "Avalanche" should have alerted me from the outset that this

172

wouldn't merely be a subtle blob of jam on a light slither of pastry. From what I could work out from looking at it, it had fudge pieces, with *fudge sauce*, and toffee lumps, and *toffee sauce*, and chocolate bits, and *chocolate sauce*, and then a thick coating of icing sugar. It was a little tricky to determine this accurately however, as the thick layers of grease masked the toppings and made it all look blurry. You therefore won't be surprised when I tell you that it tasted sickly. *Sickeningly* sickly. It felt wrong eating it. It even felt wrong *looking* at it. I'd actually go as far as saying that this brown, sugar-sludge massacre looked and tasted more wrong than if I'd eaten an *actual* beaver's tail. Although this was probably a little less bristly.

As I sat tentatively chewing on the greasy pastry, getting some of it in my mouth but also a substantial amount on my hands and down my t-shirt, I noticed a very strange sight out on the water. Silently cutting its way through the calm waters of Halifax harbour was a submarine. Was Canada going off to war? It was very subtle if they were. I could see men on the deck too – submarinists I imagine, but they didn't seem in too much of a hurry, and I'm guessing that the u-boat wasn't going to be diving under water anytime soon with them on top, so maybe it was a training session, or just a simple, quick battle - like the fifteen minute one that had happened in Québec City.

Thankfully I didn't find myself thinking about this for too long, which was good, because I wasn't having very sensible thoughts. This was because I was quickly done with the *Beaver Tail* and so I could head off and see about getting hooked up to a de-greasifier pump. Strangely, as I stood up and threw the wrapper away, it *stopped* drizzling and the sun even came out. War vessels and Beaver Tails; was this just a brief dark interlude in daily Halifax life?

I set off along the waterfront towards the hostel, but soon I was stopped in my tracks by a man standing on the edge of the promenade.

'Do you play guitar?' he shouted across at me, while pointing an incriminating finger in my direction.

This was strange; I didn't think I had a fan base this side of the Atlantic. Or *any* side of the Atlantic for that matter.

'Err…yes…?' I said, intrigued. Maybe I had a guitarists' face, or maybe he caught sight of my sturdy left index finger that smacked of virtuosic fret-board operation.

'A *Washburn?*' he pursued.

This was a very specific line of questioning coming from a complete stranger. Sadly for him his psychic powers had failed him on question two, because I *don't* play a *Washburn* (which for the non guitar-playing community is a make of guitar).

'No.' I answered abruptly. Maybe a little *too* abruptly, as he seemed quite disappointed by this.

'Oh. So you're not the guy I was playing guitar with yesterday?'

He *definitely* seemed a little upset now.

'I'm afraid not,' I replied as sympathetically as possible.

'Oh. You look a bit like him.'

'I see.' I said, wondering how I could really be held responsible for that.

'But you *do* play guitar?' he started up again.

There was a hint of an emotional recovery in this line.

'Well…yeah…' I hesitantly agreed.

I was a little concerned. Did the person he had mistook me for owe him *money?* Where was this *leading?* Had he been *wronged* by this mystical *Washburn* player who evidently had no distinctive features as to be accurately recognised again? Was *I* going to be a substitute for the indiscretions of a *Washburn* player? This wasn't fair! I'm *far* nicer and more trust-worthy than a *Washburn* player! Why should *I* take the hit for this person? *I* play *Fenders* for god's sake!

'Here you go,' he said, walking over to me and offering me his guitar. His mood had lightened considerably.

'Oh…thanks,' I said, slightly taken aback.

And I took the guitar, and I strummed out a few chords and played a few bits and pieces. It had been around three weeks since I'd last played a guitar, and so to be getting a go on one was brilliant – however unusual the circumstances.

Jeff was a very cheerful man, and what he lacked in teeth, he certainly made up for in enthusiasm and spirit. Apparently he had busked across Canada, having taught himself a few chords and songs along the way. He specialised in making children smile, by emitting the most bizarre 'duck quacking' noises you'll probably never have the pleasure of hearing. He aptly demonstrated this as a small girl trailed passed behind her parents. Upon hearing the noise, she looked back at him with the kind of expression you may expect a six-year-old girl to make when looking at a strange middle-aged man with only four teeth who was making duck/suffocation noises.

While I wasn't entirely convinced of his place as a child-entertainer, I was quite impressed by his trip (being a fan of unusual quests and all that) and also his self-taught capabilities. He had also let me have a go on his guitar for which I was very grateful, and so I put a few coins in his bag. If he kept this up then soon he would be able to afford a *Beaver Tail*, and then he could clear the rest of his mouth of inconvenient teeth.

I continued along the waterfront where I saw a large number of people heading into Halifax's convention centre. I very cleverly concluded that there must be an event on, and because I'm a sucker for following a crowd, I went inside to see if anything good was on.

There wasn't. It was wrestling. I carried on back to the hostel.

* * *

I was passing through the kitchen a little later that evening when I got chatting to a lady. Charlotte was from Vancouver Island (where I was making my way towards) and she was heading home having been travelling on and off for ten years. *Ten years*! That's a *long* time to be travelling, and as a result she had loads of interesting stories about the places she had visited, and how she went about travelling. This included a recent freighter ship voyage she had done across the Atlantic from Le Havre in France to the east coast of Canada.

I was fascinated by everything she was saying. I think this is one of the great things about travelling; everyone you meet has come from different places and is heading off somewhere else – all with different reasons for travelling. Some people are travelling to see specific places, or to meet friends or family. Others travel as part of an education course, or combine it with working abroad. And then there are others like myself, who travel as part of a special mission; a quest of discovery that will *itself* create tangent experiences such as those I was encountering.

I then moved on from the kitchen, and replaced deeply set travel philosophies with low-grade television in the hostel lounge.

I sat in the corner of the room (on a seat – it wasn't the naughty corner) and took in some of the days hype and drama from the news. On the other side of the room from me was a rather ragged looking middle-aged man with wild, untamed greying hair, who, for the third consecutive evening was slumped across one of the sofas, making occasional and incomprehensible outbursts directed at the television set before passing out for the night. I was about to give up any hope of finding anything worth watching on television when a familiar face walked into the lounge. It was Anita, the Irish girl I had met in Québec City. She had found her way to Halifax a bit sooner than expected after visiting a few other places in the region, and she was now staying at the hostel while she looked for work. She also had news on the sandwich front, having received some important information regarding the infamous 'Tayto Sandwich'.

176

According to Anita's sources, the 'Tayto Sandwich' is best created through a series of "fill and squash" stages of production, in which crisps (cheese and onion flavour being a favoured selection) are added and compressed within slices of (ideally) fresh bread, with the addition of other fillings, with ham and cheese proving popular choices. Ham and cheese certainly seemed to be the staple fillings for a classically made sandwich.

Some even described the sandwich as a "cuisine", which is praise indeed, and clearly an example of the place this lunchtime filler has in the hearts (or at least stomachs) of the Irish.

Other variations included the addition of condiments (mayonnaise, ketchup, etc) and even carefully selected beverages that should be drunk with it. The Spacebook page created as a dedication to the sandwich only further emphasises the significance of this apparent bread-encased wonder.

This certainly sounded like a sandwich I should try, although with so many opinions and seemingly important guidelines on how to create the perfect example, I would need to seek expert assistance before setting about making one myself.

I continued to chat with Anita about our various excursions since we last met until the conversation was suddenly halted by the arrival of another guest. An *all too familiar* guest. A *rudely interrupting* guest. It was the pin-striped cowboy…

I know by now it's probably the correct social etiquette to refer to him by name, but I never found it out. This was down to the fact that I could never pay attention long enough during his inane, dreary ramblings to discover what it was. I had also carefully decided that I didn't want to be pen friends with him. To do this I would also have to return to the seventies when this was fashionable, and that would create logistical difficulties based upon the time validity of my rail pass.

Anyway, the point is that he went off on another makes-you-want-to-bash-your-head-against-the-wall-until-you're-unconscious style speech about...oh, I don't bloody know - until eventually I couldn't take it anymore, and so I said I was going out for a walk. Anita then asked if she could join me, and so soon we were both escaping into the night to release the tension of being stuck in an enclosed room with that mind-numbing idiot, and to take in the fresh, bracing sea air that I would not be feeling again until I made it to the other side of Canada.

* * *

The next morning I got up and packed up my now completely dry (but still slightly grubby) clothes that had been finishing drying across the bunk bed frame, and then I left for the station. It was time I *properly* set-off on my westerly travels, starting with a twenty-two hour train journey back to Montreal. As I left the dorm room, the cowboy was packing up *his* bags. Apparently *he* was leaving today too. What a lovely coincidence! This worried me.

'Where are you heading?' I asked nervously.

'Oh...well...I'm   like...first...I'm   like...meeting...—' his response began painfully. But I didn't have the time or inclination for another drawn out speech.

'Listen. Are you going to Montreal on the train? I interrupted impatiently.

'Well...like...no, I'm like...—'

'Great! Have fun!'

And with that I closed the door.

Chapter 24

Ice to meet you...

(Return to) Montreal, Quebec

"Fine words butter no parsnips."

Now I can't say I've ever heard of this proverb before, but I feel that with some slight grammatical adjustments I can make it more appropriate. Here goes...

"Fine words! Butter, no parsnips."

The train journey from Halifax was as expected. Mainly because it was the same train that I had arrived on three days previously, and it was also taking the same route as before, just in reverse and with a three-hour extension on to Montreal. One important difference though was that I was nominated as the fire exit door operator! This was a proud moment, and a real sign that my status in Canada was on the up.

The journey included some more bizarre middle-of-the-night stops where I could see shadows moving about in the dark. But on the plus side I did manage to secure a double seat this time. This meant that I could compress myself into a semi-horizontal position for the night time leg of the trip. This proved helpful in bumping up the amount of sleep I got, although this could have equally been put down to the boring film that I stood watching in the 'television car' that evening.

* * *

It was early morning when we pulled up at Montreal's station. I liked Montreal, and it was nice to be back. It was also very convenient to know exactly where I needed to head for the hostel, although as I suspected I was not able to check-in until early afternoon, and so I had a few hours to kill first. Thankfully the lady on reception let me through the swipe-key activated door to the inner corridors of the hostel so that I could stow my backpack in one of the lockers. I also cheekily took this opportunity to grab a shower in one of the washrooms after my night on the train.

So refreshed and with less baggage, I set off back up the hill to Parc du Mont Royal, where I sat on a wall in the mid-morning sun and took in one of my favourite views in Canada so far, whilst listening to music and drying out my towel from the shower I'd just had. You might think that this was an unusual thing to do, but I don't think it was any stranger than the number of people who arrived at the top of the 'mountain' in spandex and then promptly stuck one of their legs up on the wall overlooking the view. This was either some bizarre French-Canadian custom or a hot spot for belatedly stretching joggers.

After sitting up there for about an hour, I took another casual stroll around the hill, and slowly wound my way back down to the city. I conveniently found myself in the Latin Quarter at lunchtime. I couldn't resist paying *Schwartz's* another visit – just to make sure I hadn't just caught them on a busy day before.

I hadn't. It had been a Friday when I had last come here, but I was reasonably confident that today was a Monday (a combination of travelling and overnight train journeys make it a little tricky to know what day it is sometimes) and once again there was a large gathering of people waiting to eat smoked-meat sandwiches. I joined them, and I ended up being given the same seat at the counter as before. I am a man of variation though, and so this time I also had a coke.

Having finished the sandwich I made my way back through the city to the hostel, where I was now able to check-in. I was looking forward to having a restful afternoon followed by an early night, as I knew I'd be spending a lot of time without a bed in the coming days so I wanted to make the most of having one tonight.

I'd *literally* just sat down in the dorm room having sorted out my bags when the door burst open beside me.

'Hi! Do you wanna go ice-skating?!' the figure in the doorway practically shouted at me.

This was a little scary. I was well and truly caught off guard. This guy had just piled through the door as if he was being chased by a gang of angry leaf-punchers, and now he was suddenly staring at me, wide eyed, and asking if I wanted to go ice skating. There was no introduction or small talk; he just cut straight to it. He wanted to go ice-skating, and I appeared to be the first human being he had found since deciding this, so I was the one he wanted to go with.

I stared at him for a split second while I took all this in, an expression of fear mixed with bemusement frozen onto my face. I'd just had a long and restless night remember, and so I was pretty train lagged. (Montreal is a whole hour behind Halifax, so my head was all over the place.)

'Yeah, sure,' I replied, in a casual but pleasant way.

I played it 'cool' because I am a masterful social weapon, but you know what? I actually thought this was *great*. This is what I love about travelling; the unplanned, spontaneity of how things can happen. There's no messing about arranging dates three weeks in advance, no setting up Spacebook events and groups and contacting people by phone/text/email/wax-sealed letters to find an appropriate

181

time or activity that everyone wants to do and can make – you just have an idea, and you go with it. You live in the moment. You grab the bull by the horns! You dive straight into the snake pit! You iron your socks for the party!…

Okay, I'll calm down.

Thankfully the guy had now run off again, and so he wasn't still in the room to see me rise to my feet ceremoniously, place my hands on my hips and stare purposefully out of the window in a powerfully adopted 'world-conquering' type stance. And yes, I *did* once iron my socks. It was a spur of the moment thing before a university sports awards evening. I had the iron out and my socks were in the vicinity (rest assured I didn't iron them on my feet though). And you know what? I don't regret it either - it made my feet feel all warm and fuzzy.

Five minutes later and we were striding off towards the ice-rink. Bruno (as I later found out his name was) was Brazilian, and he had just spent three weeks studying in Montreal as part of a business course he was taking back home. He had just finished and was heading back to Brazil in a couple of days, staying at the hostel until his flight. Bruno had never been ice-skating before, but he'd decided that he wanted to try it, and he'd also managed to get some free tickets from the hostel reception. I, on the other hand, happen to be a beautiful ice-dancer, and completely at one with the ice. He'd chosen a good ice partner to lead him on his quest to find elegant skating extravagance…

Yeah all right, that's not *completely* true. I'd been a few times before, but I was by no means a competent skater. However, what I lacked in ability, I made up for in blind-enthusiasm, and so we were soon at the indoor rink trying to convince a very grumpy man that the tickets we had meant we were entitled to skate for free. He was not at all keen for us to get away with not paying (which for the record I found very un-Canadian of him) but in the end there was little he could protest about once he had studied the small print on the tickets.

Minutes later we were stepping tentatively out onto the ice. There were only two other people on the rink, and both were skating as if...well, as if they had been lots of times before. They were skating backwards, twirling around, and making flamboyant hand movements that suggested they had aspirations of high level ice...display...event...performing. Well anyway, it was safe to say we wouldn't be stealing their thunder any time this afternoon.

The location was quite unusual. The ice-rink (that was laid out to accommodate hockey too unsurprisingly) was set in the large, central, open foyer of an office block, with suited office workers milling about the edges and up escalators as we skated.

We slid about on the ice for over two hours, by which time Bruno had begun to skate without clutching on to the side walls, and I had started overlapping my feet in what I (probably wrongly) considered to be a highly sophisticated manoeuvre. We were trendsetters though, as by the time we slumped down on the neighbouring benches to relieve our bruised feet of the unforgiving ice skates, there were around twenty people on the ice. Word must have got out that a specially qualified and spontaneous 'train fire exit door operator' was in town, and with that they must have sensed an opportunity for safety-endorsed fun.

On our way back to the hostel Bruno asked if I wanted to have dinner with him.

I said I didn't think that would be appropriate.

He then rephrased it, and suggested we cooked together.

This sounded more appealing.

He asked what I fancied eating, to which I said I didn't mind.

He said that as he had some left, we could have pasta!

I sighed, and said that sounded good.

So we cooked pasta, each taking on different tasks of the meal making process. I prepared bits of chicken and messed about with some herbs, while Bruno chopped up broccoli until it was almost broccoli powder, the likes of which I had never seen before in my long history of broccoli consumption. We also included virtually every other vegetable under the sun we could find in our respective food bags as part of the meal. Except parsnips. I'm not a fan of parsnips.

As a result of our team effort we had everything cooked up and ready to serve in no time at all, and soon we were munching away on this surprisingly extravagant pasta concoction. We both found it slightly amusing that a Brit and a Brazilian had just cooked an Italian meal in the French-speaking part of Canada. Now *that's* multiculturalism!

After dinner Bruno asked...well, essentially everyone in the hostel - if they fancied coming out for some drinks. I suggested a place that I had walked past when I was last here, and that I was keen to visit as it said it had a live jazz band on. Montreal and jazz are pretty synonymous, so I was keen to hear some while I was in town.

Having rallied together some troops (a few aimless, wandering backpackers) we set off up the road to the bar. I say bar, but having looked more carefully through the windows we could see a rather posh looking *restaurant*, where everyone was eating. More significantly though, was the complete lack of a band. We moved on elsewhere.

Soon after we found an Irish bar, which also had live music on, but it wasn't very 'jazz'. It was pleasant enough though, and so we stayed there and had a few drinks. I didn't get to bed until around 2am. So much for an early night.

Chapter 25

Sandwiched up for the week

Quebec to Ontario

*"An Englishman's home is his...*train seat."

I woke up tired the following morning. I don't therefore know *why* I woke up, especially as I'd beaten my alarm by a good couple of hours. Still, there were things to be done, so I got up, showered, and packed up my bags. I then headed down to the kitchen to do some important food preparation, because I was going to be spending the next three days on the train.

When I sat off on this trip I had no real idea where I was going to go once I arrived in Toronto, other then that I needed somehow to eventually end up in Vancouver. Because of my easterly excursions I was getting short of time as I had a return flight booked back to London from Vancouver for the beginning of June. This meant I had to move fast to get across the country, but I wasn't prepared to fly.

For a start flying is expensive – I can't just go around buying flights to visit places so I can have a sandwich! That would be reckless! Who do you think I am? But *far more* significantly was that I considered flying to be *cheating*. You can't claim to have been across the country if you fly – you miss everything! No, this just wasn't on. I wanted to see as much of this country as possible, so I used my rail pass to book an economy seat for the trip across The Prairies, through the Rockies, and on to the west coast. I'd be doing this on the cross-county train known as *Train 001 – The Canadian*!

It was going to be a two-part trip, with a two-night stop-over in Winnipeg. First however, I had to get to the starting point of the train – Toronto! And *guess* how I was going to get there? Yes, okay, I'm not very imaginative - I was going to get the train. Well, if I gained one thing this trip it would be a sound knowledge of the Canadian rail network.

So, with three continuous days of being stuck on a train ahead of me I was going to need some supplies, not least some food. I'd heard they provided meals on the train, but I'd also heard that you'd have to be the type of person that lived in a palace and who wore gold shoes to be able to afford them. Or at the very least you'd have to have a job of some kind...

Anyway, I didn't fit any of these criteria, and so I was going to bring my own food onboard. There obviously wouldn't be cooking facilities on the trains, and so I think you can see where this is heading. That's right! I was going to make sandwiches. *A lot* of sandwiches. When I'd been in the supermarket yesterday I'd picked up a loaf of bread and some (you guessed it!) ham and cheese, and so here I was making up the entire loaf (and it was a special Canadian extra-long loaf) into ham and cheese sandwiches. The hostel kitchen was very well equipped, and having made up a large pile of sandwiches, I could then very conveniently cling-film wrap the sandwiches into packs. Cling film - what a great addition to kitchen facilities! I now had special packs of sandwiches for every sandwich-needing occasion I faced on the train! How brilliant was that? This was *surely* backpacking at its finest.

As I was finishing wrapping up the final pack, another hostel resident strolled into the kitchen and caught sight of my impressive tower of neatly packaged sandwiches.

'Wow!' he said, almost dropping his jaw (have I used that phrase correctly?) 'You must really like sandwiches!'

'Oh if only you knew,' I replied, in a slightly cryptic tone and whilst smiling. And then god help me, I *think* I also winked.

Why on *earth* did I wink? Did I think I was in a film and I was making the gesture in an ironic fashion to the viewing audience as part of some kind of 'in joke'? What was I *thinking*? As if it wasn't weird *enough* that I was overtly implying to a complete stranger that I had a sandwich fetish, surely winking would only *confirm* to him that I was indeed a bread-obsessed nutter! I just hope that someday he gets to read this book so that he'll finally understand.

I got out of the kitchen quickly. It was a good thing I was leaving today if I was going to be doing stupid things like that. I'm sure *he* shared the same sentiment too.

* * *

Looking back on it I realise that I mentioned sandwiches quite a lot in those last few paragraphs. While you'll be aware that there is little I can do about this given that sandwiches are a pretty pivotal theme throughout the book (and therefore your complaints seem a little unfounded as you are no doubt reading this book *knowing full well* of the sandwich plot) I do realise that I risk overwhelming you with sandwiches talk and issues. Therefore, as a brief yet generous respite, I shall temporarily avert the focus from *sandwiches* to *socks*.

I know I have made you fully aware of the debilitating problem of *Traveller's Hot Foot*, but in the past couple of days it had really come to a head. When I had been packing up my clothes in the hostel in Halifax I had found one particular pair of hiking socks to be in such a disgraceful state I had opted to transport them in an external mesh pocket of my backpack. This just *couldn't* continue. I had thin 'base-layer' socks – which were crap. And I had thicker hiking socks – which *again* were crap. What I needed were some socks that didn't claim to be good.

I set off for St Catherine's Street where all the shops were, and then I strode purposefully along the busy sidewalk in search of an appropriate retailer. Unfortunately it wasn't yet 10am, and so most of the shops were closed. However, I did find a small, grubby-fronted 'touristy' shop, and after having a quick look around I saw just what I was looking for in a glass cabinet.

Before I had time to look up to see if there was a sales assistant around, a voice spoke up in front of me.

'You want socks?' he spoke sharply. There would be no small talk here, evidently.

'Yes, I would actually,' I replied – hoping that he had just been hyper-alert and had seen me briefly eyeing the socks, as opposed to making a bold assumption that I was merely the type of person who looked like they *only ever* bought socks from glass display units.

'Each pack is eleven dollars,' he said informatively, holding up the two packs of *Montreal Canadiens* ice hockey socks.

These sports socks looked ideal, and it would be a good souvenir given the time I had spent over the past two weeks watching Montreal play in the hockey playoffs. I was just about to get out the money when he spoke up again.

'Or you can have both for twenty dollars.'

I looked at him slightly confused. I had *intended* on buying both packs (I *really* needed new socks) but I certainly hadn't expected the opportunity to haggle. Not in a proper shop in Canada. He was entering into dangerous territory, for I was a keen haggler, and so a rye smile formed across my face.

'I'll give you fifteen,' I said in a dark, dramatic tone whilst staring hard into his eyes. Not in a romantic way you'll understand – in an *intimidating* way. Not that I particularly *wanted* to intimidate him, but anyway.

'But I have a family to feed!' he suddenly pleaded.

Oh for god sake. What *was* he playing at? You don't kick off a haggle and then on your second line deliver *that* lame and amateurish sentence! You can't flick from hard-edged haggling to desperate pleading in three seconds! This was poor form on his part. His shop was full of overpriced and unofficial (and no doubt fake and illegal) merchandise, so if he was going to play dirty, then so was I.

'Well I'm a backpacker and I have grubby feet! I'll pay eighteen.'

He was about to come out with some whiney reply when I turned to walk off.

'Okay! Okay!' came his feeble response.

We had a deal.

Back at the hostel I changed into a pair of my slick new sports socks. As I did so, the Chinese man who had also been staying in the dorm room was heading out. It had been a coincidence to find him here, as he had also been in my *other* dorm room when I had been in this hostel a couple of weeks back. He had a peculiar air to him, largely based around the fact that when I had been here previously, he had once showered three times in the same day. And this was only during the time that I was *in* the room – which wasn't very much. (I was in the dorm room, not the shower room – that would have been inappropriate.) He wasn't showering now though, he was walking out of the door, but as he did so he made one last confusing contribution to our shared time here. He said "thank you" as he left. This was very strange, as all I was doing was sitting on the bed. Maybe he had encountered some of my horrible socks, or *maybe* he had caught sight of my stylish belt buckle and this had restored his faith in European waist fashion, having possibly thought this was lacking in recent experiences of European trouser-waist enforcers. Perhaps he was just generally a very grateful person. Well, whatever - he was quirky. I respected that.

The five-hour train journey from Montreal to Toronto was a very 'business' affair. The train was full of suited men and women who spent the duration of the trip engrossed in newspapers or conversing on their blackberries, tirelessly discussing "those reports that needed doing". There was one group at the back of the carriage that stood out, as they were clearly a tour group. Every few minutes I heard a man (who I took to be the guide) point out something he had seen out of the window, and this would be quickly followed by a smattering of subtly-enthused shuffling and the clicking of camera shutters. I'm not entirely sure what they kept seeing that was particularly worthy of all the tourist explanations and photo opportunities as we spent most of the journey passing through relatively uninteresting farmland and small villages where neatly white-clad wooden houses with large terraces sprung out of the grasslands.

After a couple of hours I pulled out my netbook so I could make use of the free wi-fi that they offer on these corridor train services between Toronto and Québec City. I checked my emails, made some 'business' type expressions so those suited passengers around me would see I was one of them, and then I remembered that I wasn't wearing a suit, and as normal I had removed my shoes. It was no use. I wasn't fooling anyone, so I had a game of solitaire. I then remembered something I had to do, and so I quickly finished my game and clicked my way onto some airline web pages.

A few minutes later and I was sitting with a big, important smile on my face. I had just booked a flight. I was a backpacker, sitting on a commuter train surrounded by business-folk, with a computer on my lap that I had just used to book a flight. How flash was *I*? That's right, very, I think you'll find.

Now I know what you're thinking; after the big lecture I gave earlier about flying being "cheating" you'd accuse me of being a hypocrite. Well I'm not. Not really anyway. This flight was an additional trip that I could only embark on thanks to the glorious speed of air travel. I shall explain more later, but rest assured that it wouldn't be affecting my east coast to west coast, cross-country voyage – that would still all be done via the trusty rail network.

I was just finishing up my prolonged smiling session that had been triggered by a bold message that had appeared when I was booking the flight saying "Warning! This flight does not include our new plane interior!" when I noticed the appearance of Lake Ontario out of the window. I could tell it was this, because silhouetted on the rapidly reddening late-evening horizon was the distinctive skyline of Toronto. I didn't think I'd be hugely keen on seeing that place again after my last incident in the city, but with this stunning sunset view, and with the heart-warming thoughts of how *Air Canada* were so concerned that I would be outraged by the lack of modern upholstery in their current flight services - all my problems of Toronto accommodation had been forgotten. I was just excited to be embarking on the next leg of my adventure...

Chapter 26

"Hey ma! I got me some magic beans!"

Ontario to Manitoba

*"A fool and his money...*can both be exchanged for magic beans."

It was nine-thirty and I was standing in the queue for the train getting bullied by a group of Canadian women. There was an hour gap between trains, so after a quick leg-stretch I was back in the underground foyer of Toronto's Union Station waiting to begin my three-day trip to Winnipeg, Manitoba.

I had got chatting in the queue with this multi-generational family of females, and when they found out I was English they found it hilarious, and kept trying to imitate my accent. As I've found with *every other* Canadian who has tried this, they just sounded like Jane Austen characters, seemingly under the slightly worryingly impression that all English people were brought up in the eighteen hundreds. Still, it passed the time, and soon there was a loud announcement that "Train *001*... [dramatic pause]...The *Canadian*, to Vancouver" would now begin boarding. Yet another example of the grandeur this country held over rail travel. Why it was train "*00*1", and not just train "1" is beyond me. I was also surprised to discover that the train went all the way through to Vancouver. I thought you had to change at Winnipeg, that's why I had only bought a ticket that far. Interesting...

The economy section consisted of two carriages of seats at the front of the twenty-six carriage train. It was quite different from *The Ocean* train that had delivered me to and from Halifax, and at first glance it didn't look as comfortable. The interior looked much older (and they hadn't had the courtesy to mention this on their website unlike *Air Canada*) and the seats were smaller, and didn't recline backwards as far. They also didn't have clever under-seat storage, but instead they had fold-out extensions that you could prop your legs up on. These were important issues to discover early on, as this seat was going to be my home for the next thirty-five hours.

After settling everyone in, a few members of the train crew came along and handed out pillows and blankets. They then gave a safety talk, which alarmingly informed us that we had to wear shoes when moving around the train, as it had been known for people to have their toes chopped off by the moving floor-plates between the carriages. I wasn't alarmed by the toe-chopping element though, oh no! *I* was alarmed by the fact that I was expected to *wear* shoes on the train, given my travel-habits and the fact that mine were *already* neatly stowed away under the seat in front of me. This journey was already proving challenging. At 10pm the train slowly edged out of the station. It was by now dark, but there was an air of excitement and anticipation hanging around our economy lodgings as we set off on the long voyage into out-back Canada.

* * *

It was a long night, but I did manage to get some sleep. I achieved this by rotating between two different positions throughout the night, in an attempt at limiting the damage to my limbs and spine as I was bent up across a pair of seats and their accompanying fold out leg rests.

I soon got chatting to Jess and Kailey, who were in neighbouring seats to myself on the other side of the centre aisle. They were

Vancouverites returning home after a short holiday to Montreal. I imagine that's what people from Vancouver are called anyway. I suggested we played cards, and so we did what good train passengers do and we put our shoes on, and then we headed to the next carriage along, because this next carriage was special. It was the 'dome' car, or the *space lounge* as I periodically came to refer to it as. This was an area of seating with tables, with a narrow staircase leading up into a glass-domed seating area, from which you could see out in all directions. It was a bright sunny day, and so we whiled away a couple of hours playing cards as the Ontario countryside drifted past us on either side.

A train employee stuck his head up into the *sky dome* (as I sometimes chose to call it) to tell us that lunch was now being served in the dining car, one car along from where we were up on the *space deck*, as I occasionally described it. I took this opportunity to ask him about the severely cracked window that was facing forwards in the dome, in this *360 viewing platform* (as I occasionally described it), complaining that it was disrupting our view out. I wasn't being intentionally rude, just a little cheeky, as these Canadians seem to tolerate it well.

'Oh, I hadn't seen that one. It must be a new one,' he said casually, whilst looking behind him at the damaged pane of glass, 'Yeah, we get kids out in the prairies shooting at the train.'

There was silence as our expressions changed from playful happiness to mild horror.

'People shoot at the train...?' I managed to choke out.

The train employee continued nonchalantly, 'Sadly, yeah. When it happens we radio into the local police and they try to pick them up. Luckily most of them are stupid enough to hang around so they get taken off to station.'

I'm not sure that this came as much of a relief now that we knew we were sitting ducks lined up for target practise.

After we had absorbed this new insight into Canadian cross-country train travel, we tentatively continued with our card games. The Vancouverites taught me a frenetic game that involved far too many simultaneous card-placing actions for my poor male brain to cope with, and so after I had thoroughly confused myself we decided it was lunchtime, which meant a return to the relative safety of our low-level seats to collect our pre-prepared food. This was where I consumed sandwich pack one. The bread was dry and the cheese was rubbery. I wondered how I would feel about them by the time I got to eat pack *five*.

It was mid-afternoon as the train pulled up in the fantastically named Western Ontario town of Hornepayne. This was pretty much our first real opportunity to get off the train for some fresh air since getting on over seventeen hours ago. Most people got off and headed towards the primitive looking building that seemed to form the hub of the town. It was a dust bowl. The hot, humid afternoon hit us as we stepped down from the carriage, with the dry breeze whipping up the sand and dust into our eyes as we made our way over to a mini-market; the worryingly named 'Val-u Mart'. There were a few people wandering around the haphazardly built township that I assumed to be residents, looking every bit the archetypal small-town dwellers with their wide-rimmed hats and boots. The boots weren't wide-rimmed, they were actually typically bootlike – I hope that's now clear.

I immediately decided that this was the type of place where you could purchase 'magic beans', and so as others searched the sparse shelves for extra train provisions, I studied the small rack of seeds and bulbs that I had rightly predicted would be inside the shop. It didn't take long to find the most likely packet for containing magic beans, and so I purchased them. At least now when I returned home I wouldn't have to worry about getting a job with these powerful bargaining tokens. You never know, I might even exchange some for a cow! I could call it…*Mazy*!

Once back outside, we got our first real opportunity to see the true length of the train. It was *incredibly* long, stretching almost as far as the eye could see, although with the constant barrage of dust blowing about this wasn't quite the remarkable feat that it may have initially sounded. I turned to avert my eyes from another wave of dust and I noticed a sign stuck on the neighbouring shop window. It read, "Moose Licenses have arrived."

Brilliant! This place was living up to all my expectations of what a middle-of-nowhere town should be. Now I didn't know if this sign meant residents of Hornepayne could now collect their licences to hunt moose, to *own* and *ride* moose, or whether the licenses were *for* moose, enabling them to legally drive cars. To be honest it wouldn't surprise me if any of these were true.

As I was revelling in this fantastic window posting, a man appeared behind me, making me jump slightly. He was another passenger on the train, although he was a fancy 'sleeper class' traveller – frowned upon by us economists. He was American, and probably in his sixties, and he was travelling alone to Vancouver as part of a holiday. It worked out that he was spending most of his holiday…sorry 'vacation', travelling to and from his destination. I couldn't really comment though, as I was *always* on the move.

He seemed pleasant enough, although he spoke in quite a disconcerting manner, asking me a lot of slightly peculiar questions about the fact I was travelling alone. It was turning into the type of questioning that made you shiver and want to pull your jacket more tightly around you. But it was hot, and I wasn't wearing a jacket, so instead I politely told him that I must now leave to return to my peasant dwellings at the front of the train. This dry, arid climate would have been playing havoc with my new socks, so I needed to get my shoes off and air them. I obviously didn't tell him this last bit, but in retrospect maybe I should have.

That evening, having munched my way through sandwich pack two, I went to the bathroom to change into my evening wear. Sadly I had misplaced my ball gown, but I had a spare t-shirt and some lightweight trousers that I eventually conceded would suffice. As I washed my face I was just considering how spacious these in-train washrooms were, when the train suddenly jolted, causing me to slam my head into the mirror in front of me. This was uncalled for – I was being *positive* about the train for god's sake! I managed to pull myself back into a more dignified shape, and then I opened the sliding washroom door and stumbled mildly concussed back to my seat. This was unfortunate, as I had some serious thinking to do, and a sore head was not going to help matters.

A popular reaction to me telling people that I was going to Winnipeg was, "why?". My new carriage-companions – Jess and Kailey, were also quick to question why I wanted to stay there for two nights. To be honest I didn't really know, but as it was on the way I thought I'd better have a look. That was pretty much my philosophy throughout my Canadian travels. Also I had originally been under the impression that I *had* to stop-over at Winnipeg, but having since found out that the train carried on straight through to Vancouver I had started to question my plan. I wonder if I could switch my tickets? I'd had success before at ticket refunds and exchanges so *maybe* I could do it again. I could actually use the extra time in Vancouver as I had some special missions planned, not to mention the all important ferry trip that I *had* to get right. But then did I really want another three days on the train? That's *four consecutive* nights without a bed. *And* I'd have to cancel my Winnipeg hostel booking and somehow find accommodation in Vancouver, and there was no wi-fi connection out here in The Prairies. This was tough, but we were due to arrive in Winnipeg early the next morning, so I had to make a decision.

* * *

I got a similar amount of sleep to the previous night. While I had the unexpected bonus of finding a third sleeping position to throw into my night-time rotation, I was also disturbed at getting on for midnight by the American man I'd met earlier that afternoon at Hornepayne, when he had suddenly appeared behind my seat in the shadows. It nearly made me jump again. Why *was* he here? He asked me a few more slightly odd probing questions as I exchanged worried looks with my neighbouring passengers. I sunk lower into my seat (which was some achievement given how thin the cushions were) until eventually he drifted off into the darkness. This was all very peculiar, and inevitably it was another factor that I needed to include in my decision making process as to where I got off the train.

When morning came I was ready. In between sleep position rotations I had weighed up the pros and cons, but then I was eventually swayed by my adventurous/reckless nature. I sensed an opportunity here, and this was something I couldn't let slip. If I could make this work then I would be creating time for more west coast antics, and so I decided to go for it! This was aided by the information I was given from Jess that the train had a four-hour stop-over in Winnipeg, which should be enough time to enable me to do the necessary administration to make the various switches, bookings, and cancellations. It was risky, but there was hope. And after all, I'm a whiz at administration, so my previous job experience should really pay off here!

The train pulled up at around half eight that morning. I was excited! But this was short lived, as we then got an announcement saying that we would have to wait onboard the train until the intended arrival time of nine o'clock.

What? We weren't allowed *off* the train because we had arrived *early*? What kind of an outrageous procedure was this?

They justified it by saying that the station's staff "would not be ready" until nine.

Wouldn't be ready? For what?! People to get off the train and walk past them to carry on with their lives?! This was absolutely *ridiculous*. I would like to highlight this as one of the more bizarre sides of Canadian rail travel. But we had no choice, and so we sat there until nine o'clock until we were allowed out. I then set off on my mad dash around Winnipeg.

I started at the ticket desk in the station, where the lady managed to switch my tickets with ease. She then took my backpack that I had just taken off the train, and put it *back on* the train again. In my brief reunion with the bag I noticed it was incredibly dusty. This was odd; maybe it had got off at Hornepayne too. Looking for a moose license no doubt. It all went smoothly though, and soon I was off again, and onto the streets of downtown Winnipeg. The station was on one side of the city, and the hostel was across on the *other* side, and so I ploughed across the grid system towards the point I had marked on my map.

I arrived at the hostel less than half an hour later. I was making good time, but I was paying the price with my cleanliness, as although it was only mid-morning, it was already hitting thirty degrees. This was a level of heat that I had not experienced so far in Canada, and it wasn't great timing seeing as I was hoping to spend another two days without a shower on a train.

The man on reception in the hostel was grumpy and hugely disinterested in those he served, but this didn't matter, as he was also quite efficient, and within seconds he had cancelled my two-night booking. Great! I then took a seat in the lobby and set up my netbook, where I managed to book a dorm room in a well-located Vancouver hostel for the extra nights. This *was* going well. I then moved on to the next leg of project journey-switch, which was a visit to a supermarket to pick up some more provisions for the extra days on the train. This *again* proved straight forward, as I found a suitable shop just a couple of blocks from the hostel. I was all set, and I'd got all this done in under and hour and a half. Time for some tourism!

As I headed slightly less hurriedly back towards the station I caught sight of a guitar shop on the other side of the road. I couldn't resist. I crossed over and pushed my way through the door. Racks of guitars lined every wall, with more spilling across the narrow floor space in between the glass counters that housed other musical implements and accompaniments. A loud booming voice then broke the silence that had only been interrupted previously by the tinkle of the door chime as I had entered the shop.

'You know the rule here...' he began sternly, 'you *play* the guitars!'

The man's face softened into a smile, mirroring mine. This was good. Very good.

So I spent the next hour being handed various guitars and then taking them for a metaphorical spin. (I don't want you thinking I'm the type of guy who spins guitars around thoughtlessly in confined spaces.) I then noticed a small acoustic guitar at the end of one of the wall racks. I picked it up and had a look. The man asked if I liked it, and I explained that I was in the middle of a five day train journey, and how I'd always wanted to travel with a guitar. I think you can see where this was heading.

I wasn't seriously considering buying it, because I just couldn't justify another guitar – I already had quite a few back home, but then the shop owners kept knocking money off, and they *even* rummaged in the basement to find me a case for it – which they threw in for *free*. They were incredibly friendly. I was sold. *It* was then sold. To me, for next to nothing, and with a free case and plectrums too. I liked the people of Winnipeg. Winnipeg was cool.

I left the shop clutching the over-sized case containing the travel guitar, and I set off back towards the station with a big smile on my face. I had less than an hour until we were needed back at the train for boarding, but I still wanted to do some tourist stuff.

If you look up Winnipeg in a guidebook it will say that the main tourist attraction is 'The Forks'. Conveniently this was situated just behind the station, and so this was my destination.

Fifteen hot minutes later and I was there. I was at *The Forks*. Do you want to know what *The Forks* is? Of *course* you do, because you love learning about foreign lands and also because I've intrigued you.

The Forks is the confluence of two rivers; the Red River, and the Assiniboine River. Yup, that's it. Two very brown rivers that meet up to form... *one* brown river. I kind of began to see why people thought it was strange that I was going to be stopping here to visit. Granted there were some nice sculptures and parklands alongside the river, but c'mon, back home in Watford we have *three* rivers, and while they don't join up in an exciting fashion, neither do they get promoted as a significant tourist draw.

I meandered around a few of the nearby pathways before crossing through *The Forks Market*, which were some more open spaces with some pretty closed up looking shops and huts. I then made my way back over to the station in time for boarding.

I'd had a successful visit to Winnipeg; I'd sorted out all the necessary administrative business, I'd had fun strumming a range of guitars as well as a securing a potential source of entertainment for the next leg of the journey, *and* I had seen the sights! This was one of the finest and most efficient whirlwind visits I had ever carried out – *this* was *Tornado-Tourism!*

I got back on the train in very high spirits. Not *only* had I penned a new and exciting phrase for my style of travel, but *also* my seat had been reserved for me! Everything was working out *great.* Bring on another three days on the train!

…and then the American man appeared behind my seat.

Fuck it. I'd forgotten about him.

Chapter 27

We'll be strumming through the mountains as we come

Manitoba to Alberta
(via Saskatchewan)

*"Two's company, three's...*an awkward train debate...or a sing along!"

The train pulled off once again, and I broke the news to my co-passengers that they would be blessed with my company for a further three days. They were all ecstatic, as I'm sure you can well imagine. This also included my favourite American friend, who very kindly offered to share his hotel room in Vancouver with me as he had a spare bed. As nice as this was, it was also exceptionally creepy, and when I politely declined he went on to ask me another series of questions based upon who I'd be meeting in Vancouver and what I would be doing once I got there...and probably something else about heart-shaped chocolates.

Thankfully he disappeared soon after – possibly to sharpen some knives, who knew? It did seem unfair that 'sleeper-class' passengers were allowed to stroll up and down the train, whereas us 'comfort-class' folk weren't allowed beyond our dining car, as one of the other economy passengers had discovered when they were stopped by a member of the train crew after they went for a wander. If we weren't allowed to have a sneaky peak at the upper-classes, then *they* shouldn't be allowed in *our* section. Equality. That's *all* we ask for.

A little while later there was an announcement over the in-train PA system. The staff were good at providing information about various places we passed on the journey, and they were taking this opportunity to alert us to the fact that soon we would be passing through Portage, Manitoba – home to *the world's largest coke can*! This sounded massively exciting, and so to make the most of this a few of us decided to head down to the *sky platform* (as I sporadically described it) to get the best view of this eighth wonder of the world. We managed to snap up the last few remaining seats in the *roof gallery* (as I intermittently called it) where we waited in an ever-increasing puddle of anticipation. The train then slowed right down, and came to a grinding halt. Was it here? Should we be able to see it? What was going on? TALK TO US TRAIN STAFF!

No. We weren't yet at the world's largest coke can. We had just stopped as the train sometimes does - normally to let a four-hundred mile long freight train amble slowly pass us at a cross-over point, which usually took around twenty minutes.

The passenger rail network in Canada is not an especially profitable business. This is probably because it is pretty expensive unless you have an off-peak season rail pass like myself, and even this is only worthwhile if you plan on covering a lot of distance in a short period of time. As a result it is not a popular form of transport (which strikes me as catch 22; not much demand for rail travel – train prices go up to compensate in revenue – high price of tickets – less appealing for potential passengers) and so the far more profitable freight trains get priority on the tracks.

So after a frustratingly long period of stationaryness, the wheels began to turn once more, and then a few minutes later we saw it; *the world's largest coke can*!

It was disappointing. *Really* disappointing. In fact I hadn't been this disappointed since I found out that cow tipping was a myth. Ironically a research project based around cow tipping was carried in none other the University of British Columbia in Vancouver. Aren't these nice little tie-ins and links wonderful? Yes, I thought you'd agree. Oh, and cow tipping is the act of pushing over a sleeping cow, and *not* the act of giving money to a miserable waitress. While the latter is possible, it is considered unfair to the nice, hard working waitresses, and therefore you'd be ill advised to do it.

Anyway, *the world's largest coke can* is not much of a spectacle. My main point of contention with it, is that it doesn't even *look* like a drinks can. It is apparently cylindrical in shape (although it was hard to tell from our angle) but it certainly didn't resemble any drinks can I've drunk from. It was more or less just a large billboard with the *Coca-Cola* logo on it. It's definitely not something to write home about, although I felt its inclusion in this book was appropriate – not least as a warning to those of you considering a fizzy-drink pilgrimage to Portage, Manitoba.

Further down the tracks we stopped in Rivers, Manitoba – the halfway point on the Toronto to Vancouver, *Canadian* journey. I decided to celebrate this by getting another sandwich pack out from my bag and taking it down to the tables below the *space deck* (as I haphazardly named it) for consumption.

While I tucked into the chewy four-day old bread and rapidly warming ham slices, I overheard some voices talking place behind me. Two men and a women were having quite a serious discussion about various key historical events, with one of the men claiming that they were all conspiracies. He covered all the classics; assassinations, wars and bomb plots, but then it got to the moon landing and the conversation got quite heated. This man had very strong views on how everything was faked and that there were major cover-ups. I started to wonder if he had some kind of background in top-end space science technology as a foundation for these theories, but then I turned around to look at him, and based upon his decrepit appearance and the can of cheap, high-volume lager he was swigging I decided that he was probably just a drunk with too little else to occupy his brain with, so I finished off the remaining scraps of sandwich and headed back to my seat.

* * *

The hours began to drag by, and the landscape during this stretch of the journey only added to the monotony of train life. Fields stretched out endlessly on either side of the train as we cut through the green countryside of Southern Canada. Occasionally we would see a herd of cattle grazing near the tracks, paying no attention to the long silver train as it noisily rumbled past them. At one point we passed through a rift in the land where there was fiercely burning vegetation beside the tracks as a result of the hot and unforgiving conditions of this part of the country.

As evening set in, the fertile lands of Manitoba were turning a more arid brown as we crossed into Saskatchewan. The incredibly flat landscape meant that the sun took an age to set, with no topographical undulations on the horizon to disrupt its warming rays. Did you like that concise paragraph of evocative description? Thanks.

I sensed that this sparse province that we had just entered was the butt of many jokes in Canada. A view enhanced by Kailey's deadpan assessment of this mammoth journey.

'[One the train] time stands still. There is no distinction in time other than day and night… Saskatchewan doesn't even have this.'

As you can tell, things were getting slightly melancholic and philosophical, but thankfully there was an interruption, as it was announced that a film would be showing in the dining car.

To the dining car! And so we went to the makeshift cinema where we sat on uncomfortable metal-framed chairs and watched a film on a tiny television that popped out of a cupboard that I didn't really pay any attention to.

It was an hour or so into the film when the squealing of brakes disrupted our cinematic experience. We had arrived in Saskatoon, Saskatchewan! I'm not really sure that warranted an exclamation mark, but I saw anything that broke the monotony of staring at the small screen in front of us as something to get excited about, and so the film was paused and we all hurried to the end of the car to de-board the train. It was around 10pm, and so it was dark. It was also spitting with rain as we stood about on the platform next to the small station building. Saskatoon is the most populous city in Saskatchewan, and apparently home to the nineteenth busiest airport in Canada! What a place! I was feeling restless after sitting watching the film (and the three consecutive days on a train may have also contributed) and so I wanted to get some exercise. I said I would sprint the length of the train and back, to which Jess said she would time me. Unfortunately I *still* hadn't grasped just how long the train was, and combining this with slow realisation that I hadn't significantly moved my legs for several days meant that it was quite a painful experience. I made it back to the group around three minutes later, pretty exhausted, and having received many curious and slightly concerned looks from those passengers who had remained on board as I ran past.

* * *

It was early afternoon the following day when we pulled up at the station in Edmonton, Alberta. Another night of intermittent sleep on the increasingly uncomfortable seats had been survived, with the acquisition of yet another sleeping position doing little to improve the experience. I can't be too precise about the exact time we arrived

207

as the train spent two hours moving backwards and forwards between the platform and nearby sidings. Maybe this was some kind of Alberta train ritual, I wouldn't put it past the train company to instigate something peculiar like this given what I'd experienced already on the journey. During one of the stops we neatly aligned with the platform, and some people got on. Invaders! Edmonton was one of the major stops on the trans-Canada trip, and this meant us pre-existing passengers had to fight to defend our seats that had been ours for the past four days. It's weird how you get so protective over something you essentially despise.

After the daunting re-shuffle of new passengers and bags we set off again, luckily with no one having to switch their seats. This was a relief, as many of us were progressing rapidly through the early stages of our (by now well-established) train routines, and any enforced change to these could probably have wrecked us. Speaking of wreckages, a short while after we left Edmonton we passed a goods train that was smashed up in the woodland right beside the railway line. There was no disguising it, this train had derailed and was in an awful tangled mess. This did not bode well, and the site of this crumpled mass of iron and…train bits made us train travellers feel slightly tense about being on the same track that had caused this. The only mildly comforting thought was that the train went so bloody slowly we'd probably never get enough speed up to have a serious accident. Another strange sight that we could see out of the window was snow. There was quite a thick covering of snow on the fields and trees in the countryside of mid-Alberta. This seemed very strange, not least as it had only been the previous morning in Winnipeg where it had been thirty degrees. There's no avoiding it – Canada is climatologically inconsistent, and therefore very hard to pack for as a backpacker. Thankfully the mono-seasoned microclimate of the train meant I could get away with wearing the same clothes throughout the trip. Yes, okay, I was starting to need a shower.

The afternoon was spent chatting with our new carriage-buddies and trying to avoid a large group of small children as they ran excitedly up and down the aisles. Louise was English and had been staying with friends in Edmonton before boarding the train for the west coast. Henrik was Swedish, and was heading out to Vancouver having spent a few weeks working in an Ikea in Toronto. And that's not a rude stereotype joke – he actually had. I took this opportunity to bring out the guitar I'd bought in Winnipeg and have a go on it. Other people joined in, singing along to provide some welcome and apparently much-appreciated entertainment for the carriage as we made our way into the increasingly mountainous terrain of Western Alberta.

It was early evening when we pulled up in the Rocky Mountain town of Jasper, on the Alberta British Columbia border. We were five hours behind schedule thanks to the station antics and procrastinations in Edmonton and a few enforced stops while goods trains passed by. It was a fantastic setting as the sun was dropping behind the snow-capped mountains that encased the town. This was a popular destination and so was the final stop for many passengers. Thankfully the rest of us were allowed off the train too. Actually we were asked to get off while they cleaned the train and did various maintenance jobs, but this was fine, as it gave us forty minutes to have a wander around the town and to get something to eat.

Jasper is a very quaint town in Jasper National Park. It consists of many smart and stylish little shops, cafes and restaurants that lead back away from the station. It's very much a tourist hotspot with its dramatic setting in the heart of the Rocky Mountains, but as it was in between seasons (the winter ski season having finished but the summer camping and hiking season not yet up and running) it was quite quiet and there was a very relaxed feel to it.

The group of us strolled slowly up the road while our legs adjusted to this strenuous exercise that they had been deprived of lately. It had been decided that we should get a few alcoholic beverages to celebrate as it was our last night on the train, and so we stopped off in a bottle shop and bought a few select drinks. As we left the bottle shop I noticed a sign above one of the neighbouring shops. "The deli sandwiches are: two pieces of bread with heaven in the middle". I think this was a sign. Well I *knew* it was *a* sign, but I also knew it was a *sign*. Luckily the rest of the group were up to speed on my sandwich quest, and so as soon as they saw what I was staring at they very kindly suggested we got something to eat here. I was literally licking my lips. Not only was this seemingly the perfect place to get something to eat, but it would also rekindle my appreciation of proper sandwiches after five days of the dry, boring ham and cheese sandwiches that I had thrown together. We shuffled inside the small deli and assessed the variety of fillings. The man behind the counter was the co-owner, and a very charismatic man. He was loud and brash, and when I explained how important this sandwich was, he told me he'd make me 'the best sandwich I'd ever tasted'. Great – that saves me making a decision.

After he had skilfully put together five personalised and individually labelled sandwiches for us all, he handed me his business card, and then we headed back to the station as it was time to get back on board the train for the final leg of this epic cross-country journey.

Next stop – Vancouver!

Chapter 28

Are we nearly there yet?

Vancouver, British Columbia

*"Home is where...*ever you lay down your travel pillow."

Once back on the train we quickly adjourned to the *sky capsule* (as I inconsistently labelled it – it's okay I'll stop with this now) where we sneakily brought out our contraband and carefully wrapped sandwiches. We then consumed them whilst carving our way through the darkening mountains that towered up on either side of the train in the failing evening light. It was incredibly dramatic, with the occasional shout of 'bear!' from various other sky-capsulites getting everyone eagerly peering through the thick glass windows as we sought to catch a glimpse of these native creatures as they ambled along through the nearby vegetation.

The sandwich itself was nothing short of masterful too. I feared that with all the hype the creator had laden on it that it might end up being disappointing, but no. Although it was a bit on the pricey side at $7.88, the vast array of fillings including meat, cheese, pickles, peppers and various condiments enclosed in a thick, multi-grain seeded roll was excellent. Combine this with the surrounding views of the Rocky Mountains, the good company, *and* the fact we were on the home straight of the train journey, and it all added up to a brilliant evening. The guitar was then summoned, and as darkness fell we carried on the group entertainment until everyone slowly fell asleep.

* * *

As I struggled to straighten myself out after a fourth consecutive night of being scrunched up on a train seat, I lifted the window blind to reveal lush green mountain sides lining the route of the train. Having packed up my travel pillow for the last time on this train, I sat watching the mountains slip in and out of the low-lying clouds until they began to give way to small rural communities, quarries and scattered buildings. As we followed the river towards the coast these grew in size and proximity to each other, until we were chugging our way through the outer suburbs of Vancouver.

The train seemed to slow as we crossed over numerous bridges and wound around the foothills towards the city, signalling to those of us on board that we should start packing up our belongings in preparation for the seemingly imminent arrival at Vancouver Pacific Central Station.

It turned out not to be as imminent as expected. We actually spent a hugely frustrating hour going painfully slowly, *backwards*, or simply *nowhere at all*! I suppose we should have learnt from five days of this, and we could have guessed that a smooth and speedy arrival would not be on the agenda. What was odd though, was how despite being five hours behind schedule in Jasper, we were now only *one* hour behind. And if the train had consistently gone forwards for the last couple of kilometres instead of stopping and reversing every few minutes then it may have been even less then that! How we had made up the time was a real mystery. I certainly had felt no indication of any increased speed during the night. It was all very odd, but then days on the train felt longer than normal days so it was all very odd anyway.

Actually the days *had* got longer since being on the train. The journey went continuously west, passing into a different province most days, which often meant a change in time zone. In the past week I had gone from *Atlantic* Time in Nova Scotia, to *Eastern* Time in Ontario, to *Central* Time in Manitoba and Saskatchewan, to *Mountain* Time in Alberta, and finally to *Pacific* Time in British Columbia. Practically each day we gained an hour, so most days were twenty-five hours long. It just screws you up. This final delay did however provide a bit of time to reflect on the journey though, as this was to be my final train destination in Canada on this trip.

Despite my issues with the Canadian cross-country train network as a viable method of travel, it had been a fantastic experience. Granted it is at times upsettingly slow and irrational in its procedure, but it is essentially reliable in terms of timings, and the grandeur of the whole train-travelling process does add to the occasion for the inquisitive foreign visitor.

While the UK train network is a quick and more often than not effective form of travel that encompasses the length and breath of the land and therefore making everywhere highly accessible, it is more functional, and it is used merely as a means of getting from A to B. This is in contrast to Canada, where aside from the comparatively short distances between the eastern corridor cities from Toronto up to Québec City (where trains are quite frequent and more commuter in style and clientele) the cross country services are a real experience, where you can pass through massively contrasting landscapes and provinces. As I found from those I met on board, the train journey *itself* is very much part of the trip away, and despite the bruised limbs and stiffness that us economy folk had to endure in, we had also had a lot of fun along the way through those we met and the places we passed through. I said that flying across the country would have been cheating, and now I even more firmly stand by that having seen the land in between the urban centres that are usually left unseen by visitors.

Sadly this rather philosophical in-head analyses of the train journey *still* didn't manage to fill all the time left by the final tentative movements towards the station, and just as we thought we were pulling up at the platform, we stopped and moved backwards again. These rail-based procrastinations were increasingly irritating to our tired and weary bodies, and as a result the nostalgic thoughts of train travel subsided, giving way instead to a thrilling discussion about plug adapters. By the time we eventually did stop at the platform I think we all knew that we needed to spend some time away from the train. And plug adapters.

Just as we were about to leave the train, after eighty-three hours on board, an announcement interrupted the hustle and bustle of luggage movement, with the voice asking 'Mr E. John. That's a Mr Elton John to please remain on the train.'

A few of us smiled, assuming this to be a coincidence or another oddly delivered joke by the quirky train staff, but having heaved our bags into the main station building, Louise overheard an irate man in a suit berating a train official, apparently expressing Elton John's anger at having his presence on the train announced to everyone.

So it *was* Elton John – a fellow Watfordite! Had he been following me all the way from Watford? Was he a massive sandwich fan and so was trying to covertly find out my destination and beat me to the prize? If only we had known he was onboard – he could have joined us for a sing-a-long last night! I bet he would have *loved* that! He was probably just frustrated that the train had travelled at a snails pace when he was more of a *Rocket Man*. Poor old Elton.

* * *

Having split up after getting off the train and going back to our various homes and hostels, we met up again that evening across the road from where I was staying on Granville Street – the main tourist centre of downtown Vancouver. The street was buzzing with backpackers and street entertainers as people slipped in and out of neighbouring bars and cafes in this highly cosmopolitan visitor hotspot. We were all in high spirits – not least because at least for some of us it had been the first time we had showered in nearly a week, but in general it was nice to have finally arrived in Vancouver. We had a few drinks and then headed off to an Irish bar in the trendier Gastown neighbourhood, near the waterfront, guided by Jess and Kailey.

The bar was filling up as we strode in, and soon a band took to the stage to perform a series of Irish themed songs in between dj tracks to create a fun mix of music throughout the evening. By one o'clock we were finding it increasingly difficult to stand upright, but not so much from alcohol, but more because of the tiredness incurred from five days without a bed. The thought of being able to stretch out horizontally was very appealing, and so we all decided to head back to our homes and hostels.

* * *

I got up the next morning after a much-appreciated sleep. As an added bonus the hostel booking included breakfast, which was a fantastic array of bread, muffins and cakes. Luxury. I also was entertained by the 'eleven-step guide to washing your hands' that was stuck to the washroom wall. Who knew there were so many stages in the hand washing process?

At nine o'clock I met up with Louise and headed up to the waterfront where we met Jess who had said she would show us a nice touristy bridge as she had the day off work. We took the ferry from a jetty close to the Vancouver Convention Centre, and from there it was ten minutes across the water to North Vancouver. From here it was a fifteen-minute bus ride up to the Capilano Suspension Bridge – a narrow footbridge that spans one hundred and thirty-six metres across the Capilano River, seventy metres below. It was raining quite heavily, but then I'd heard this was a popular feature of Vancouver, and it also rather suited the rainforest that we now found ourselves in. We watched a trio of musicians who were all dressed in themed clothes (although I'm not sure what that theme was) while they played some folk music to an audience of about five that were sat out by the coffee trailer, trying to restore some heat with a hot beverage as they hid from the rain. We clapped in support of their fine efforts (the musicians, not the coffee drinkers – although I was secretly impressed with how expertly they were drinking these caffeine drinks after my mess up back in the Hemel Snow Centre) and then we stepped out across the swaying bridge, getting pretty wet in the process. The other two had opted to wear the complimentary yellow plastic rain covers, but I had politely declined this fashion accessory, as the yellow clashed with my eyes…or because I had a perfectly adequate waterproof jacket. Yes, that's a far better reason!

On the other side of the steeply curving bridge we got to go around a series of raised wooden platforms and walkways that wound around the tree tops, proving an alternative and interesting view of the forest canopy. It was all very pleasant, if a little expensive, but that was nothing to the gondola further up the road at Grouse Mountain. Here they wanted $42 for the privilege of going up to the top of a cloud covered mountain where there was nothing to see or do. Great. No thanks! So instead we headed back down to the ferry and crossed back over to downtown Vancouver.

Vancouver is a city that very much appears to have grown significantly over recent years, with endless high-rise apartment blocks sprouting upwards from the downtown area. Vancouver is one of the most densely populated cities in North America, and this ties in with it also being very high up on the list of places to live with the highest quality of life. It is also therefore predictably expensive.

Granville street runs through the heart of the city, and is lined on either side with shops, restaurants, clubs, and bars that get increasingly seedier as you head south towards the bridge over to Granville Island. As a passer-by along this street you find yourself being constantly pestered by the high number of homeless people that roam this area. Apparently they migrate here from the east as the climate is more tolerable, and obviously the city's popularity with visitors draws them in. You will also find the odd desperate backpacker trying to secure a few pennies as they've messed up the budgeting for their trip.

The city is a stark contrast to many other Canadian cities with its eclectic mix of inhabitants, many coming for the job opportunities from the spiralling growth of the city, but also as the quality of life is supposed to be very high here, and the surrounding natural features are a fantastic asset. It is understandable why people would want to come here, with its setting amongst dramatic mountain ranges, rainforests, and the Pacific Ocean all providing a wealth of activities for all seasons; there is skiing in close proximity to the city during the winter season, mountain biking and hiking in the summer, and a lively sports and entertainment scene all year round. This is why many travellers you meet across Canada have usually spent significant time in Vancouver, living and/or working, especially since the Winter Olympics came to town just a few months earlier.

Many of the events of the recent Olympics were held in a resort around eighty miles north of Vancouver called Whistler. Recognised as one of the best ski resorts in North America, and after the extensive coverage and hype that it got during the recent Olympics, this had been somewhere I had very much wanted to go on my trip, and so having arrived a couple of days early in Vancouver I thought I could probably *just about* squeeze in a fleeting visit tomorrow. This meant it was time to make the switch from train to bus.

217

Chapter 29

Time for an important board meeting

Whistler, British Columbia

*"Many hands make...*gloves more difficult to attach."

I was glad that the views from the bus were dramatic as we meandered around the winding coastal road, because it was a pleasant distraction from the bitterness I was feeling at having missed breakfast this morning, having left before it was ready in an attempt to pull off my visit to Whistler. While this was hugely irritating, I was looking forward to exploring the mountains and the Olympic village. I'm sure there would be other free blueberry muffins and orange juice somewhere on the horizon anyway.

The mountains grew increasingly snowy along the two-hour journey, and it also seemed to be getting brighter as we headed further north, and when we pulled up mid-morning outside Whistler Village Visitor Centre it was positively sunny.

I took this opportunity to go in and get some information about the area so I could find out what I could do here, and which were the best routes for heading up into the mountains. The helpful lady behind the desk immediately pulled out a map, which is always a good start, and then she started circling things on it with her biro. This was exactly what I needed.

There was a gondola in operation that took summer ramblers up Blackcomb Mountain behind the village. There were also plenty of bike hiring shops, and pathways and cycle routes through the valleys for visitors to explore. This all sounded very nice, but just as I was walking off she said something very intriguing.

'Of course it's also the last day of the snow season.'

I stopped and turned around. I had secretly yearned to take my recently acquired snow-skills to a mountain setting, but I had feared that I would be too late in the year to do it on this trip, and not having been on a snow holiday I imagined I would be well out of my depth. I also presumed the costs might be out of my budget. This was a real teaser though – the *last* day of the season. Was it a sign? I'd had a few so-called 'signs' on this trip, and not all of them had worked out. I was *so* tempted though, but how did I go about it? 'One snowboarding please!' Is that the correct phrasing?

The lady took the map she had previously scribbled on and added a few more black pen marks next to relevant snow hire shops and kiosks, and then I set off into the heart of the village.

Whistler Village is a series of curving pedestrianised walkways around various clothing outlets and eateries. Set beneath Whistler and Blackcomb mountains it is quaint yet even at this time of day and in the off-season it was beginning to buzz with outdoor adventure enthusiasts. Top-of the range mountain bikes were lined up in huge numbers outside shops, and people dressed in brightly coloured waterproof protective clothing strutted around the pathways lugging skis or safety equipment behind them. I found one of the shops that had been circled on my map, and went inside and down to the basement.

'Hi. Can I have some snowboarding…stuff, please.'

Yes, I was hardly speaking like a pro, but thankfully I had done enough sessions on the indoor slope back in Hemel Hempstead to know that I wasn't 'goofy' (a right foot first rider), and that I knew how I wanted my bindings angled. I was totally down with the cool kids in my board spec.

Soon I had a board and some boots, and I also got some waterproof trousers, although unfortunately I had to wear them over my jeans as they were pretty loose. I asked if they had gloves. They said no. So I asked if they had goggles. They said no. Luckily I had some sunglasses and my own gloves, although they were far from ideal, but then this whole attempt was a bit scrappy in its formation.

Geared up, I made my way out to the main forecourt at the foot of the mountain. I queued up to buy my lift pass, but as I did a man came over to me and offered me his pass at a discounted price as he didn't need it. Ideal! It was then a quick stumble in my boots over to the gondola, and up I went.

I fumbled about with my hat and gloves as I made my ascent up Blackcomb, and soon it was time to get out. Luckily I remembered to take my board off the outside rack of the gondola car too – otherwise I may have found the snowboarding bit a little tricky. I then strapped in my left boot to the board bindings, and slid over to a chair lift. I didn't really know where I was going, but I knew that the best snowboarding was done on snow, and as there wasn't any left at this first drop off point I guessed thanks to my fantastic knowledge of altitude-temperature correlation that I would need to go higher up the mountain to find snow. So I did, smoothly flopping back onto the bench of the lift like I was a regular snowster.

A few minutes later and I was smoothly disembarking next to a green arrow. I really should have done some more research into this, but I was pretty sure 'green' meant a more basic run, so that would probably be a good starting point. I clipped in my other foot, and slid off down a deserted alpine slope.

It was fantastic. The snow was good (although I'm not sure what I was basing that on) and to be continuously boarding down a series of long, winding routes through the trees was phenomenal. You have to take into account that my only previous boarding was going down a single straight slope that lasted no more than twenty-five seconds and was surrounded by adverts and corrugated steel, so to be carving through the thick snow for over ten minutes at a time, *and* with this stunning setting of one of the best ski resorts in the world was brilliant.

As my confidence increased, so did my speed, and soon I was tearing down various blue routes (sometimes because gravity was insistent on leading me astray) getting air off ridges and just generally being reckless as snowboarders are supposed to be. I barely saw anyone else on the slopes as it was the last day, and that made it far more exciting to be in this white and green wilderness, and far safer as occasionally I over did it and ended up face first in the snow, or precariously dangling over ridge edges. People who saw me were probably terrified by my sheer speed and fierce appearance as I was dressed all in black; hired black trousers, black jacket, black boots, board and bindings, black gloves and a black hat. People would probably have called me "stealth…something", which I would have laughed off patronisingly, but secretly it would have been *great.*

On my third run I was heading down a route that led past a chairlift boarding station, and not wanting to be lame and come to a miserable stop on the flat, I pointed the nose of the board straight down the fall line of the slope and hurtled full-pelt towards the edge of the next part of the run. Sods law then made an untimely appearance, and in my attempt to avoid an undignified and slow stop before reaching the next slope, I speed-stacked it into a bump, and triple-somersaulted across the snow in front of all the other snow-goers who were in the queue. Well if you're going to screw it up, you might as well do it in style. This was coincidently the very same moment that I discovered that neither my gloves nor my jacket were waterproof. But despite cold, wet hands, damp clothes, and ice down my back and trousers, I picked myself up and ploughed on. It was still pretty damn good.

I did a couple more runs interspersed with a few scenic stops for photographs and to fumble about with my gloves as I tried to regain some feeling in my fingers. I then checked my watch and realised it was time to head back down the mountain to catch the bus back to Vancouver. I headed up a nearby chairlift and set off for one last run.

It was all going great as I peddled the board through the snow, but then as I tried to flick off a pile of snow, I clipped the edge of the board on the mound and stuffed it into the side of the mountain. Another dramatic but thankfully pain free tumble followed, but I felt my foot come loose. I looked down to see that it was still strapped in but the bindings had come off the board. This was not good. I took off my gloves and tried reattaching it, but despite repeated attempts I achieved nothing other than making my hands go numb. My mountain adventure was over.

I trudged through the snow and down the mountainside for ten minutes carrying my board until I reached a gondola that would take me back to the village. Despite this less than fashionable final descent I was very happy with how the day had worked out so neatly. I made it back to the hire shop and dumped the gear by the desk. One of the employees then picked up the detached bindings and studied it for a few seconds.

'Hmmm. Looks like it's broken,' he said decisively, nodding his head and scratching is non-existent beard.

Really?! F**k me, I hadn't realised!

'Yes, it *does*,' I replied calmly.

'Okay, well I'll refund the cost of your gear then.'

'Oh…right. Thanks.'

It hadn't occurred to that I might get a refund. I suppose they weren't to know I had to be leaving now anyway, so this had all worked out *very* well – discount lift pass *and* free gear hire! Brilliant! I took my wad of cash out of the shop and headed over to the bus stop where I sat in the sun to drip-dry. It was time to go back to Vancouver. I wasn't even going to *try* and get a sandwich in Whistler. A trendy, hyped-up resort like this was guaranteed to have prices to match. Besides, it was almost sandwich judgement day, so that all important ferry terminal sandwich had my focus...although I had one last opportunist mission I wanted to carry out.

The journey back was relaxing, but that was largely due to the amount of rush-hour traffic we experienced coming into Vancouver that meant we weren't moving very much. At one point it took us half an hour to drive fifty metres down a hill. It was a nice hill though, so I didn't complain. Once back I changed out of my damp clothes, showered and then met up with Louise in the hostel over the road, where we had a roast dinner for $5. This was stupidly cheap, but surprisingly large and tasty. I also had a coke as I was by now severely lacking in energy, and when the bill arrived it turned out to be free for whatever reason. I then asked for *another* one (I was *seriously* low on energy) and as I tried to hand over some money for this the bargirl said 'No, it's a free refill.'

A free refill on a free drink? This didn't sound like a sustainable business model, but what the hell! Today had just been endless discounts and freebies. Maybe I should go out and explore this run of fortune further...or I could just go to bed because I was shattered. I did the latter. Sorry for being boring.

* * *

It was eight o'clock the next morning, and I was back at the bus station and waiting to board the *greyhound.* I was once *again* frustrated at missing breakfast for the second morning running, but then this was my last opportunity to try this exciting sub-mission.

'Have you got your passport?' the bus driver asked.

I showed him my passport.

I was off to the *United States of the Americas*!

223

Chapter 30

Don't mock me – mocha coffee!

Seattle, Washington (U.S.A.)

*"Ignorance is…*a fast track to being pushed down an escalator."

I was thinking about maps. I like maps, and I like *looking* at maps. But I didn't have any maps to hand, so I had to settle with just thinking about them.

I was several days into the long westward train journey, and with little else to occupy my mind I had began thinking about my destination – Vancouver – and where it lay in geographical terms. I knew Whistler was in striking distance, but then my attentions turned to the south. Specifically towards the Canada-US border, and beyond this to Seattle. Yes, I have a very good brain map, and it's good of you to notice.

Seattle has some strong connotations; it's the origin of grunge music and *Nirvana*, it's the birthplace of *Starbucks* Coffee, it's where aeroplane manufactures *Boeing* and that little computer firm *Microsoft* began, and it is of course the setting of US sitcom *Frasier*. What a place! But what was *really* on my mind were sandwiches. This may or may not surprise you depending on how much attention you've been paying throughout this book.

It had suddenly occurred to me that I might be missing a trick. Here I was ploughing along the southern edge of Canada trying

sandwiches, and I hadn't once stepped over the border to America –
'the land of food'! ...Or is it 'the land of the free'? Hmmm, My
brain-maps are considerably better than my tag-line knowledge.
Anyway, I'm *reasonably* confident that the U.S. is known for it's
snack food consumption, and sandwiches can *sort of* drop into this
category. I certainly remember having some large and spectacularly
filled sandwiches on previous visits. I therefore thought that maybe I
– the sandwich hunter – should step over the border and sample an
American sandwich to gain a bit more perspective on my sandwich
quest. This all depended upon whether I had time, but thanks to my
train schedule adjustment I worked out I could just fit in a fleeting
visit south of the border.

So here I was, stepping out of Seattle's bus terminal, having endured
a four-hour trip stuck talking to a man who had less charisma than a
beach pebble. Customs had been the usual fun and games, and
although the second half of the journey had seemed longer (thanks
to road signs being in *kilometres* in Canada, but having switched to
miles in the U.S. and so I couldn't understand why the distance
numbers suddenly started going down at a slower rate) we had
arrived on time, and I was ready to begin my American adventure!

I actually had two goals while I was here; I wanted to eat a
sandwich, and I wanted to go up the tall building that I was aware
Seattle had. First things first though; I wanted to find the hostel I
had booked yesterday and get checked-in. The only map I had
secured of Seattle was a hostel leaflet, and it only showed the small
area surrounding the hostel. This did include the main train station
that was near the hostel though, so I thought it would do.
Unfortunately I arrived by bus, which as you may have already
guessed is not a type of train, and as it happens the bus station is
nowhere near the train station (unlike in Vancouver and many other
places where they are part of the same building), and so essentially I
had no idea where I was. This wasn't a great start.

I crossed over a few streets to see if I could get my bearings or recognise anything, but as I'd never been to Seattle before and I had done absolutely no research, it didn't prove fruitful. But *then* I caught a glimpse of something through the gap between two office blocks. It was the very distinctive shape of the tall building! Made familiar by its outline on the starting credits of *Frasier*! Excellent. So I decided on a change of plan, and instead I would guide myself towards this icon by tracking it by eye. This was made possible as I'd left my main backpack in a locker back at the hostel in Vancouver so I could travel with just my day bag. It's like that old saying that I've just made up; staying one night – travel light. I'm not especially proud of that on refection, but I'm sure you get the point. Technically this also meant that I was *sub*-backpacking – which was hugely exciting in itself.

It took me around twenty minutes to negotiate my way around the city streets until I reached the base of the building. This had included a brief stop to get some 'greens' from an ATM I happened to pass on the way. That's 'dollars' by the way. I'm actually wondering if I made up that slang term for them. Anyway, I now had some legal currency, which always helps when you're in a place that's in a country that uses money.

The 'Space Needle' was built for the 1962 *World's Fair* in Seattle. It's *quite* tall, but (quite literally) not half as tall as the *CN Tower* in Toronto. It's very distinctive in shape however, and it does look like a…space…needle. Whatever one of those looks like. Well it's definitely pointy on top.

I followed the signs around to the entrance, which actually led me right around the base and back to the front of the building again. This was all very silly, but if it made them happy then that's fine. Once inside I bought a ticket with my recently acquired dollars, and got in the lift to the viewing deck. The viewing space was impressive. Many tall buildings have good views, but they don't make the most of their opportunities. The *Space Needle* had an indoor area with screens that showed live camera footage that you can rotate round three hundred and sixty degrees and zoom in and out of. It also had a screen with a view from the tower looking out over the city that you could adjust the time of, meaning you could scan through a whole day and night scene to see how the view changes. It was all very clever and exciting and interactive. I also appreciate the diagrams and comparisons of other tall buildings, so you can see where it lies in the grand scheme of high-upness. There was also an outside viewing deck, and this had a few telescopes spread around it, pointing out in different directions that were free to use! This is unheard of – usually they try and rip you off for using these. One frustrating thing about Toronto's *CN Tower* is that they have none of these things, and they don't even tell you what you can see, *even though* there are loads of interesting things that you *can* see. I mean it wouldn't take a lot of effort to put a few boards up with labels on. It's one of the highest viewing platforms in the world and yet they don't bother giving visitors a little insight into what they're looking out at. Wasteful – *that's* what it is.

So I was very impressed with the *Space Needle*. It was well equipped and well laid out. The only slight downside was that the views out weren't quite as interesting as some tall building locations, but that's not its fault really. It did however allow me to plot a very rough route through the city to where I thought my hostel was, as I knew from my tiny map that it was near the stadiums, which I could see in the distance from the viewing deck.

Having finished playing about with the interactive screens I got in the lift to go down. It was quite full, and as usual with these 'express elevators' you have a guide with you in case you get lost. This woman was a lively host, and she told us a joke on the way down to help pass the forty-three second journey.

'A snail was attacked by two turtles. When the officers asked what happened the snail said "I don't know. It all happened so fast!"'

Silence…

Nice try lady, but *talking snails*? I don't think so…

The lift opened out into the gift shop – a cunning ploy designed to lure visitors into spending loads of money on *Space Needle* paraphernalia, such as plastic moneyboxes and bright green fleeces. I didn't have enough money to warrant a moneybox, *let alone* a plastic one, and it was *far* too hot to need a fleece (and green clashes with my eyes) so I negotiated my way around the stands and sales desks until I found the exit. The truth was that I didn't want to spend what little money I did have on souvenirs – I wanted…no, I *needed* to spend it on a sandwich! But where should I go? How could I choose a worthy one? I'd had signs up until this point leading me to my choices, but how could that happen here? I needed one *right now*!

Maybe god heard me. I'd been starting to wonder if he had been installing power in me, or maybe sponsoring me in some way, because these sandwich opportunities kept arising. Was it fate that I found out unexpectedly and at the last-minute about the Montreal, Halifax and Jasper sandwiches? Was *he* responsible for the original *Google* search results that led me here? Suppose it had been *him* who had tried phoning me in Toronto airport! *Dammit*! If only I could have worked out how to answer the phone! He may have been trying to contact me to warn me about the boat trip salesman! The sun also seemed to be following me on my trip…but then there was also the homeless Toronto issue, and the zip-breaking incidents, as well as the few odd people I'd met along the way. *Perhaps* he was testing my resilience – seeing if I was committed to my cause. Well I was! And surely skipping a nice *free* breakfast to travel to another country for the night just to try a sandwich so I could prove I was being thorough had shown this? He may have been less consistent lately, but he must now have realised my level of dedication, because just then he shined a brilliant light down from above to guide me once more. And the light was red…

I was just walking out of the *World's Fair* complex when I was stopped at a road crossing by a red light. As I waited patiently I noticed just behind the light was a window with a sign stuck on it facing out at me. "Voted Seattle's best burger!"

Now I know what you're thinking so just don't, okay? Yes it said "burger", and I was looking for a 'sandwich', and I had specifically said that 'burgers' do not count as 'sandwiches', but think about it; in America they refer to 'burgers' as 'sandwiches'. And while that directly contradicts my official sandwich quest guidelines, I had also stepped over the boundaries by coming to the U.S. So I had drifted into a grey area of sandwich research, and was now being presented with the perfect opportunity to have the perfect grey area 'sandwich' to fit. Well, I don't care what you say – I've justified it in my head and there's nothing you can do about it. So deal with it.

This was brilliant! I was less than thirty metres from the *Space Needle* and I had found the perfect thing to eat. When the light turned green I crossed over and hurried round the building to find the entrance. It was a sports bar, cleverly named "The Sports Bar", and it was very large inside, but quite empty. The walls were decorated with glass cabinets filled with autographed sports memorabilia. A smartly dressed waiter seated me, and then he handed me the menu. I didn't really need it, I knew *exactly* what I wanted to have, but it seemed impolite not to flick through the laminated pages anyway.

I soon placed my order, and then sat back to watch the *French Open* tennis that was being shown on the numerous television sets that hung from the walls. This was a nice bonus too, although I was being made to pay for it. This burger-sandwich was $14. It had better be nice if I had to use up most of my remaining US currency on it.

It arrived quickly, and it was nice. That was probably largely down to me having missed breakfast and so I was hungry. It was pretty much just a hamburger, but it came with some very straw like chips that were thankfully far nicer than the last chips (or "fries") I'd had – the gravy soaked mush that made up my Québec City poutine. It also came with a crisp salad. That's a fresh salad, *not* a salad of crisps. Crisps *and* chips would not be promoting healthy eating. Anyway, it was job done in America, and I'd only been in the country two hours! This was efficient even by my high standards, so I now had the rest of the afternoon to kill.

I decided it was time to find the hostel I'd booked, so I headed along 5th Avenue towards the central downtown area of the city, where I soon found myself in a busy shopping area surrounded by high-rise buildings. I was quite happy ambling along the streets in the direction I guessed would eventually lead me to my accommodation for the night, but just as I was dodging a determined afternoon shopper as she stormed along the sidewalk I was stopped by an excitable lady in a bright jacket. I must have screamed tourist, as she pounced on me as soon as she caught sight of my rugged backpacker appearance...or it may have been my clueless expression as I spent far too long looking up at road signs.

'Where are you headed?' she asked enthusiastically.

'Oh, a hostel on King Street, but its fine I—'

'Great, well what you need to do is come down here...' she began, while trying to drag me by the arm back along the street - away from the direction I wanted to go.

'No really,' I said, 'I'm quite happy walking,' I protested.

'Don't be stupid, it's free anyway!'

There was no arguing with her, this transport employee (at least that's what I assume she was) was determined for me to experience the delights of the Seattle public transport network.

She then pointed up at the sky and said I could get the train, and then she pointed at the ground and said I could also catch the bus.

I definitely thought she was crazy at this point. I am a wise man, and I know that trains do not travel through the sky, and I also know that buses do not travel underground.

Just as she was mid speech there was a loud metallic crashing sound, and I looked round to see the large metal connector rod of a bus drop off the overhead electric wires and smash into the side of the bus.

She must have seen the bemused look on my face, and probably felt a little up against it having given me this fast-paced spiel about all these different wonderful forms of public transport when this accident happened. She quickly brushed it off though.

'Oh don't worry about that – it happens all the time.' And with that she led me into the large entrance of a building and pushed me down an escalator.

It had all happened so fast, but a few seconds later I found myself in a large underground tunnel with a wide platform. No sooner had I taken a quick glance up and down the platform to get some form of indication of where I needed to be, when there was a shout from the platform on the other side of the tunnel.

'Hey you, come here!'

I looked up slightly startled, and saw a lady staring at me. What the hell? I'd only just got here! Who *was* this? Actually I didn't care, because just then a bus, yes, that's what I said, a *bus* pulled up by the platform in front of me.

Sod this, I didn't want to stick around to see what this bizarre and slightly aggressive woman wanted, so I jumped through the open doors and we were off.

I was slightly dazed by the quick-fire antics of the last few minutes, but nevertheless, here I was on a bus that was running parallel to trams in an underground tunnel. There were also trains that ran on raised tracks above the city, and electric buses on the roads. This was public transport heaven! *And* it was free, as the woman had said. Not only that, but after checking the onboard map, I got off a few stops later to find myself right outside my hostel in China Town. It may have all been a bit odd and a little frantic, but it had worked out well in the end.

231

I checked into the hostel with relative ease once the man on reception had found my booking under "Chris Imbrose", and I found my bed in the largest dorm I'd ever been in, with seven bunk beds (that's fourteen beds if you're struggling with the complex maths). I then had to mark the bed I'd been assigned using a velcro poker chip, which I found very novel. The only problem with my efficient delivery to the hostel was that I now had even more time to fill. I had planned to wander through the streets, casually making my way here over the afternoon to use up some time, but now I was already here I needed something else to do. I left my bag in the dorm room and set off over to the nearby sports stadiums where I could peer inside and watch the nearby trains go past. I then walked up a main road towards the 'International District' when I saw my first *Starbucks* shop. I know, I know, I was in Seattle – *Starbucks* on every corner, right? But because of my underground arrival I'd *missed* all the corners, so this was the first one I saw, and I quickly made a brave decision.

I deduced that I couldn't really afford to buy an aeroplane (the exchange rate just wasn't that favourable), I probably wouldn't bump into *Nirvana* or Dr Frasier Crane, and computers usually get the better of me. This left me no other option than to try a *Starbucks* coffee in order to gain a true Seattle experience. Oh, there was a baseball game on that evening, but baseball isn't as synonymous with Seattle as these other things are, and also baseball is boring.

Now it may surprise you to hear that I'd never been to a *Starbucks* before. In fact I've never had a coffee from *any* coffee shop before. I've probably only had around *three* coffees in my life, and at least one of those was by accident. This is largely due to me not being a trendy teenage girl, and so I don't meet up for coffee on lunch breaks, or as a brief bag-resting interlude on shopping trips. But I *had* been practising drinking coffee at the snow centre back home, so maybe this - the home of coffee shops - *should* be the place I finally put all that training into a real world scenario.

232

I was nervous as I pushed my way through the large glass doors. I immediately found myself by the counter, with its vast array of cups in all different sizes, and the glass cabinets with wide selections of accompanying cakes and slices. What did all these shiny metal machines do? I imagine it was a similar situation to what trainee astronauts experience when they first sit in the cockpit of a space shuttle.

My eyes were wide as I took in this alien landscape. Men and women in suits adorned the stylish round tables that were dotted around the open shop floor. I then looked up at the board behind the counter that showed the menu. Why were there so many words on it? Why wasn't there just one big word saying "Coffee" on it? *Surely* that's all that was needed? Just then one of the mission commanders from behind the master control panel spoke.

'Can I get you anything?

Shit. I'd been too busy procrastinating and trying to come to terms with the place that I hadn't even got close to knowing what I should ask for. I was smart enough to know 'a coffee please' wouldn't cut the mustard.

'Errrm, no it's okay, thanks. I'm just looking,' I replied sheepishly. By that I really mean I spoke *reservedly*, I didn't 'baaaa' at her.

Hang on… "Just looking"? Why the *hell* did I say that?! This wasn't a car showroom or a carpet sample warehouse! Oh god, I'd *properly* screwed this up.

I smiled at the space-waitress. Nope, it was no good; there was no recovering from this now. I'd revealed my coffee shop amateurism. There was nothing else for it. I had blown my chance of getting a coffee with any sprinkle of credibility. I turned around and walked out of the door. This had been the Apollo 13 of coffee purchasing attempts.

This had obviously not gone well, but I am not a quitter! Oh no! God had tested me before on such matters, and I would once again prove that my sturdy determination would get me through.

Back in Vancouver I had passed two consecutive streets with *Starbucks* shops on the corner. This had made me smile as it fitted the cliché. But here I was, for the first time in my life *actively looking* for another *Starbucks* and I couldn't bloody find one anywhere. But this is *Starbucks city*! There should be *two* on every corner! But there were none. I passed lots of corners, and all of them were *Starbucks*less. This was hugely annoying, but I couldn't very well go back to the other *Starbucks* after I'd acted so unprofessionally in it. I had to do this smoothly, like the yuppie I had practised being in London all those weeks ago.

Eventually, having now made my way into the central 'International District' of the city, I saw the trusty *Starbucks* sign poking out from a shop front. This was it.

I paused, straightened my belt buckle (well I wasn't wearing a tie…) and strode confidently through the door.

I immediately took up a prominent position in front of the counter, and straight away I began eyeing up the list of coffee options on the board behind. I wasn't going to be fooled into looking at my surroundings this time! I would *not* be phased!

The man behind the counter looked over at me, so I quickly started stroking my chin with my index finger while crossing my other arm over my chest. I'm pretty sure this portrays the look of a confident yet selective coffee drinker. And yes, if Hollywood ever does a film requiring this role then I *will* be expecting a phone call.

I thought about this logically. I wanted something *cheap*, but also something that suggested I had an acquired taste. Basically it had to be under $3 and it couldn't have a sweetcorn topping or pollyfiller expanding foam on it. Then I spotted one.

'Yes, can I have a "Caffé Mocha" please.' I spoke in my most formal English – or 'Fenglish' if you will.

'Would you like whipped cream on that?'

Gah! It's more of those sodding options again!

'*No thanks,*' I said firmly.

And that was it. I took a seat at a nearby table, and to my absolute delight it had a copy of *The Seattle Times* on it, so when my coffee was brought over to me half a minute later, I sat holding my coffee whilst reading the newspaper. I was a *true yuppie*! I then sipped my coffee and burnt my lips. Well *almost* a yuppie.

And I think that 'mocha' means chocolate.

Chapter 31

Sleepless in Seattle

(Yes, I'm still living it up in)
Seattle, Washington

*"Beggars can't be...*escaped from with politeness. Sometimes you just have to hide."

I walked out of the coffee shop sensing I had entered a new era. A new era in which I could operate competently as a member of the suit wearing community. Now I just needed a suit. Oh, and I suppose a job that I could wear the suit to. Well I'd definitely taken the important first step at least.

I walked back to China Town. Actually it would probably be more accurate to describe it as a 'scurry'. As I'm not a regular coffee drinker the mocha-coffee had hit me hard, and so I was all jittery and wide-eyed as I shot through the streets of downtown Seattle - completely whacked off my face on caffeine. I got back to King Street and walked into the door. That's right, I didn't walk *through* the door, I walked *into* it. This sobered me up somewhat. This wasn't right – why hadn't it opened? Doors are *supposed* to open when you push them! Unless they are 'pull' doors, but I was *sure* this had been a 'push' door earlier.

'Are you looking for the hostel?' a man standing beside the doorway asked me.

'Erm…yeah.'

I obviously screamed 'backpacker' from my rustic, worldly eyes.

But hang on, why was he asking? I was *clearly* trying to get into the hostel! That's what doors usually facilitate, and especially doors at the front of hos—

'It's next door.' The man said with a grin creeping across his face. His big, stupid, mocking face. 'That's a taxi firm shop.'

Bugger.

Yes, okay, in my sleep withdrawn, caffeine high state I had got the wrong entrance way. But they *did* look similar, and after a month of constantly being on the move between different hostels and entrances it was getting increasingly difficult to remember which doors I was and was not supposed to be trying to get through. I swiftly spun around and pushed my way through the correct entrance and went up to my dorm room. I sat down on the bed, and then I realised that I didn't *want* to be in my room, because after all my afternoon procrastinations it was now gone seven in the evening and so I thought I better get something to eat. So I stood up, went downstairs and walked out of the door again. It was a 'pull' door from this direction. Yes, I had it sussed now!

I was pretty tired by this point, and I was on a post-caffeine come-down. It had been a long day, and I was looking forward to getting a good night's sleep tonight after a week of disruption on the long train journeys and early starts in Vancouver. Because of this I didn't want to go too far to find something to eat. The hostel was in China Town, so I thought that this would be the perfect place to find some reasonably priced, interesting cuisine. I set off walking around the nearby streets. The sky was darkening as night time beckoned, but also the clouds were drawing ominously across the sky. There was no shortage of options. On every street there were lots of pokey little shop fronts with red and green neon lit signs offering various types of Asian delicacies. They all seemed to have a rapidly disintegrating menu stuck haphazardly to the window, featuring a

237

few faded photographs of the food they offered that were probably taken in the early 1980s. Needless to say none of them looked very tempting. They were pretty run down and deserted, and whenever I paused for too long outside of one, homeless people would approach me wanting money. I walked round for a good twenty minutes until one particularly persistent street person wearing a thick jacket with a large hood over his head started following me and shouting. This caused me to quicken my pace and dive down a narrow street in an attempt at losing my pursuer. It was getting very dark by now, and the clouds suddenly let rip. The streets were very dimly lit, and so all this combined with the unquestionably alluring sight of the glamorous zips on the pockets of my jacket attracting the attention of the local undesirables I dived into the next neon-lit entrance way I found.

It was a small, grubby little empty restaurant, but hey, I had made a decision - albeit a slightly forced one. I took a seat at a small wooden table by window, where a rather decrepit looking flower hung wearily in a small cracked vase in the centre. It was an artificial flower, which made the fact it looked dead all the more remarkable. A menu was quickly thrust into my hands by a small lady. She then stood next to me, pressurising me into making a choice. It was tricky. I had one eye on the lady and her unnecessary continued presence, and one nervous eye peering out of the window in case the street people had tracked me down. As you can probably work out this left me with very few remaining eyes with which I could use to look at the menu, but somehow under the circumstances I managed it, and I quickly ordered a meatball, noodle and vegetable dish.

It was eerily quiet in China Town, with only the sound of the distant fuzz of a television with poor reception in a neighbouring room and the occasional car splashing through the puddles outside interrupting the silence. It therefore made me jump slightly when the little lady suddenly appeared again in silence beside me, delivering a bowl and then leaving again without saying a word. Maybe speaking was bad etiquette, I still muttered a 'thank you' though, and I hoped I wouldn't be punished for it. Despite ordering what sounded like an appetising array of Chinese cuisine, what I now had in front of me was a bowl of grey water with a couple of uncooked-looking balls (that were equally as grey) floating in the middle. I jabbed at one of the balls with my fork and this seemed to disturb the sediment at the bottom of the bowl, and a few straggly, blackened leaves and wormy noodles surfaced. I tentatively slurped at the grey water and chewed on the solid bits that arose from beneath. I was almost starting to sense that I wasn't in the most gentrified neighbourhood of the city. Soon two very large and shifty looking men came bustling through the door and took a seat on the other side of the room. They leaned across the small table and began muttering quickly in hushed undertones. I averted my eyes, and focused instead on my map of Seattle that I had just taken out of my pocket. From trying to have eyes everywhere, and I was now doing my best to avoid looking *anywhere*. This included my food, as I found it easier to digest it without inspecting each mouthful too closely.

Suddenly one of the shifty men got up, pulled his jacket collar tightly around his face then pushed his way out of the door and with his hands in his pockets, set off hurriedly down the street, while the other man packed a bowlful of beige dripping noodles into his mouth. I'd had enough. I quickly pulled the last few dollars and cents out from my wallet, scattered them on the table and headed out the door. My hostel was only just down the street, and so thankfully I was soon back in the relative safety of my dorm room.

In was ten o'clock, and I was lying on my bunk reading my book and considering going to bed, as the idea of being unconscious for a good eight hours was a very appealing idea. I had recently returned from the washrooms where I'd had a bit of a struggle with the paper towel dispenser, and so I was feeling pretty drained.

I had been washing my hands in the washroom opposite my dorm room when I noticed the hand-drying machine that had a label on it saying 'NO TOUCH SENSOR'. I thought that this was a rather peculiar warning, as I'd never come across a hand towel dispenser that *did* have a touch sensor, so the label seemed a little unnecessary. However, when I reached over to pull down a paper towel, the machine made a sudden loud whirring noise, that caused me to step back in alarm and knock the bottom of the machine in the process, which dislodged some of the plastic casing. A few sheets of paper towels then came grinding out of the slot. Right. So what the sign should have actually read was 'NO-TOUCH SENSOR', or even better, '"NO TOUCH" SENSOR'. Or *even* 'AUTOMATIC TOWEL DISPENSOR'. I mean for god's sake there were loads of ways this could have been labelled more effectively and thus preventing me damaging the machine! What was worse was that now whenever I reached over to try and fix it, it just dispensed *more* paper towels! I stepped away from the front of the machine and then made darting hand movements to the side of it to try and repair the unit, but this didn't work. It just whirred and spat more paper towels out at me. Stop it! I couldn't win – there was no way of getting close enough to it without getting towelled. Soon I had become highly agitated and extensively covered in paper towels. *And* my hands were still wet. Eventually I threw my hands in the air (which actually helped dry them a bit) and gave up in a fit of despair, slipping out of the washroom before anyone could spot me and discover the paper towel atrocity that had occurred within it. I got back to my room and dried my hands on my trusty travel towel.

It was soon after I had settled down with my book that two girls burst into the room. Anna and Parisa were from Montreal but had just arrived in Seattle in the early stages of a cycle ride down the west coast of the U.S. Soon after an Irishman by the name of Hugh arrived, and after chatting for a while I was informed we would now be going out for a drink. I was in no position to argue, although I did a bit, but failed miserably, so we all hit the streets if China Town. I'm not sure if any of us had completely thought it through as there was nothing open at half eleven, and as I'd recently experienced - China Town wasn't exactly the type of place where you'd want to be wandering aimlessly. After twenty minutes we gave up, and returned to the hostel and played cards and drank tea instead, accompanied by a couple of other people who had appeared in our dorm, but whose names unfortunately exceeded my daily quota for learning, and therefore I regret to say I cannot remember them. They were all very nice though, and we all had a fun time up until a completely hammered English girl who was all wired up and blabbering incomprehensibly about conspiracies rudely interrupted us. Why do conspiracy theorists have to ruin it for everyone else? It was by then some ridiculous hour in the morning though, and so we headed to bed. Another opportunity for some sleep-recovery missed, but it had been worth it just to bare witness to the frantic card-based game of spoons that had united our group of international backpackers in the kitchen.

* * *

I had to be up early the following morning to catch the bus back to Vancouver. It was six in the morning, but I had one last visit to pay while in the city that sometimes sleeps. Last night the Canadian girls had mentioned a market that they had visited, and this had instantly triggered a memory in my sleep-deprived brain.

When I was about thirteen years old I had been in a geography lesson at school where we had watched a video about a market where they threw fish about. I have absolutely no idea how this bore any relation to the geographical topics that we were studying, but the image of the fish-throwing had stuck in my head. I had completely forgotten up until the girls had mentioned it that this world-famous attraction had been in Seattle. I was initially

241

disappointed having thought that I'd missed the opportunity to go and see it, but then thinking it through I guessed that fish-markets were probably morning-based affairs anyway, and so I might be lucky enough to catch it on my way to the bus station. So having packed up my stuff I set off on the underground bus towards the city centre, where I emerged into the morning drizzle and jogged down a couple of blocks to the waterside.

Pike Place Market was in the early stages of being set up when I arrived. A collection of makeshift looking buildings lined with counters span along a steep hill beside Pike Street near the docks, and here the early preparations for the fish were being made. Unfortunately there weren't many people *or* fish about, and no matter how long I stood there expectantly, I didn't see this changing in the small amount of time I had.

I willed them on in my head – go on! Just throw *one little fish*! But they didn't, and I didn't want to be the person who asked them to throw a fish in case they made me buy one, as I think it would have been a struggle to get it through customs. I *did* see a man throw a cardboard box, but in all honesty it wasn't quite the same. My dreams had been crushed. Okay, so I'd almost missed out on coming here at all, but having been reminded of the name of the market I had instantly recalled that distinctive fish-throwing video from all those years before, and so I had got quite excited at being in the actual place where it happened years later, with the thought of fish flying over my head in all directions sending me into a weird nostalgic daze. Perhaps this reckless disregard for hygiene and bizarre fish-preparation etiquette didn't really work in the real world of fish sales anymore. Anyway, it was time to stop hanging around staring at fishmongers – I had to get back to Canada, for tomorrow was sandwich judgement day!

On the bus journey home a nosey woman started grilling me. Well, she asked me a lot of questions at any rate.

'So what were you doing in Seattle?' she asked, poking her head through the gap in the row of seats in front of me for another bout of distracting enquiries.

'I was having a sandwich,' I replied bluntly, whilst removing my earphones as she clearly hadn't taken the hint that I was done talking to her.

'Oh, then what did you do?'

'...I got on the bus back to Canada.'

'Oh, is that where you're from?'

I glanced down at my United Kingdom of Great Britain and Northern Ireland passport that was on my lap.

'Erm *No.* I'm from *England.*'

Why couldn't she just leave me alone?

'Oh, so what are you doing in Canada?'

'Having a sandwich.'

'Oh...okay.'

Chapter 32

And so it was Judgement Day ...but also it was Thursday

Tsawwassen to Swartz Bay, British Columbia

*"Time spent wishing is time...*that could have been spent carrying out a little more internet research."

The bus pulled up in Vancouver early afternoon, and after ditching my bag at the hostel I set off for the large green expanse that forms Stanley Park on the north-west peninsula of downtown Vancouver. I had a mini-mission to wrap up while I was in town. A couple of people I met on the bus from Seattle wanted to come along too, and so did Kailey from the train, so the four of us set off in the rain, looping around the perimeter of the park on the waterside pathways. When we reached the far end of the peninsula, I stepped down over a concrete wall and touched the Pacific Ocean. That was the east-west link up done!

We continued on around the park until we were back in the city, where we walked along a street that had bright pink bus stops and lampposts. You'll never guess what part of town it was...

That evening I set aside some time to plan the important events of tomorrow, but after a few seconds of careful deliberation I realised that other than getting a bus to the ferry, then a ferry to the ferry terminal, there was very little else I needed to plan, so instead I went out for a drink with someone from my dorm. It was only after I'd left the next morning that I realised I never found out what his name was, which is a shame because he had lots of interesting travel stories.

* * *

I got a good night's sleep, and better still I got up at a reasonable hour so that I could finally have the inclusive breakfast that I had missed for the past three mornings. This had been a good start to the day, and I was therefore in the perfect mental state to head for the bus station once again. Not that I'm suggesting that without breakfast I would have been a little deranged and lacking in all concept of direction, but a well-sourced freebie gets me in the right frame of mind for important missions, and lets face it – there weren't many bigger ones on this trip than today's one.

I trod the route that had become so familiar over recent days; along Granville Street, turning right down Smithe Street, then round the perimeter of the large concrete structure of BC Place Stadium, along the water front, under the Skytrain track, and then over the road to Vancouver Pacific Central Station. I stepped through the doors and into the large hall of the station, and made my way over to the bus ticket desk, with a slight feeling of apprehension building inside me. What if there were no buses today? This was my last day in Vancouver – it *had* to be now or never. What if the sandwich kiosk was *closed,* or had *run out* of the sandwich? What if they didn't even *sell* the sandwich anymore?! I wasn't sure what I could do in the event of any of these issues, so instead of getting all worked up about it I just went for it.

'Hi,' I began calmly, 'I'd like a return ticket to Victoria on Vancouver Island please.'

'No problem, we have a bus leaving in about half an hour,' the lady behind the window replied cheerfully.

'Great!' I sighed a big sigh of relief.

Hurdle one overcome.

She started tapping things into her computer.

'Is the return trip for the next day?' she then asked.

'No, same day – today, please.'

'Oh,' she suddenly looked a bit concerned. Please don't tell me I wasn't allowed to only go for the day... 'That's a bit tight for time. You won't get much time in Victoria if you come back today.'

'That's fine.'

I knew this wouldn't leave me much time to explore what was by all accounts supposed to be one of the nicest cities in Canada, but I didn't have a choice – I only *had* one day.

And then a worrying thought suddenly occurred to me. Initially, when I had first found the website back in England I had presumed that the ferry went from Vancouver itself and docked *in* Victoria, but I had since learned that both ferry terminals were about an hour from each of the respective cities. What if it was the same coach that took us to the ferry and then took us off to Victoria on the other side? That could mean I miss the terminal building and can't get the sandwich! I *had* to make sure that I would have time to stop off in the ferry terminal on Vancouver Island so I could buy it!

'Erm...will the bus be stopping at the terminal building when we get to Vancouver Island?' I nervously asked.

She looked at me puzzled, 'Well...not *really*, only if it needs to pick up any passengers, and even then it would only be a few seconds.'

'Right...but if I need to get off and quickly do something at the terminal...would that be possible?'

'Errr...no, probably not.'

She was *very* confused by now, but there was no way around it. I needed to make sure I'd have a window of opportunity to get to the sandwich shop.

'Okay then. Can I just have a ticket to the ferry terminal then, please? ...It's because I need to...meet someone...and exchange something...'

Brilliant. Here I was confusing a bus ticket sales woman, who by now *already* thought I was being slightly odd and mysterious, but now must have thought I was outright creepy and probably trying to arrange a drug deal. Well played, Chris. Why didn't you just shut up and settle for being slightly odd and mysterious?

'...Yes, I *can* do that for you, although you probably won't have time to visit Victoria and get back to Vancouver in the same day.'

'No, that's fine,' I quickly retorted. I'd already realised and accepted that I wouldn't get to see Victoria – but sometimes sandwich quests force these big decisions on you.

'Okay,' she said, finally agreeing to my request, although she was still eyeing me like I was a grade A nutter. But then that was fine too; because explaining my situation and the real reason for my unusual demands would do little to detract from that image anyway.

The clouds were beginning to break apart as the coach bounded along the road heading south towards the ferry terminal at Tsawwassen, close to the U.S. border. The coach was about half-full (as I was feeling positive, otherwise I may have described it as half empty) and around an hour after leaving the bus station we were pulling up on the vehicle deck of the large white ferry.

The BC Ferries service from Tsawwassen to Swartz Bay takes around an hour and a half to cover the twenty-four nautical miles. Most of this is spent weaving through lush green-covered islands with smart housing and private boat ramps dotted along the shorelines that rise out of the deep, greeny-blue waters of the Georgia Strait. According to the maps on the passenger decks of the

247

ferry, the voyage crosses through US waters, such is the arrangement of the border, but thankfully we didn't have to stand outside and wave our passports about. It got quite blowy out on deck, so this would have been risky.

I passed the time at sea stumbling around the outer decks as the vessel negotiated the sometimes choppy Pacific waters, before retreating to one of the large indoor seating lounges, where I sat thinking about the impending sandwich, and where it had led me.

It had been exactly a month since I set off on this mission across Canada, and I'd had an eventful time. I thought back to my early visit to Niagara Falls and my mixed feelings towards its setting. It seemed so long ago now. I thought back to my problems in London, Ontario, and my resulting homelessness in Toronto, and then onto the hot evenings in Ottawa spent having barbeques and drinking beers. From there I had moved further east to Montreal, where I had encountered the obsession this country had with ice hockey, and where I'd discovered that internationally renowned sandwich. After that I'd been to Québec City, where I'd first met my travel nemesis, and where I had been charmed by the old town, with it's dramatic setting on the hill and its elegant winding streets and architecture. I had then gambled on travelling to the far east of Canada, where I had yet more sandwich success, and had completely screwed up my laundry. It had then been the epic seven day train journey across the country, meeting interesting characters and seeing the dramatic changes in landscape and scenery that Canada has to offer. I'd had ice invade every part of my clothing whilst snowboarding in Whistler, and I'd visited the United States and been outwitted by a hand-towel dispenser. And now I was here – somewhere in the Pacific off the coast of Vancouver, and just minutes away from the thing that had led me on this adventure – *the sandwich* that had enabled me to experience all this...

Of course you would have been spared this piece of nostalgic reflection had I remembered to bring my mp3 player.

248

At around half two everyone began collecting up their belongings and making their way down to their vehicles or towards the foot-passenger exit as our arrival in Swartz Bay was imminent. I hung back, as I didn't feel the need to stand in line stuffed into a tight metallic corridor. Besides, I wasn't planning on going that far once we were released onto dry land anyway.

Soon the gates had been opened, and everyone started to make their way along the gangway to the ferry terminal. Swartz Bay ferry terminal – this really was *it*! I walked slowly, yet purposefully down the ramp, with my head held high as I tried to give the occasion the symbolic gravitas that I felt it warranted. The Canadian train company would have been proud.

As the other passengers dispersed out into the forecourt I wound back around the network of footbridges and into the terminal building, where I walked above the large rabble of pre-ferry passengers waiting to board the ferry for the return trip in the concourse below. Not like an air-walking Jesus impersonator – but on the upper mezzanine level. I glanced around this waiting area to make sure the café wasn't in this section. It wasn't. I then continued along the sloping walkway of the ferry terminal until I reached a set of glass doors, and then…

Hang on. I was *outside*. This wasn't right.

Where were all the shops?

Chapter 33

I ferry nearly missed it…

Swartz Bay to Tsawwassen, British Columbia

*"It's not over until…*you've gone past it, realised you've messed up, then gone back and found it."

I stopped on the edge of the kerb for a few moments looking out at my surroundings. I felt like Macaulay Culkin in *Home Alone* when he steps out into New York City in a bewildered state with so many possibilities at his fingertips. Except in this slightly less glamorous real world situation I just had the dull, grey tarmac parking area of the terminal building ahead of me. And *very few* possibilities. There certainly wasn't any smartly turned out chauffeurs here to take me to Canada's finest sandwich shop. There wasn't even a triumphant orchestra to shroud the miserable silence. This was all very disappointing.

As I stood forlornly outside the ferry terminal I tried to work out why I wasn't currently stuffing a reasonably priced sandwich into my mouth. There were clearly no food outlets or facilities of any kind in the terminal building, but maybe there used to be? Had they closed them? No, that was stupid – they sold *reasonably priced food!* It would have gone down a storm! There's *no way* they would have closed it! Perhaps I'd got the location wrong? But no, *Swartz Bay* terminal – *that's* what the website had said! I had read it myself several times. It was written just below that alluring photo; that seductive image of a seating area overlooking water with a hilly landscape on the horizon. I looked behind me at the view from the terminal building. There were no outdoor seating areas or alluring views from here – we were in an inlet.

And then it hit me. I suddenly remembered watching passengers queuing up at a food counter on the ferry. I thought about the open deck area – the one with the seat benches – where I had tried to look casual while taking a photo looking into the mirrored glass windows so it looked like someone else was taking a photo of me because I'm super-cool and a photographic master. It couldn't be…could it? Had I made a fantastic mess up? It slowly all started to make sense. That photo on the website must have been taken from the ferry looking out over the islands. The man who had eaten the sandwich had travelled *from* the Swartz Bay terminal! Shit! The sandwich must be *on* the ferry! My whole trip had been based around this sandwich and it now appeared I'd screwed up the basic requirement of knowing where I could get it! This was not smart, but there was nothing else for it. I turned around and went back into the terminal, and I walked up to the ticket counter.

'Hi, can I have a ferry ticket please.' I asked, slightly embarrassed.

'Sure. Are you okay to leave right now?'

I looked around me and sighed, before replying, 'Yup.'

'Great! Because actually you're in luck – there's one leaving in a just a few minutes!' he replied excitedly.

Wow, what were the chances! I chose not to tell him I knew this as I'd just got off it.

'That *is* convenient!' I said, mimicking his enthusiasm.

And so I bought a ticket, joined the crowd in the departure area, and then re-boarded the ferry. I had been on Vancouver Island for six minutes.

Back onboard I headed straight out on deck to confirm my suspicions. Yes! Suddenly those benches looked familiar! They were just short of a few parasols but then it wasn't the summer season yet so that was understandable. And then I remembered how quickly the queues had built up at the food counter on my outward journey, and with the fear that the sandwich would sell out I rushed inside and joined the extensive queue that I found trailing out from the lower passenger deck eating area. I kept twiddling my fingers and rocking sideways as I stood in the queue in an impatient fashion. I could see a food cabinet that had a sign with 'Bread Garden' written above it. Yes! That name was familiar! This *must* be it! As the queue crept forward at a painfully slow rate I began to see the different packages that were housed on its metal shelves. There it was! I could now see two sandwiches on the second shelf! C'mon, c'mon! Hurry up people! Then I realised that all these people were queuing for hot food. Hot food! *I* didn't want hot food! I wanted a sandwich! A *reasonably priced* sandwich! Get out the way! I broke from the line of hot food appreciators and shot over to the cabinet. And there it was. The Ham and Swiss Sandwich. I was literally shaking as I reached out to pick up the sandwich. It looked *just like* the one in the photo. I know it *should* have looked the same, based on the fact that it was intrinsically the same thing, but it nevertheless seemed strange.

Three months ago I had stumbled upon a website that had a photo on it of an unassuming sandwich. This image had single-handedly caused me to drop everything and come on this quest. A quest that had broken the monotony and aimlessness of my recent existence. A quest that provided me with many eventful moments and adventures, and that had shown me some brilliant places and people. And now, three months on from that moment of enlightenment at a boring desk in an office in Hemel Hempstead, here I was, standing in the self-service section of the food court on board a ferry off the west coast of Canada, holding that very same

252

sandwich. I was very grateful for this sandwich. Because lets face it - if this sandwich had been sold at the snack kiosk on Platform 2 of Harrow-on-the-Hill train station then I fear this story would have been a little shorter and less eventful.

I took the sandwich (which was actually a roll, but that's still legitimate) up to the till.

'Seven thirty-four, please,' the lady said.

I stood there for a moment.

Five dollars. *That's* what it had said on the website. The *reasonably priced* sandwich was supposed to be *five* dollars. This could be problematic. The price was kind of a key issue, and at *over seven dollars* this was a pretty high price for a sandwich...

I paid anyway, although I handed over those final two dollars pretty grudgingly. I took the sandwich over to a table on the other side of the lounge, sat down and looked at it. The label said it was served in a Portuguese bun. It hadn't said *that* on the website! I looked around me, hoping that maybe there would be someone to share this symbolic moment with. But no, everyone else was stuffing their faces with chips and lasagne. They didn't appreciate the wonders of chilled, breaded snacks. Philistines!

So there was nothing more left to do. I carefully undid the plastic wrapping and took a bite.

It was mission complete.

* * *

The ham, cheese and lettuce were fine. Nothing outstanding, but then that wasn't really the point. It was about being *reasonably priced.* The bread was surprisingly nice; a good quality roll that was soft and floury, but at $7.34 it was pretty expensive. This was less of a surprise having found out that it was sold *on* the ferry though, as this was a monopolistic food sales environment, so it *would* be priced higher. I therefore felt slightly frustrated, as despite it being predictably priced for its sales location, I couldn't claim it was a *reasonably priced sandwich* based on everyday lunchtime consumption needs. As it was sold on the ferry it also wasn't going to be a sandwich that a regular lunchtime diner could access, as lunchtime trips across the water were unlikely to be a regular commute for anyone.

So in many ways I had failed in my mission. I had come all this way for a sandwich that hadn't fitted the basic criteria that had caused me to come all this way. I'd also callously turned up a week late after my mix up with the *British Sandwich Week* dates.

But to be honest it wasn't any of this that was bothering me. The truth was that I was sad. As I sat there, picking up the last few crumbs of bread from the plastic packaging with the tip of my index finger I couldn't help thinking once again about everything that had happened since I'd conducted that *Google* search back at the beginning of March. Yes I'd had a fantastic time in Canada, but even the time before I had flown out here I had felt lifted by the impending journey. I suddenly had a purpose – whether considered trivial or not – that had distracted me from the dullness of temporary employment, and that had inspired me to plan a spontaneous adventure that had objectives and a sense of direction. Even those I'd met along the way had embraced my quest and had been keen to have their input, offering advice and sharing information, or they'd simply wanted to come along for the ride and be a part of it. I knew I loved travelling, but now I realised how much better it is when you have a goal, as this pushes you to discover things and have experiences you wouldn't otherwise of had. And *that's* what this sandwich that I had just eaten and been about. It was a perfectly ordinary and everyday item, but its mere existence had been a finishing post of a journey that had been of far more significance.

And that was what was making me feel deflated now - it was the *finishing post.* I'd *completed* it. I would now have to return to

England and drift back into a world of purely functional sandwiches that were priced in whatever fashion the vendor felt was appropriate, while I attempted once again to slip into the harsh, bleak reality of the real world.

It was *over*.

Chapter 34

I heard it has two golf courses!

Edmonton, Alberta

*"Treat others…*only if you are a medic."

My phone beeped in my pocket. It was a text from Jess who I'd met on the train. She was asking if I'd found the sandwich. In the coming days I would get countless messages and emails from friends back home and those that I had met on this trip asking if I'd found it and what it had been like. I guess this all just reaffirmed the positive response and overall nature of the mission I'd been on.

I tapped out a reply to Jess, and then a voice came over the ferry tannoy system.

'Would the owner of the grey Mitsubishi please return to your vehicle, your car alarm is…alarming.'

A murmur of appreciation rippled through the seating lounge in response to this light-hearted message.

That's what I really like about Canadians; despite formal procedure, there's always a personable character behind it with a cheerful, good-natured spirit that could lift your mood. Although granted by the eighth repetition of the announcement it began to wear a little thin.

* * *

It was the following morning, and having checked out of the hostel I was now making my way down Granville Street to the Skytrain station. I was heading to the airport...but I wasn't flying home. I had come to the end of my sandwich mission, but I hadn't reached the end of the adventure.

When I had arrived in Canada I'd got in contact with a couple of people I'd met in South America last summer. They lived in Edmonton and had said that we should meet up, which I was certainly keen to do. At the time I had planned on stopping by on my journey across the country, but upon hearing that they had important exams for their medicine course up until the 28th May this seemed like it would be difficult as I didn't want to disrupt their studying. I then worked out that I could probably just about fit in everything I wanted to do before the 28th, (and this would also have fitted in well as I'd originally thought that I'd need to be in Vancouver for the 24th for the culmination of *British Sandwich Week* before I'd realised I'd messed up the dates) and so I should have a few days left to come and visit before my fight home on the 6th June if that suited them. They said it did. This also worked out nicely as it meant I would still had some Canadian adventures to look forward to beyond the completion of my sandwich quest.

Well, today was the 28th May, and so I was on my way to the airport to fly over to Edmonton, Alberta, to meet up with Paula and Alex in their post-exam celebrations. You may remember that I wrote about booking a flight on the train journey between Montreal and Toronto from the comfort of my seat. Well, this was it.

I arrived at the airport and went to check-in. It seemed that personal contact was something that this airport wanted to avoid, having positioned a long line of electronic check in machines in front of the baggage desks. It had taken me three months to build up the courage to use the self-service checkouts at the local *Asda* supermarket when I was at university, but now I was a little older and wiser, and in the spirit of adventure I strode confidently up to

257

one of the machines. A few seconds later and I had incorrectly told it how many bags I had with me, and so it had in turn spat out a copious number of baggage tags that I proceeded to attach to every conceivable handle and strap that my backpack had. I then took it proudly over to the baggage drop counter, where the lady frowned at me, removed all but one of the labels, and then sent me and it off in our separate directions.

Well, at least I'd given it a go.

It was then on through security, where once again I was subjected to a frisking based upon my irresistible figure…or my shifty face - it's hard to tell which. Whatever their reasons, this process involved me removing my belt. A tricky task, seeing as my belt is lined with countless pairs of metal rings so that the wearer can adjust the size of the belt depending on whether they have just been compressed between lift (elevator) doors, or if they have just eaten their bodyweight in high quality puddings. It's a level of adjustability I have found very useful in recent weeks. Having said this, manoeuvring the strap through the numerous belt loops of my jeans is an arduous and not remotely dignity-maintaining activity, and one that left me having to waddle wide-legged through the metal detection arch to prevent an untimely jean-descent, and a possible resulting incidence of indecent exposure.

Soon enough I was re-belted and crunching on the heavily-salted courtesy snack provided by *Air Canada* as we flew across the sky on the our way to Calgary. Oh yes, that's right – I was supposed to be going to *Edmonton.*

Well, when I was booking the flight on that train journey I had found that it was £1 cheaper to fly via Calgary! This may involve dragging out the journey by an extra two and a half hours, but this also meant I could visit Calgary (which I hadn't been able to so far) even if it was only going to be for forty minutes. I felt it was important anyway. Also the overall trip was only going to be around four hours, which is still *twenty-three* hours less than it would take on the train.

I got chatting to the man who was sitting next to me on the flight. He had just been on a business trip to Vancouver and was now heading back home to Calgary with his suit and his business accessories. When I told him I was going to Edmonton he laughed.

'Ha, what happened? Did you lose a bet?' he said. Which was rude.

No, I *hadn't* lost a bet. Strangely he also found *everything I said* absolutely hilarious, and no, before you ask, I hadn't mentioned the whole sandwich thing. In fact all I'd told him was that I'd been on the train and visiting places. I didn't get what was funny. Maybe I just lack a sense of humour. He did however offer to buy me a beer, which was very nice of him, but seeing as it had only just stopped being morning I politely declined.

We landed in Calgary amongst the clouds. This somewhat inhibited my view of the city as we flew in, and therefore pretty much ruined my reasons for flying this elongated route. Well, I suppose I still had that extra £1 coin in my bank account – so the last laugh would be mine when I got back to England and bought a discounted loaf of bread…or a first class stamp.

After all the antics of the previous week I was feeling a little lazy, and so I asked at a nearby airport information helpdesk for the whereabouts of the gate I needed for my imminent connecting fight. The gate number was strangely coded and there appeared to be no signs for it. The man immediately gave me some hand signals (no, not like that) and in a very pleasant manner directed me to where I needed to go. I wasn't convinced, but I cautiously followed his pointing anyway. Within a few seconds I was back at the gate where I had just arrived from. This kind airport information man had successfully navigated me back to the flight I'd just got off. I still liked Canadians – but sometimes I just wish that they would back up their friendly enthusiasm with accurate knowledge. Never mind though, I soon found the correct gate on my own, and it wasn't long before I was bouncing around inside the tiny propeller driven plane to Edmonton. Judging by my wayward time awareness thanks to the various time zones I kept crossing through, I incorrectly worked out that the flight was eight minutes long. It didn't matter though, because just as I was picking up my bag from the carousel in Edmonton's airport terminal, I turned around to see Paula and Alex.

We happily chatted about what we'd all been up to since the last time we had seen each other in Buenos Aires, and then in the evening we went round to one of their friends houses, where a large group of post-exam medics had collected for a barbeque and drinking games. Understandably the conversations revolved heavily around medical things, and so to demonstrate I wasn't completely out of my depth I threw in a highly out-of-context and unconnected comment about the bicuspid value. This seemed to earn me a point. I could then return to my state of blissful ignorance. Oh, and my beer. Shortly after we headed out to a bar in the city, which was rammed. Rammed full of medics in full celebration mode. If I ever I was going to have a drinking related accident – *this* was certainly the time and place to have it. There were medics *everywhere*. Actually judging by the way some of them were knocking back shots it may not have been so wise to rely on them for precise medical assistance, so it was just as well I didn't require any help, and it turned out to be a very enjoyable evening.

* * *

I had the next day to entertain myself. The others had things they had to do, and so Paula suggested I visited *West Edmonton Mall*. *The West Edmonton Mall*. This was a big moment. Whenever Edmonton had cropped up in conversation since I'd been in Canada, it almost always triggered the mentioning of *West Edmonton Mall*. This was party due to its location – *in Edmonton*, but also because

260

(as the legend goes) it is very big. It is in fact the largest shopping mall in North America, and the fifth largest in the world (and it was the largest up until 2004) with the complex being home to *over eight hundred* shops, *two* golf courses, and apparently quite a lot of other things...

As I'd gone along on this trip I'd kept a list of everything people had said was in the *West Edmonton Mall*. I'd brilliantly called it the *Things What People Say Are In The West Edmonton Mall* list. And here it is!

Things What People Say Are In The West Edmonton Mall

- An ice rink
- A cinema
- A swimming pool
- A ship
- A water park
- A bungee jump
- A theme park
- A Lebanese shoe shop
- *Two* golf courses
- Sea lions

So I set off into the Edmonton rain, quickly finding a bus stop and catching the number 4 bus to the mall. It was exciting, which is strange really, because a day out at a shopping centre isn't something that would usually appeal to me.

The bus ride was about twenty-five minutes, and as we pulled into a large passenger drop off area I could just about make out a very large grey and white building through the drops of water that were slipping down the window of the bus. I jumped enthusiastically off the bus (after it had stopped and the driver had opened the doors of course) and made my way through the sheltered car park to the entrance. But it wasn't just *any* entrance. It was *Entrance 48!* If this wasn't an early indication of how big this place was, then...well, perhaps the massive indoor swimming pool that suddenly appeared on my left having stepped through the entrance

261

door was. It was big, as the scriptures had said it would be. Shops lined the edges of the two levels, but it was in the middle where the unusual features were. I could see the distinctive shape of a ship's mast on the retail-horizon. I headed closer, passing a large viewing window that overlooked the indoor water park, with its large wave pool, collection of colourful slides and a bungee platform. That was four things ticked off already! When I reached the area where the ship was I noticed there was also some mini boats that could fit two people on, and you could motor around the small pool shooting other boaters with the onboard water gun. Another part of this pirate-themed area had radio-controlled boats that could be operated from the upper walkway. Beside this was a tiered seating area in front of another pool of water, where a crowd was gathering. I took up a place on the bridge that overlooked the arena, and before long a lady appeared with a headset microphone and a ball and frisbee. I sensed some kind of a show. My powerful detective intuition had served me well, as within a few seconds a dark, slimy creature slid out from behind a gate, dragged itself up to a platform, and then promptly flopped off into the pool below. I concluded that his was the sea lion show, so I stuck around and was surprisingly entertained by this impressive free display of…sea…lioning.

After the sea lions had finished splashing everyone I moved on to other parts of the mall, where I found the theme park, the ice rink/hockey arena, a mini golf course and an *apple* shop, where I wasted half an hour playing about on the new *iPad* that had been launched the previous week. All this going around seeing things in between fighting my way through all the hoards of shoppers turned out to be pretty exhausting, and so when I found myself in the shopping mall's own China Town I decided to get something to eat to re-energise. Yes, I had Chinese food – not a sandwich! I *know*, it was a scary moment for me too!

I spent the afternoon exploring the remaining wings of the complex, passing a section that was home to three radio stations and another part that housed a multiplex cinema. However, no matter how much wandering around I did I still couldn't track down the second golf course. Maybe I'd been misinformed? It was hugely disappointing though, as it meant I couldn't tick it off my list. Oh, and I didn't find the Lebanese shoe shop either, but then to be honest I didn't look very hard as shoe shops aren't really my thing. Strangely I also couldn't see any sign of a cathedral, a blimp flight centre, or a mountain ski resort. I decided that it was probably time to leave the shopping mall as I was starting to find it a bit limiting with this apparent lack of facilities. Well I suppose there's always going to be areas where they can expand...

Chapter 35

Hot rock socks

National Parks, Alberta

*"Sticks and stones…*make for a warmer night's sleep."

The rain and snow that had been spitting from the skies above Edmonton over the past couple of days was beginning to subside as we set off on our road trip. Having finished her exams Paula had a few days free, and said she'd be happy to show me the National Parks of Alberta, something that I had jumped at being as I am a massive fan of lakes and mountains. When *Google* had first instructed me to go to Canada I had carried out a bit of research, and this had consistently drawn out stunning pictures of the Rocky Mountains, glaciers and expansive blue lakes. I couldn't wait to visit these areas, and I felt it would be the perfect high point (literally!) on which to complete my visit to Canada.

The first day was spent driving south to the town of Lethbridge. From here we visited Writing-on-Stone Provincial Park – a fantastically isolated expanse of land (thanks to it not being on the way to anywhere) that is home to a collection of ancient markings that have been etched onto the sandstone river cliffs. Unfortunately the name of this park has been taken by some lesser people as an invitation, and inspired them to leave their own writing-on-stone. There is little remaining of the original historic battle inscriptions and drawings, and sadly the dominant carvings are that of people called 'Dave', who apparently "woz ere" at some point during last year. Thankfully the large amounts of graffiti don't excessively detract from the interesting rock formations that the river has left through its own carving nature, and you can hike amongst these thanks to a series of walking trails that guide you through the more interesting areas and viewpoints. The park also has a smart, new visitor centre, with interactive displays, videos and a discussion area to help inject some life and understanding into the park and the people that used to occupy it. The landscape surrounding the area also impressed me, with the flat land stretching out for miles until it hits the hills of northern Montana, as the U.S. state border lies just to the south of the Provincial Park.

After this visit we drove west, and on to Waterton Lakes National Park at the southern end of the Canadian Rockies. As we neared the park entrance the flat rural land suddenly broke apart, with mountains springing up around us from behind the low-lying clouds. This National Park is set apart from its two northerly neighbours by virtue of the fact that it does not have the immense tourist influx that Banff and Jasper have to endure. As a result (and aided further by it being between seasons) it was largely deserted, and the twisting roads and calm lakes make this a very special location for a foreign visitor like myself to see. We drove out to Cameron Lake, a large expanse of blue and white as at this time the water was completely iced over, and is surrounded on all sides by steep snow-covered mountains. Here we each ate a sandwich that had been prepared by Paula's mum. It was a really good sandwich too, and eaten in a fantastic location, added to further by the discovery that the far end of the lake – only a few hundred metres away - was actually over the border in the U.S. The isolation of this lake gave the surroundings a hugely dramatic and almost eerie feel to it. We sat on the rocks by the shoreline gazing out over ice, with only the occasional crunch of crisp lettuce from the expertly crafted sandwiches breaking the silence that engulfed this vast, mountainous cauldron.

Sandwiches eaten, we headed back towards the town of Waterton, stopping on route as we spotted black and brown bears lumbering through the woodland. Once back in the vicinity of the town we visited a small waterfall, before taking a short hike up to the stunning viewpoint of Bears Hump. This bare rock platform juts out from the mountain side, and while balanced precariously on the edge of the rocks you can see down to the town below, with the lake beyond it that leads down a valley. What made this point even more serene was the complete lack of a breeze that you would expect from such a high up and exposed location. It was a brilliant introduction to The Rockies, and having returned to Lethbridge for some more fantastic hospitality courtesy of Paula's parents, I was even more excited about our impending trip up through the heart of the mountains that would begin the next day.

* * *

We set off in a north-westerly direction early the next morning, passing through Calgary on our way towards The Rocky Mountains. Having missed out on the aerial views of this former wild-west town, I could now see Alberta's most populous city from ground level, although now it appears to be a classic tower bock filled modern city, and is home to many large firms – especially those related to oil thanks to the rich reserves that Alberta has provided of this much demanded fossil fuel. Industries have broadened out over the past thirty years, and Calgary is now said to be one of Canada's fastest growing cities. I bet you're impressed that I got all that from looking out of the window aren't you? Clever, eh?

Once we had made it through the busy city roads we passed along side the site of the 1986 Winter Olympics, with the distinctive structures of the ski jumps and sled tracks balanced on the hill to the left of the highway. It then wasn't long until the snow-capped peaks of the Rockies began to emerge ahead of us, and soon we were passing the wooden huts and hoardings that signified the beginning of Banff National Park. By now the mountains were towering above us on all sides. Some were lined with alpine trees while others were bare rock. The sun was increasingly finding gaps in the clouds in which to enhance the brilliant white of the snowy peaks.

We stopped off at the small town of Canmore where we stocked up on provisions for our trip, before making our way further along Highway 1 as we wound our way through the mountains to Banff Town – the tourist hub of the Canadian Rockies. Banff is a vibrant town with a picturesque setting between the mountains, and its main street – the imaginatively named Banff Avenue – is lined with expensive cafes, restaurants and hiking and sports gear shops. We stopped off briefly at the tourist information centre before heading over to Sulphur Mountain, where the less adventurous visitors (but the more wealthy) can reach the summit via the (again brilliantly named) Banff Gondola, for a mere $30. Being the adventurous types though (and the slightly impoverished), we chose to hike up the mountain, zigzagging along the gravel pathways through the trees beneath the subtle whirring of the gondola as it delivered tourists up and down the mountain overhead. At first it seemed quite a straight forward hike in the cool afternoon temperatures, and we even stopped off at a semi-frozen waterfall for some real mountain-filtered water, but as we got closer to the summit the path became increasingly icy, and thanks to our relatively inappropriate footwear we began to slide about a bit. We made it up within two hours though, and as a reward we were treated to spectacular views out from this snow-covered peak of Banff Town far down below, and across to the surrounding valleys and the highway that cuts through them. A wooden mountain top promenade also allows you to walk across the ridge of the mountain to gain a few extra metres in altitude and get a little closer to the snow. As we made our way back towards the gondola station (you can ride back down it for free!) I saw that they sold sandwiches. In all that I had learnt about how a sandwich should be judged, it seemed like an opportunity I shouldn't miss. The sandwich looked dull and plain, and at $5 it further resembled the sandwich I'd eaten back at Watford Gap Services six weeks earlier, and in any ordinary situation I would regard this as a completely unreasonable lunchtime indulgence. But here, after a good hike and amongst the snow and Rocky peaks it was worth it. Crap sandwich – stunning location. It's all about balance…

From Banff we travelled further into the National Park until we reached Lake Louise where we camped. The campsite was surrounded by an electric fence, either to prevent bears getting in, or sleepwalkers getting out. The campsites throughout The Rockies are very well laid out and equipped, with each pitch featuring space for tents/RVs, a bench, and a fire pit, with communal wash facilities and firewood piles. A big attraction of camping is making a fire, but after the satisfaction of chopping up some wood with an axe we struggled to get it lit. Thankfully a German man came to the rescue…with a giant pinecone. We had a look around the forest for more of these fire-starting pinecones for future use, but there were none. I know Germans are efficient, but he hadn't honesty brought these with him from Germany had he? Well wherever he sourced then - they did the trick, and soon we were cooking away as dusk fell in the valley.

That night was cold. I had brilliantly chosen to go camping with a zero season sleeping bag. Granted it was nice and small so it slipped tidily into my backpack taking up very little space, but now the time had come for me to use it and it proved about as effective as non-stick glue. So I spent the night shivering away whilst dressed in every available piece of clothing I had with me, including my hat and fleece neck warmer. It was good to be camping again…

When the next morning eventually presented itself, we packed all our gear up and hiked over to Lake Louise. Here the trials of cold-weather camping were forgotten, as we were treated to one of the countries finest lakes. The clear, blue waters of Lake Louise calmly lap against the foot of the surrounding mountains on one side, while a pathway leads the many visitors around the other side to marvel at it's shimmering surface from a variety of perspectives.

Just north of Lake Louise Highway 1 splits off and heads west as part of the Trans-Canada Highway. We continued north on to Route 93 – The Icefields Parkway. This is two hundred kilometres of tarmac that has to be one of the finest roads in the world, cutting through the heart of The Rockies with snow-covered mountains, alpine forests, vast glaciers and clear blue lakes lining either side. There are lookouts and hiking trails scattered all along the route, and it's a case of picking the ones that are open (the snow meaning many trails and campsites were still closed) and that you have time to visit.

We trekked through knee-deep snow to catch a glimpse of the magnificent Peyto Lake – the bluest lake I have ever seen, thanks to the glacial rock flour. 'Rock flour' is the fine rock sediment that forms by the moving glacier grinding down the rock and depositing it into the lake below, with the sediment reflecting the light to create its vivid turquoise colour. Further along the route we stopped at the spectacular Athabasca Glacier that flows down from the Columbia Icefield. This gigantic sheet of slowly creeping ice finishes between the mountains just a couple of hundred metres from the highway, and after scrambling over some gravel and scree slopes we could get right up to the edge of the ice.

The second night we camped in the less facilitated but equally tranquil Jonas Creek campground, two thirds of the way up along The Icefield Parkway and in Jasper National Park. We had stopped off earlier in the day to pick up some additional aids to try and create a warmer night of sleep. I had two small sachets that apparently got hot when the outer layer was broken open, but in actual fact they just made my feet feel fuzzy, and had *absolutely no effect* on the rest of my cold, shivering limbs. I also picked up a foil-type shiny silver sheet (try saying that three times quickly!) but having wrapped myself up in it I quickly decided that it wasn't providing me with much heat, the highly reflective nature of it also meant that I was constantly blinded whenever I switched my torch on, and I also couldn't live with the shame of how noisy it was, as every time I moved an inch it rustled uncontrollably. And I had noticed that when I looked down at myself wrapped in it I looked like a turkey ready for roasting in the oven. If I was to die of hypothermia, this was certainly not the way I wished to be found.

So after another very cold and uncomfortable night under canvas, we pushed on to complete the final stretch of this fantastic highway route. On the way we stopped off along the Athabasca River at Athabasca Falls, a waterfall that has calved a narrow gorge through the rock and caused a series of blowholes and inlets that narrow rocky footpaths guide visitors around. From here we carried on to Jasper, where we set up in large campsite just on the outskirts before heading into town for a wander around.

As we walked along beside the railway track where I had been nearly two weeks ago, we noticed a board outside a shop that offered various activities. One in particular stood out to both Paula and myself, and that was for a zip-line. It sounded fun – flying through the mountains on a twelve hundred foot line, so we went inside and booked it, with the lady mishearing my name and booking it under 'Imbrose'. An hour later and we were on our way out along the highway to an area of deserted scrubland just beside the road. Here we had to wait for the zip-line team to arrive, in which time we had a visit from a lady from a nearby radio station who was passing by, but who pulled over and stopped when she saw us and asked us a few bizarre questions about the zip-line before offering us a newspaper and then leaving again.

Soon after she'd gone, a truck pulled up with two men in it. These were the zip-line operators, and after a quick briefing where we had to sign a disclaimer where my name was once again misheard as 'Imbrose', then we went to the starting point on top of a wooden cabin on the hillside. That's three times in the last week and twice in the last hour I'd been misheard as 'Chris Imbrose' – yet this has *never* happened before anywhere else. I'm thinking of changing my name just to make any further bookings out here more straightforward.

Paula went first, and she stepped up to the launch runway and after being strapped into the harness she confidently ran forward and threw herself off the building. She…zipped along (I guess that's the best way of describing it) until the wind slowed her, and then she was lowered back down to earth. It was then my turn, and the quirky instructor asked me if I'd been zip-lining before. I told him I hadn't but that I'd been hang gliding. He said that this would be a step down from that, which to be honest was a little deflating, but I guess it made sense. Anyway, as he now (wrongly) assumed that I was some kind of horizontal flying pro – he lowered the tension in the zip line above so that I fell more, and he told me to run off at an angle so I could swoop sideways like a predator bird. You'll notice I haven't used quotation marks there, and that's because *I* made up that simile, because that's what I *assumed* I'd look like. What actually happened was I ran enthusiastically off the side of the building then swung about in an uncoordinated fashion just as a strong gust of wind hit me, so I was just flapping about like a sky-dangling idiot. My sidewards departure and the strong headwind meant I didn't go very far, and certainly not the twelve hundred feet that the poster had claimed I would.

As we trudged back up the hill to collect our belongings we both agreed that it had been a pretty expensive activity given how far we hadn't zipped, but when we got to the top the man said he was impressed with my "hang gliding skills and experience" (yes, those

271

are intentional and accurately deployed quotation marks) and so he said that if I wanted some work then I could help out at the zip-line centre. This was amazing; back home I'd spent eight months sending endless emails, covering letters and CVs to companies and yet within a few minutes here I'd air-flapped my way into a job offer! Canada is great.

Back at the campsite that evening I took a shower having not been able to the previous couple of days. As I made my way back from the wash facilities I was stopped in my path by an elk. It didn't actually ask me to stop, but we had been warned when checking into the campsite that it was elk calving season, which sadly didn't mean there was an elf-based buffet being served every evening, but that female elks were being very protective of their newly born elklings (no, I doubt that is what they're called either) and so they can get very angry and attack campers who come near them. So I took a few well-distanced photos, and then undertook a slight detour to avoid being bashed up by an elk hoof.

Back at camp we got a fire going with ease, because by now we were pros and didn't require giant imported pinecones *or* Germans to get the flames...flaming. To celebrate our final night of camping on this trip we cooked marshmallows, and then Paula had an intriguing idea of how to warm up our sleeping bags. We filled our water bottles with hot water that we had heated over our raging campfire, but we also found some large stones and rocks from around the campsite that we put on the grill above the fire. These then got very hot, and so we wrapped them in our spare socks and put them in our sleeping bags. Hot rock socks!

That night, as I crawled into my sleeping bag, I was warm and comfortable, and after three days with barely any sleep I fell unconscious within minutes. Unfortunately I then woke up an hour later, and as is the way with hot things - they cool down, and so I was then left shivering once again for the rest of the night. It had worked a treat in the short term though.

I awoke the next morning buzzing. Sleep deprivation had finally driven me to the point of insanity. But as I emerged from the tent and emptied my socks of rocks (other campers must have thought this was very strange behaviour) I noticed a group of forestry workers cutting down nearby trees with a chainsaw. This accounted for the buzzing (which was a relief) but I still didn't feel it was a justifiable method of waking campers. I would have set an elk on them if I could have found one.

After breakfast we packed up our stuff and set off back to Edmonton, passing a town called 'Nojack' (which sadly didn't appear to have a car repair garage - because 'Nojack Car Services' would have been great...) as we left the Rocky Mountains behind us. Tonight was my final night in Canada, and Paula had said that we were going to meet up with a group of her friends as they had got free tickets for us to go somewhere this evening. This sounded good - how better to celebrate the last few hours of my trip in this country than by going to a Canadian event with a nice group of Canadians!

I asked Paula what the tickets were for.

'Baseball,' she said.

'*Sackgasse!*'

'Sorry?'

'Nothing.'

Chapter 36

And so it ends. Twice.

Vancouver Airport, British Columbia

*"Good things come to those...*who turn up early and ask."

Baseball. My entertainment nemesis. So this is how my Canadian adventure would end - in the same manner in which it began; with three and a half hours of mindless bat-swinging boredom.

At around seven o'clock a few of Paula's friends came round and we headed up to the roof of her apartment building where we had an impromptu barbeque in the evening sunshine. We had only been gone a few days, but in that time the thick coats and umbrellas that had been worn by those making their way along the streets of this city in the cold rain and snow had been replaced by shorts and flip-flops as the hot sun now enforced its presence. They weren't a direct replacement of course, because people don't wear shorts on their upper body or hold flip-flops over their head – not even in The Prairies - but I'm sure you get my meaning.

After the classic array of sausages and salad had been cooked and consumed we headed over to the baseball stadium. You could clearly see the stadium from the roof of the apartment building (and a lot of the rest of the city too) and once we were seated in one of the small stands we could see the apartment block. It was also the first time I'd properly seen and appreciated just how green this city was, with vast blocks of green canopy dominating the surrounding area. Soon the two teams came out and began throwing and catching the ball, and every so often a more daring player would hit the ball, and everyone would get frightfully excited and clap a little bit. People in baseball paraphernalia walked around the stands selling drinks and snacks, and it was quickly decided amongst our group of eight that this was something we should invest in.

'Four Canadians?' the vendor asked us, as he appeared next to our block of seats having spotted the opportunity to offload a few 'Canadians' – a popular, low-cost beer – to a row of four guys.

'Actually it's three and a Brit,' I replied sharply, to which everyone laughed, and I was happy and remembered once again why I like Canada so much.

So we sat watching the baseball and "crushing beers" (as I was told was the correct term). We laughed and joked, and I occasionally shouted phrases that I'd heard shouted at the last baseball game I'd been to in Toronto, and therefore assumed would help me fit in.

'Step up overbay!' I projected powerfully in my finest Canadian accent.

I thought upon hearing this that everyone would swivel their heads and give me a knowing glance and maybe a nod in recognition of my well timed and highly appropriate message to the teams, but instead I just got a few raised eyebrows and some disparaging sniggers.

Jeff (who had secured the tickets for the game and who was sitting next to me) then informed me that "Lyle Overbay" was actually a player for the *Toronto Blue Jays*, and therefore my enthusiastic instruction was a little…well, stupid, and lacked context or relevance.

Pah! That was just a minor technicality, and so I continued to throw out motivational phrases to the illusive 'Overbay'.

As the sun set across the valley I can honestly say I had no idea what was going on in the game. Maybe this was connected to the number of (well-priced, I might add) beers that were being rapidly consumed, but I like to believe that it was mostly due to the banter that was in constant flow between the group of us. I felt warmed, not only by the sun, but by the fine company that I was now present in. Everyone was relaxed and having a good social time with friends, and that's when I suddenly realised what baseball was really all about.

I've always been used to going to football matches, (that's "soccer" for you Canadians) where everyone is one hundred percent focused on what is happening on the pitch (except for when I was four and I used to hide under the seat and play with my watch light – strangely I found it massively entertaining) but here it was different. Baseball – especially these lower league matches – was about getting together with friends and having a good time; "crushing beers" and enjoying each other's company in the setting of team-spirited sports competition. I got it now, and I really liked it.

The beer vendor was by now hanging around our area as he realised the positive financial repercussions of doing so, and in between t-shirt throwings and melodic, synth-organ led musical interludes, the crowd engaged in various call and response exchanges with the stadium's MC and participated in all the obligatory chants and gestures that are encouraged at these sporting occasions. In between bat-swings a bizarre Rastafarian-bird creature thing (that I was assured was the team mascot) would run about in the stands and entertain the younger fans, and another baseball-attired man would walk around shouting "I've got fuzzy mangoes", much to the amusement of many of us. For the record; I think they're sweets.

The sports-mad Jeff even handed me his business card, saying that he thought I should have the contact details of a professional curling instructor. It's true, I *didn't* previously have the contact details of a professional curling instructor, and to be quite frank my wallet has felt a more secure place since I slipped that card into it.

Finally, when the game was over (I couldn't tell you what the score was) they put on a fireworks display. They must have known I was leaving tomorrow. It was a very impressive array of colour and bangs, and it was much appreciated.

* * *

The next morning I was treated to a fantastic breakfast at Paula's sister Tara and her husband Mark's apartment. Along with their visiting aunt I got to indulge in my first taste of Canadian maple syrup – something that I'm sure would have been held against me had I left the country without doing so. Aside from the brilliant array of waffles, eggs, bacon and fruit that they put on, it was really nice to be included in such an occasion, and as a final act in Canada it really summed up the hugely kind and welcoming nature that I had found Canadians possessed. As I said goodbye to Paula at the airport an hour later, I was genuinely sad to be leaving, and hoped that it wouldn't be long until I got to return to this country that had provided me with so many adventures and experiences.

I used the electronic check-in machine where boarding pass and luggage tag were successfully printed and delivered to my hand. I took them over to the baggage counter, where I'm sure the lady gave me a subtle, proud look having realised I'd used the service correctly. No, I *wasn't* drunk. Having said this, upon checking my ticket she suddenly looked concerned, and told me that my flight was delayed, but that she would try and fit me on the earlier flight that was also delayed. I was then ushered over to a man behind another counter, and soon a new ticket was thrust into my hand and before I really knew what was going on I was sitting in the back row of an aeroplane as it powered down the runway. Somehow the delay to my flight had worked in my favour, and I was now airborne just forty minutes after arriving at the airport. This *was* efficient, and now I was a couple of hours ahead of schedule too!

My glee (if that's even what I was showing – which I actually doubt) was short-lived however.

'Would you like a drink, sir?' the male flight attendant asked as he clumsily manoeuvred the trolley beside my seat, interrupting my film watching.

'Yes, could I have a lemonade, please.' I replied.

The man turned to the female flight attendant who was maintaining order at the other end of the trolley, repeated the word 'lemonade' in a mock-posh accent and giggled.

He turned back to me and said, 'do you mean a *Sprite?*'

I was irritated by this mocking attitude.

'*No, Sprite* is a brand!' I returned sharply. ''Lemonade' is the drink – or if it *is Sprite*, then it's 'Lemon and Lime'.

If they were going to be rude then I was going to fight them with consumer knowledge and political correctness.

'Oh.' The man looked slightly taken aback – as you would after being proved wrong, so very wrong. 'Oooh! Are you British?'

Don't change the subject!

'Yeesss…' I said, glaring at the seat ahead of me.

Just give me the damn *Sprite*.

* * *

The plane docked at Vancouver International Airport on time. Well, the *flight time* was accurate – we were actually quite late, but then this was an earlier flight…so I was actually very early. I'm also aware that planes don't really 'dock'. Oh, leave me alone. Because of my early arrival in Vancouver I now had over five hours until my flight back to England, but this didn't hugely affect my first objective. I carried my bags over to the check-in desk that I was pleased to find already open despite my early arrival time, and I dropped my bags beside the counter and handed over my passport.

'Is there any chance of being bumped up to business class?' I enquired. No longer did I approach these issues with subtle tact or a smart outfit, as I think I've made it clear that I have no shame in the endless pursuit of freebies and upgrades.

'I'm afraid *Air Canada* don't offer that,' the baggage attendant replied.

He seemed affable enough though, so time for the big one.

'Okay, how about volunteering? Is the flight overbooked?'

The good people of *British Airways* had been striking lately, and much to my encouragement I had noticed that the *BA* flight to London that left shortly before the flight I was booked on had been cancelled, presumably due to the strikes. This was my best chance of getting bumped off the flight as there would now be lots of extra people trying to get to London.

'Lets see,' said the man, tapping a few keys on his computer. 'Well, it appears that the flight *is* overbooked, but only by one seat, so it's very unlikely you'll be needed to offer up your seat. I can put you down anyway though, if you want?'

I did want.

The man put a special yellow sticker on my backpack and then he shoved it onto the conveyor belt and it was gone. I then headed through security with the usual belt-removal hassle, and then settled into the departure lounge; shoes off, bag down, guitar out.

The hours rock 'n' rolled by as I sat about strumming my guitar in between wanders around the departure area, using up my last few dollars on a few presents for people back home. Eventually it was time for boarding, and I watched as everyone else was gradually called up by seat block to go through to the plane. Finally the last few passengers made their way through the gate and I was left alone in the seating area; shoeless and playing my guitar. This was it. I put my guitar down, slipped on my shoes, and walked over to the desk to find out whether I was flying home or not.

'Actually we would like you to volunteer if that's okay?'

Yeah! Damn right it's okay!

'Yes, I think that will be okay,' I responded calmly and philosophically.

The lady in charge of...the flight, or the airline...or something, then came over looking very serious, and she apologised for the overbooking and thanked me very sincerely for offering up my seat.

Was she kidding?! I knew this meant I got to stay on in Canada and that they would put me up in a hotel and give me flight vouchers. I was getting *paid* to stay on in Canada! This was brilliant.

The airport crew made a few phone calls and did a few administrative bits and then came over to me with my flight, hotel and meal vouchers. I was being put on the same flight the following day, and in the meantime I was being put up in a flash hotel near the airport and fed.

I followed one of the airport staff down to customs, where I had a slightly difficult time trying to explain my position.

'Are you staying in Canada?' the customs lady asked while studying my passport.

'Yes, I am,' I replied cheerfully.

'And where have you arrived from?'

'Erm. Canada.'

The lady stopped looking at my passport and looked up at me with a confused expression on her face.

'...okay. So you missed your flight?'

'No, no – I was here five hours early.' I said proudly, still smiling about my prospective extended stay in Canada.

'Right. So why weren't you allowed to leave?' she was getting very suspicious of me now.

'Oh, no I *was*, but I chose to give up my seat.'

Obviously volunteering was a concept that was new to her.

'…so how long are you staying in Canada?'

'Just tonight. Well, probably – it depends if they want me to go tomorrow, really.'

She'd had enough. A deep sigh and a resigned look, and she stamped my passport. I had arrived back in Canada! …although I was pretty sure I hadn't actually *left* yet, so did this mean I was now double-stamped into Canada? That must practically mean citizenship…

I found my backpack on a distant baggage claim belt and made my way out of the airport to the shuttle bus pick up point, and within a few minutes I was being dropped off outside a very smart looking hotel. Inside I flashed my far from glamorous slip of paper that was my hotel voucher to the smarty dressed receptionist, and next thing I was pushing my way through the door of my seventh floor room. It felt odd. Six weeks of being in enclosed living quarters with numerous strangers was a big contrast to a large empty ensuite hotel room. As I tried to hang my jacket on the hook on the wall, I caught sight of the hotel price list that was pinned to the back of the door. I *literarily* dropped my jacket (the hook wasn't the best) when I saw the price of this room. Lets just say it was more than I'd spent on accommodation for the past three weeks. I was very glad the airline was paying. This was crazy.

I took out a few bits from my bags and had a shower, trying my best to make the most of the vast collection of clean, white towels that adorned the shelves and rails in the bathroom. I then changed into some clean(ish) clothes and headed down to the restaurant that was adjacent to the hotel. Here I took a seat by a window that overlooked a smart marina full of expensive yachts and sailing boats, while I studied the menu. My dinner voucher that the airline had provided was for $15, which left me with a limited choice of mainly sandwiches. But I chose the barbeque chicken. Well this sandwich thing had to end somewhere. I also asked for tap water, as with the addition of taxes and tips I couldn't afford anything more

281

exiting having only got a few cents left in my wallet. It was a very tasty meal though, and as I finished mopping my mouth with a logo-embroidered napkin I felt a sudden sense of calm wash over me. This feeling continued as I made my way back to my room and collapsed onto my bed. I suddenly realised how exhausted I was, and after flicking through my notebook I realised that I had averaged six hours of travelling a day for six weeks, and I think it was finally catching up with me.

I got ready for bed and switched on the giant flat screen television that sat on the cabinet across from the massive bed. I lay down in it (the bed, not the television) and was at first slightly disconcerted by the new sensation of horizontal space, having become accustomed to having to poke my feet between bunk bed slats or crunch myself up into a ball for train seat accommodation. Here I had six pillows (that I had no idea how to use simultaneously) and so much expanse of sheets and duvet cover I could barely see the edge of the bed. Needless to say I slept well.

The following morning I got up – after a good lie in of course – and headed down to the breakfast room. Here my airline voucher allowance was slightly more restricting than the dinner one had been.

'Good morning, sir. For eighteen dollars we have the full continental hot and cold buffet with a selection of…oh,' the waitress paused when she caught sight of the voucher I was flapping wearily in front of her. 'Right. Okay, I'll get you a toasted bagel.'

'Thanks.'

I had been prepared to check out early, but when I was asking about return shuttle trips to the airport she had asked what time I needed to leave, and having told her she said I could stay on in my room until I needed to leave. I couldn't cope with this high-class world. It actually frustrated me when a man in a suit insisted on pressing the lift-summoning button for me. I *like* pressing the lift buttons.

I was still pretty shattered, and with little else I could really do I returned to my room, switched on the television again, and crashed out on the bed until it was time for me to gather up my belongings, pocket the complimentary hotel biro, and get the shuttle back to the airport.

Once back in the terminal building I went through the now all too familiar check-in procedures. I even took my belt off in advance to preserve some dignity that would otherwise be lost during a hasty instructed removal. I was happier to leave this time, as the full-on activities and experiences of the past six weeks had finally caught up with me. I also reckoned it would get a bit boring hanging around any longer in a hotel full of shiny suitcase-wielding business folk, with their constantly buzzing blackberries and slightly too short beige trousers.

So I was quite happy as I flashed my boarding pass to the lady on the gate and proceeded through to board the plane. At the second attempt, I was now on my way home.

My Canadian adventure was complete.

Epilogue

Watford, Hertfordshire *(England)*

"Never judge a book…" Erm…maybe I'll leave that one to you.

I was back. Back in a place where the time zone doesn't change if you go into the next major town. Back in a place where buses are noisy and a regular size. Back in a place where trains travel quickly (well, some of the time). A place where the climate doesn't vary between one end of the street and the other. Sorry, I mean *road*. Back in a place where tax is included in the given price. Back in England. The country where you have to pay more to eat a sandwich *inside* the sandwich shop.

I had gone away to buy a sandwich that was supposed to be *reasonably priced*…and *technically* it hadn't been.

I had gone away to find the third *Wikipedia* Watford…which *technically* I didn't make it to.

But I had *also* gone away to escape the boredom of work and to discover new things, which I certainly *had* achieved.

And this was the *real* success. I had converted a moment of inconvenience into six weeks of fun and adventure, and that was enough. *More* than enough, actually. Sure, Canada has a few little oddities, but what place doesn't? I didn't come across a sandwich shop that charged more to eat a sandwich inside at least. Talking of which, it's probably about time I gathered together my sandwich findings.

I had naively thought that it was just a case of how much money you handed over for the sandwich that determined if a sandwich was "reasonably priced" or not. Oh, how wrong I was! I learnt from my sandwich quest that there are a considerable number of factors that need to be taken into account before deciding such important things.

There are of course the obvious factors such as taste, quality, and presentation, but there's more. Location, location, lo...ads of other things. Like the service; quirky, charismatic sandwich sales people can make the sandwich all the nicer. Think of the higher sandwich price as...a service charge, maybe? And the reputation of the sandwich. If it has some documented significance then that can also add value and justify a higher price and yet remain reasonable. Good. I'm glad you agree. But yes, location is *very* important. You could be stranded on a desert island and a grubby little man in a hat comes by and offers you a sandwich. You're starving and this sandwich keeps you alive. He charges you £10 ($14.63 approx.) for the sandwich, but it's worth it – because you *need* to eat. You see my point? The hat wasn't really significant.

Okay, okay, so that was a crap analogy, and why would a sandwich seller be wandering about on a desert island? It would make terrible business sense - but the issue is *context*. You will pay more for something if you want it out of necessity, and when you contemplate the wider picture, other issues become important when considering what you're actually paying for, and so a higher price can sometimes be justified.

Back in London I had paid more to eat in. I felt it had been unreasonable, but at least I ate the sandwich in the comfort of a heated room, and not sitting, shivering in the park where I wouldn't have enjoyed it as much. I also bet that there would be people (partly because I met lots) who would love to have the opportunity to pay £3.55 for a sandwich in London. Because they would consider just *being in London* great, because they think it is a great city – which it *is*! In the same way the sandwich I ate on the ferry in

British Columbia was a bit pricey (over £2000 if you include the bitch of a commute I had to get to it) but it was worth it thanks to all the people I met and everything I got to see and do because of it. Okay, so that's taking an extremely broad view of it, but I'm sure by now you can see what I'm getting at.

...Or on the other hand I could be talking rubbish, and you will continue to moan about paying too much for stuff. I'm certainly in no hurry to return to a London cafe for lunch, however much I like the city. But taking into account the cynical sandwich-eater assumptions *and* the wider more philosophical view - here's my sandwich quest results table that I finally got round to constructing.

I have picked out the ten most significant sandwiches of my quest, and I have named them. Not like 'George', or 'Stephanie' – that would be silly, but by the location where they were bought and another word or two that made them distinctive. I have then listed the price I paid for them, followed by four other boxes that give a mark out of five (1 being bad, 5 being very good, ...and 0 being worse than 1) and then I have totalled up the scores, giving a final score out of a possible 25. It's all very simple, really. The last column however, is a special sandwich-judging criteria; the *bonus* section! Here I have awarded special points based on more unique issues that I felt warranted consideration in regards to the reasonable pricing of sandwiches. This could be for things like extra special service, or symbolic value. Yes, sandwich judging is a serious business, as I'm sure the people at the *BSA* would confirm.

Anyway, enough explanations, here's the table...

The Reasonably Priced Sandwich plus other important factors such as Location Assessment Table

Sandwich	Price	Filling	Taste	Location	Bonus	Total
London Wholegrain	£3.55	2	3	2	0	7
Watford Gap 'PAULINA'	£3.99	1	1	0	1	3
Toronto Coffee Shop	$5.69	3	3	2	1	9
Ottawa Mix	$6.99	2	2	3	1	8
Montreal 'Legend'	$5.50	4	3	2	3	12
Halifax Award	$5.62	3	2	2	2	9
Jasper 'Heaven'	$7.88	3	4	4	3	14
Seattle Award	$14.00	2	3	2	1	8
BC Ferries Internet	$7.34	2	3	4	2	11
Banff Altitude	$5.00	1	2	5	2	10

Well, there you are! The results are in, and we have a winner! With a fantastic score of 14, the *Jasper 'Heaven'* sandwich was the most reasonably priced sandwich I had. Which is a little odd really, as if you discount the *Seattle Award* sandwich (which you may well be inclined to, given that it was a burger) it was actually the most expensive sandwich I had, and therefore arguably it goes against everything I originally believed in. But beliefs change, as the whole "the world is flat" thing demonstrated, and so thanks to my new appreciation of external factors in the consumption of sandwiches, the sandwich I had in Jasper was the most reasonably priced. This is taking into account the style and charisma in which it was created and delivered, the personalised packaging, the imaginative ingredients, and the company and setting in which I ate it. So congratulations to the *Patricia Street Deli* in Jasper, and long may you provide your sandwiches with the enthusiasm and commitment to culinary creation that you served up on that evening back in May.

Now, I should probably let you know about a few sandwich quest related things I've been up to since my trip.

Well, I've documented the journey, so you can be enlightened about the wonders of Canada, and the complicated world of sandwich purchasing and consumption. Although I'm guessing you've just read most of it, so that was probably a little obvious and unnecessary of me to mention it.

I wrote to the Mayor of London recommending the implementation of environmentally friendly "tiny buses" in London. I think that they would make great vehicles for transporting officials and participants around the Olympic site in two years time. He has yet to reply. If he keeps this up then he shall not gain any vote that I may be entitled to cast in his direction in the future. You have been warned, Boris.

I have also been in contact with the good people at the *British Sandwich Association*. They very kindly sent me a copy of the latest edition of *International Sandwich and Snack* magazine. It is nice and glossy, and full of...well, sandwiches. I guess I shouldn't have been surprised. It also mentions the awards that they gave out. I was wrong. They're *not* called "The Hammies". They're *actually* called "The Sammies"! This is still pretty fantastic.

They also took an interest in my trip, and have mentioned including some of my research in a future edition of the publication. This makes me proud, as I feel I could well be on track to becoming the *UK Sandwich Ambassador to Canada.*

Speaking of which, I have discovered that there is not a 'National Sandwich Day' in Canada. With such a creative and heritage-filled sandwich industry I think that this needs to change, and it is something I intend to pursue. National Sandwich Day in Britain is on the 3rd November, by the way. Put it in your diaries.

I was always very surprised to learn how many Canadians hadn't ever visited so many of the interesting cities and places that are in *their own* country. Especially when many of them are just a short(ish, slightly drawn out) train journey away. I then realised that *I've* never been to Manchester, which is a major English city that's only a couple of hours on the train from Watford. I am rectifying that later this month.

So I think that's it! I hope you will now give every moment of annoyance a positive spin, and *maybe* even see it as an opportunity for discovery and adventure! Of course you might be the type of person who *likes* being served sandwiches on silver trays, or you're someone who gets *lots* of job offers and so you don't need to do such silly things. You may *even* be the type of person who gets *genuinely free boat trips*, and if you are, I envy you. So wherever any odd occurrences lead you – make the most of it, but just make sure you don't get leaf-punched along the way.

Oh yes! Here are the *Anglo-Canadian* translations I promised you...

Translations

Canadian English	*English* English
10/04/28	*28th April 2010*
Eh?	*Don't you agree?*
Car	*Carriage*
De-train	*Disembark the train*
Downtown	*Town centre*
Elevator	*Lift*
Fall	*Autumn*
First floor	*Ground floor*
Fucking retarded	*A little bit silly*
Loonie	*One dollar coin/an odd person*
Mall	*Shopping centre*
Momentarily	*Shortly*
Pants	*Trousers*
Pickle	*Gherkin*
Poutine	*Chips and cheese curds in gravy*
Second floor	*First floor*
Sketchy	*Unusual/strange/best avoided*
Thank you so much!	*Thanks*
Toonie	*Two dollar coin*
Vacation	*Holiday*
Washroom	*Toilet and hand-basin facilities*

Thanks!

Paula, for your fantastic hospitality and the brilliant road trip. To Paula's friends and family, again for your fantastic hospitality and kindness. To all of the people I met along the way, for being ever entertaining, and for embracing my quest and giving me direction. *Sandwich* direction. Even those of you who said I sounded like Hugh Grant; I don't understand you, but I forgive you. To Dianne, for pointing out when I got mords in a wuddle.

And finally to Canada, for being so much more than just a land of ice hockey fanatics (although I realise that this is a pretty big part) and for being just a seven-hour, Celine Dion-filled flight away.

Just before going to print I got this through my door…

Transport for London
London Buses

Our Ref: 1007098719
Date: 05 August 2010

Mr C Ambrose

Watford

London Buses
Surface Transport
Customer Services

4th Floor - Zone B5
14 Pier Walk
London SE10 0ES

Phone 0845 300 7000
www.tfl.gov.uk/contact

Dear Mr Ambrose

RE: 'Ecolo-bus' – Putting 'Tiny Buses' in London

Thank you for your recent letter addressed to The Mayor of London, Boris Johnson, regarding the use of small 'Ecolo' buses. As I am sure that you can appreciate, the Mayor is not able to respond to every letter he receives personally. I am responding on his behalf in this instance.

Firstly, I would like to thank you for your suggestion that Transport for London (TfL) consider the use of smaller buses on London Buses' network, and understand that you feel that the type of bus used on the transport network in Quebec would prove to be successful on shorter, localised routes. Recommendations and suggestions for improvements to our bus network are always welcome.

Our buses are built to standard specifications which are intended to fulfil specific demand when new routes are planned, or existing routes are reviewed. With limited resources available, it is important to strike a balance between the size of vehicles on a route and the frequency of the service and given the large number of passengers who rely on buses to travel in London, the use of larger vehicles is preferred as the most cost effective method.

There are no current plans to introduce smaller vehicles of this nature on the London Buses' network, however, we do review all routes on a regular basis and assess the vehicle specification for each route as a part of this process.

MAYOR OF LONDON

Well at least *someone* replied, even if they're not going to help save the world *just yet* through the implementation of tiny buses. Shame.